HANDBOOK OF PSYCHOSOCIAL REHABILITATION

Robert King

School of Medicine
University of Queensland
Australia

Chris Lloyd

School of Health and Rehabilitation Sciences
University of Queensland
Australia

Tom Meehan

The Park
Centre for Mental Health and
University of Queensland
Australia

Blackwell
Publishing

© 2007 by R. King, C. Lloyd, T. Meehan and Blackwell Publishing Ltd

Blackwell Publishing editorial offices:
Blackwell Publishing Ltd, 9600 Garsington Road, Oxford OX4 2DQ, UK
  Tel: +44 (0)1865 776868
Blackwell Publishing Inc., 350 Main Street, Malden, MA 02148-5020, USA
  Tel: +1 781 388 8250
Blackwell Publishing Asia Pty Ltd, 550 Swanston Street, Carlton, Victoria 3053, Australia
  Tel: +61 (0)3 8359 1011

First published 2007 by Blackwell Publishing Ltd

ISBN: 978-14051-3308-1

Library of Congress Cataloguing-in-Publication Data

Handbook of psychosocial rehabilitation / Robert King, Chris Lloyd, Tom Meehan.
    p. ; cm.
  Includes bibliographical references and index.
  ISBN-13: 978-1-4051-3308-1 (pbk. : alk. paper)
  ISBN-10: 1-4051-3308-2 (pbk. : alk. paper)   1. Mentally ill–Rehabilitation.
2. Psychotherapy patients–Rehabilitation.   3. Community mental health services.
I. King, Robert, 1949– II. Lloyd, Chris, 1954– III. Meehan, Tom, 1957–
  [DNLM: 1. Mental Disorders–rehabilitation.   WM 400 H2358 2007]
  RC439.5.H362 2007
  616.89′14–dc22

                                                              2006021670

A catalogue record for this title is available from the British Library

Set in 10/12.5pt Sabon
by Graphicraft Limited, Hong Kong
Printed and bound in Singapore
by Fabulous Printers Pte Ltd

The publisher's policy is to use permanent paper from mills that operate a sustainable forestry policy, and which has been manufactured from pulp processed using acid-free and elementary chlorine-free practices. Furthermore, the publisher ensures that the text paper and cover board used have met acceptable environmental accreditation standards.

For further information on Blackwell Publishing, visit our website:
www.blackwellpublishing.com

CONTENTS

LIST OF CONTRIBUTORS

Trevor Crowe
School of Psychology
University of Wollongong
Northfields Avenue
Wollongong NSW 2522
Australia

Frank Deane
School of Psychology
University of Wollongong
Northfields Avenue
Wollongong NSW 2522
Australia

Helen Glover
enLightened Consultants
PO Box 7361
Redland Bay 4165
Australia

Shane McCombes
Senior Mental Health Educator
'Healthcall' Queensland Division
Pacific Highway
Pymble NSW 2073
Australia

Lindsay Oades
School of Psychology
University of Wollongong
Northfields Avenue
Wollongong NSW 2522
Australia

Terry Stedman
Director of Clinical Services
The Park, Centre for Mental Health & University of Queensland
Locked Bag 500
Richlands QLD 4077
Australia

Chapter 1

KEY CONCEPTS AND DEFINITIONS

Robert King, Chris Lloyd and Tom Meehan

Overview of chapter

The purpose of this chapter is to identify and discuss some of the key terms and concepts that will be found throughout this handbook. The aim is to enable the reader to gain an understanding of how we are using certain terms and why we think that the concepts behind the terms are central to mental health practice. Part of the chapter is concerned not just with defining terms but also with enunciating the three core values inherent in contemporary rehabilitation that inform our thinking. These values are:

- Rehabilitation takes place within the framework of a commitment to recovery
- Rehabilitation takes place within a biopsychosocial framework, and
- Rehabilitation takes place within the framework of evidence-based practice

The meaning of the core concepts of recovery, biopsychosocial, and evidence-based practice is set out here, together with a discussion of the implications of each value position for practice. The reasons why we have decided upon using the terms 'practitioner' and 'client', the two key people in the rehabilitation relationship, will be discussed.

Recovery and rehabilitation

Recovery

Recovery has become a core concept in contemporary mental health practice and has taken on some reasonably specific meaning, some of which departs from common usage. In mental health practice there are three dimensions of recovery – an objective dimension that best corresponds with common usage, a subjective dimension that is more specific to the mental health practice environment, and a service framework dimension that combines elements of both the objective and the subjective dimensions.

Recovery as an objective phenomenon

This kind of recovery implies a reduction in the objective indicators of illness and disability. It does not imply full remission of symptoms or the absence of any disability but rather objective evidence of change in this direction. By objective evidence we refer to a range of indicators such as whether or not a person continues to meet diagnostic criteria for a specified illness, scores on standardised measures of symptoms, social functioning or quality of life, changes in employment status or other objective indicators of social functioning, rates of hospital usage or usage of other kinds of clinical services, and dependence on social security. When we see evidence that a person is maintaining consistent positive progress on one or more of these indicators without evidence of reversal on others, we can say that there is objective evidence of recovery. These kinds of indicators are commonly used both to collect epidemiological data on recovery from mental illness (see Chapter 2) and to determine the evidence base for effectiveness of psychosocial rehabilitation programmes (see below and also Chapter 14).

Recovery as a subjective phenomenon

As a result of attention to the voices of people who have experienced mental illness, it has become clear that objective indicators of recovery do not always correspond with the subjective experience of recovery. The experience of mental illness is not just one of symptoms and disability but equally importantly one of major challenge to sense of self. Equally, recovery from mental illness is experienced not just in terms of symptoms and disability but also as a recovery of sense of self (Davidson & Strauss, 1992; Schiff, 2004). Recovery of sense of self and recovery with respect to symptoms and disability may not correspond. A person may continue to experience significant impairment as a result of symptoms and disability but may have a much stronger sense of self. Inversely, symptoms and disability may improve while sense of self remains weak. The mental health consumer movement has advocated for the subjective dimension of recovery to share equal importance with the objective dimension in the clinical environment (Deegan, 2003). This implies much closer attention to the psychological and spiritual wellbeing of the person with mental illness than is characteristic of the standard service environment. It also has implications for evaluation of the effectiveness of mental health services (Anthony et al., 2003; Frese et al., 2001). The subjective dimension of recovery is explored in depth in Chapter 3.

Recovery as a framework for services

Anthony (1993) called for recovery to be the 'guiding vision' for mental health services. He argued that practitioners can only assist people suffering from mental illness to achieve recovery if they both acknowledge the importance of the subjective dimension of recovery and if they actually believe in the possibility of recovery. This call for a change in service philosophy argued that traditional services, operating more within a medical model and focusing purely on objective indicators of recovery, were failing to instil and sustain the experience of hope that was central to the possibility of recovery. In other words, if practitioners are not themselves hopeful it is difficult for those who are looking to them to facilitate recovery to develop hope. In the absence of hope and a belief in the reality of recovery, services will focus on basic maintenance only and not provide any inspiration for people with mental illness to achieve and grow (Turner-Crowson & Wallcraft, 2002). Advocates for recovery as a framework for services have also looked to epidemiological data that show that recovery is a reality for many people with the most severe disorders even when objective indicators are used, and evidence that well-developed mental health services can contribute to rate of recovery (for example, DeSisto et al., 1995a, 1995b; Harrison et al., 2001; Harding, Brooks et al., 1987). Resnick et al. (2004) have suggested that the polarity between biomedical and recovery models may be unfounded, and that it is possible to provide treatment that is mutually reinforcing.

Rehabilitation

Rehabilitation refers broadly to restoration of functioning and is used widely in the field of health. Psychosocial rehabilitation refers more specifically to restoration of psychological and social functioning and is most frequently used in the context of mental illness. It is based on two core principles (Cnaan et al., 1988):

- People are motivated to achieve independence and self confidence through mastery and competence
- People are capable of learning and adapting to meet needs and achieve goals

Table 1.1 outlines some of the key features of psychosocial rehabilitation as set out by Cnaan et al. (1988, 1990). More recently, Corrigan (2003) has revisited Cnaan's principles and provided systematisation of the rehabilitation process having reference to the goals, strategies, settings and roles that are involved.

In some contexts, the term rehabilitation is used interchangeably with recovery and can be an unintentional or incidental process. However, throughout this book, the term rehabilitation is reserved for application to a purposeful programme designed to facilitate recovery. This may be a self-help or peer support programme but often it will be a programme that involves a mental health practitioner. As it is used in this sense, rehabilitation differs from recovery. Whereas recovery may take place in the absence of any specific programme, rehabilitation always implies purpose and specific goals. Rehabilitation may focus on objective indicators of recovery such as symptoms or measures of social functioning. It may also focus on subjective recovery as in recovery of a sense of self or of a sense of purpose. Often it will focus on both, and the general philosophy of this book is that it will be most successful when both dimensions of recovery are taken into account, and when rehabilitation programmes are delivered within a recovery framework whereby the practitioner has a belief in the recovery of the person with mental illness, and with generating and maintaining hope.

Table 1.1 Principles of psychosocial rehabilitation

1. All people have an under-utilised capacity, which should be developed
2. All people can be equipped with skills (social, vocational, educational, interpersonal and others)
3. People have the right and responsibility for self-determination
4. Services should be provided in as normalised an environment as possible
5. Assessment of needs and care is different for each individual
6. Staff should be deeply committed
7. Care is provided in an intimate environment without professional, authoritative shields and barriers
8. Crisis intervention strategies are in place
9. Environmental agencies and structures are available to provide support
10. Changing the environment (educating community and restructuring environment to care for people with mental disability)
11. No limits on participation
12. Work centred process
13. There is an emphasis on a social rather than a medical model of care
14. Emphasis is on the client's strengths rather than on pathologies
15. Emphasis is on the here and now rather than on problems from the past

After Cnaan et al., 1988, 1990.

Multidisciplinary service delivery: the biopsychosocial model of mental health

This handbook is designed for multidisciplinary practitioners. What do we mean by multidisciplinary and what implications does this term have for psychosocial rehabilitation?

First, let us introduce a related concept: biopsychosocial. Biopsychosocial is a term that was introduced into the field of mental health practice (Engel, 1980; Freedman, 1995; Pilgrim, 2002) to draw attention to the implications of two key characteristics of mental illness:

- Mental illness affects multiple domains or systems and not just one system. Specifically, the biological, psychological, and social systems of the person with mental illness are all likely to be implicated.
- The three systems are interlinked. They do not operate in isolation from each other. Whatever happens in one system is likely to have implications for the other.

As Pilgrim (2002) pointed out, the holistic and humanistic premises of the bio-psychosocial model have a long history in mental health care that predates the introduction of the term by Engel (1980).

A multidisciplinary approach to psychosocial rehabilitation means being able to think multisystemically. This includes being both aware and respectful of the possible contributions of other mental health practitioners who have specific expertise in one or other domains (Liberman et al., 2001). It also means having a capacity to facilitate access to services across different domains, and communicate with practitioners who have specialist skills in these different domains. In some situations it means working in a multidisciplinary team, whereby practitioners with different kinds of expertise routinely communicate and consult. However, multidisciplinary practice is more about the use of a biopsychosocial framework and development of an attitude to practice than the presence or absence of a team.

Practitioner, clinician, case manager, mental health professional

There is some variability in the term used to describe the person who is trying to facilitate the recovery process. We have decided to adopt the term practitioner throughout this book but terms such as clinician, case manager, and mental health professional could also be applicable. Practitioner is the term we have decided to use. The term is defined as 'one who is engaged in the actual use of or exercise of any art or profession'. It implies both expertise and purpose in a designated field but is very broad with respect to field. Practitioner has an honourable history in the health sciences, being used to refer to medical and nursing practice, but is also applied much more broadly in the practice of a wide range of professions, trades and arts.

The term clinician was considered but rejected because it implies a clinical service environment. Psychosocial rehabilitation can be delivered in clinical environments as part of a mix of services that might include medication, psychotherapy, and even inpatient care. However, it can also be delivered in non-clinical community services that have no medical or other clinical components. The term clinician is therefore too narrow to accommodate the range of relationships we have in mind. We do not wish to exclude clinicians and, indeed we suspect that people who identify themselves as clinicians, whether nurses, psychologists, occupational therapists or even medical practitioners, will form a major group amongst our readers. We believe that this group can also identify as mental health practitioners or psychosocial rehabilitation practitioners.

The term case manager has a wide currency in mental health and has been used to refer to both clinical and non-clinical roles – even occasionally to provision of services by peers. However there are two problems with this term. These are best captured by the objection expressed by a person with mental illness at a conference: 'I'm not a case and I don't want to be managed'. It has the connotation of a bureaucratic rather than a personal relationship and it also has the connotation of control or at the very least responsibility that does not apply in many rehabilitation relationships. Some services are adopting the term 'care coordinator' as being somewhat less impersonal. However, like case manager, this term implies that clients cannot coordinate their own services. In some cases this will be a reasonable assumption and we have no objection to services using the term case management or care coordination. However, we think that there are many rehabilitation relationships that take place outside of this framework. Therefore, while many of our readers may be designated by their services as case managers, we hope they can equally see themselves as mental health practitioners.

Mental health professional is a broader term than clinician or case manager but may be narrower than practitioner. For some the term 'professional' implies membership of a recognised profession and evokes issues of registration or membership of a professional association. While we do not doubt that many if not most of our readers will identify themselves as professionals, we expect that there will be some people who find the term difficult to identify with. For example, some community organisations employ staff because they have life or work experience that equips them to work effectively in a psychosocial rehabilitation relationship with clients who have a mental illness. In some cases these staff will not possess qualifications that provide entry into any professional association or enable registration or certification. Such people are practitioners but not necessarily mental health professionals.

Client and consumer/service user

One of the more vexing issues in mental health practice is the proper designation for the person with mental illness who is working with a mental health practitioner. The most common terms are 'client' and 'patient'. Both have drawn criticism. The term client has been criticised for evoking a different and more impersonal relationship – such as the relationship with a lawyer or a banker or accountant. It can also imply a very unequal level of expertise and a relationship in which the client is the passive recipient of information or advice or where the other person acts on behalf of the client. The term patient implies a more personal relationship but one that is even more unequal and in which the person with mental illness has a high degree of dependency. The term patient also evokes a medical model of care with focus on physical dimensions of mental illness but not on the social and psychological dimensions.

Two other terms have currency. The term 'consumer' or 'service user' is preferred by some service providers/consumers. These terms come from the broader consumer movement and imply that as a direct or indirect purchaser of services the person has rights and reasonable expectations concerning service quality. They are therefore relatively empowering compared with client or patient. However they suffer, even more than client, as a result of rendering the relationship impersonal and evoke analogies with purchasing a car or supermarket shopping. Some prefer the term 'survivor', which implies a degree of resilience in the face of the major challenges of the illness. Survivor is most popular with people who have been unhappy with mental health services. Such people often see themselves as having survived not only the ravages of the illness itself but also the mental health system.

The issue of terminology is so difficult that it is not uncommon to hear people say in exasperation, '*I am not a patient or a client or a consumer or a survivor – I am a person*'. This kind of statement suggests that none of the terms is really satisfactory and each carries with it the risk of depersonalising the relationship. However, rehabilitation implies a relationship that is specific in its purpose and the term 'person' is not adequate to convey the qualities of this relationship.

In an attempt to learn more about how people affected by mental illness saw their relationship with mental health professionals and, in particular, how they preferred to be seen, we conducted a survey in which people were asked which of several terms they most identified with (Lloyd et al., 2001). Overall, we found that client was the preferred term but that it was somewhat context specific. People in acute inpatient care were more likely to identify themselves as 'patients', whereas people in community or outpatient settings were more likely to identify as 'clients'. In a similar study, McGuire-Snieckus et al. (2003) found that people surveyed in the UK identified with the term 'patient' when the context was seeing a general practitioner or psychiatrist and equally with the term 'client' or 'patient' when seeing non-medical mental health professionals. The terms 'consumer', 'service user' and 'survivor' were not favoured in either study. We think that the terms consumer and service user are probably best reserved for advocacy, service quality improvement and service management roles where the person is representing the wider group of mental health service consumers. They are less suitable for the rehabilitation relationship, which is necessarily a deeply personal one.

Taking into account all these consideration, while acknowledging the limitations of the term, we think that client is the least unsuitable term for application in the context of psychosocial rehabilitation. We are typically dealing with a community rather than an inpatient context where services are primarily provided by non-medical practitioners. The focus is on psychosocial functioning and experience rather than physical functioning and illness. Throughout the book you will find the term client used, rather than patient, consumer or service user.

Evidence based practice, efficacy and effectiveness

Evidence based practice (EBP) is a core value of contemporary psychosocial rehabilitation (Dixon & Goldman, 2004; Drake et al., 2001, 2003). It asserts that priority must be given to practices that are either known to contribute in a positive way to recovery or at least are reasonably likely to contribute to recovery. EBP is distinguished from practice by tradition, whereby rehabilitation practices are maintained because 'this is what we have always done'. EBP emerged in part from a critical movement in medicine (Davidson et al., 2003; Liberati & Vineis, 2004; Sackett et al., 1996) that questioned the value of established procedures such as tonsillectomies and hysterectomies that were commonly believed to be helpful but had not been subjected to rigorous investigation. EBP has also been influenced by the 'scientist–practitioner' model (Chwalisz, 2003), which was developed within the profession of psychology. The scientist–practitioner employs an empirical scientist approach to practice, designing interventions based on the best possible information, measuring the impact of the interventions, and then modifying the interventions in response to information about their impact.

EBP operates from the premise that once an intervention has been demonstrated to be effective with a specific problem, it should be able to be implemented to good effect whenever that problem is present. However, practitioners should remain alert to the impact of the intervention and not simply assume it will be effective in every case. In this sense every practitioner within the EBP framework is also a scientist–practitioner, or in other words a consumer of research. EBP is developed through formal research and is disseminated through research reviews, practice guidelines and formal training. This handbook is designed to disseminate EBP.

In EBP, all evidence is not equal and there are established hierarchies of evidence (Trinder, 2000). These hierarchies provide a guide to the robustness of the evidence. At the bottom of the hierarchy are single case reports. These are better than no evidence but are weak for two reasons:

- They may not be generalisable – what works for one person might not work for another. The single case-study may depend on highly individual characteristics of the client, the practitioner or their introduction and may not be replicable for other people or in other settings.
- There may be no causal relationship between the intervention and the outcome – the change observed in a single case report may be attributed to the intervention when it was actually caused by something separate from the intervention.

Formal evaluation of interventions is designed to investigate these two issues – their generalisability and the causal relationship between intervention and outcome. Until this has been clearly established, the intervention has a weak evidence base. Near the top of the hierarchy are randomised controlled trials (RCTs). These are especially good at resolving the issue of causality. If we take a group of people who share a common problem and half are randomly allocated to receive an intervention and the other half either continues with usual care or gets a placebo intervention, then we are likely to attribute any difference between their outcomes to the effect of the intervention. If a series of RCTs with different researchers in different settings yield similar outcomes, the evidence is especially persuasive because both the causality of the intervention is established and the generalisability or robustness of the intervention is demonstrated.

Between the single case study and the many times replicated RCT are a range of evidence types that are located in the middle of the hierarchy. These include observational studies and longitudinal studies where generalisability may be reasonably well demonstrated and causality is likely but not highly likely as in the RCT.

Practitioners need to develop some basic skills to read and interpret research (Lloyd et al., 2004). There are many factors that impact on the relevance of research findings to clinical practice (Essock et al, 2003; Lloyd et al., 2004; Tanenbaum, 2003). These include:

- The similarity of the research environment to the practice environment. This is sometimes referred to as the efficacy versus effectiveness issue. Research studies often use carefully selected study groups and deliver the intervention in atypical environments. In general, the effect of interventions in a research setting (efficacy) is usually greater than its effect in a practice setting (effectiveness). An intervention is not really evidence based for practice until it has demonstrated that it remains efficacious in a practice setting.

- The nature of the comparison condition. Many interventions are better than nothing but the EBP practitioner really wants to know if they are better than what she or he is doing now. It may not make sense to change practice until it can be demonstrated that a new intervention is superior to what is often termed 'usual care', and not to no treatment at all.
- The importance of fidelity and adherence to treatment protocols. Some forms of EBP appear to be sensitive to variations in implementation. If this is the case, the practitioner has to be sure that it is possible to implement the intervention exactly as specified.
- Much of the existing research on EBP was conducted without an understanding of the recovery vision and implemented prior to the emergence of the recovery framework. This means that focus has mostly been on objective indicators of recovery and it is possible that some evidence based interventions are less effective if evaluated against recovery vision criteria.

Whenever possible, this handbook will alert you as to the state of the evidence with respect to the above issues. However, practitioners must be wary of excessive reliance on textbooks or published treatment guidelines. The evidence is constantly changing and being an evidence-based practitioner implies a commitment to remaining alert to developing the evidence base rather than assuming a static evidence base.

Conclusion

This chapter has introduced some of the core concepts that inform the approach taken throughout this handbook. These concepts are explored in relation to psychosocial rehabilitation whereby a recovery orientation, a biopsychosocial approach and evidence based practice constitute a values framework. We have briefly examined some of the terminology that is currently used in mental health service provision. The terms client and practitioner are preferred in the context of this handbook.

References

Anthony, W. (1993). Recovery from mental illness: The guiding vision of the mental health service system in the 1990s. *Psychosocial Rehabilitation Journal, 16*, 15–16.

Anthony, W., Rogers, E., & Farkas, M. (2003). Research on evidence-based practices: Future directions in an era of recovery. *Community Mental Health Journal, 39*, 101–114.

Chwalisz, K. (2003). Evidence-based practice: A framework for twenty-first century scientist-practitioner training. *The Counselling Psychologist, 31*, 497–528.

Cnaan, R., Blankertz, L., Messinger, K.W., & Gardner, J. (1988). Psychosocial rehabilitation: Toward a definition. *Journal of Psychosocial Rehabilitation, 11*, 61–77.

Cnaan, R., Blankertz, L., Messinger, K.W., & Gardner, J. (1990). Experts' assessment of psychosocial rehabilitation principles. *Psychosocial Rehabilitation Journal, 13*, 59–73.

Corrigan, P.W. (2003). Towards an integrated, structural model of psychiatric rehabilitation. *Psychiatric Rehabilitation Journal*, 26, 346–358.

Davidson, K.W., Goldstein, M., Kaplan, R.M., Kaufmann, P.G., Knatterud, G.L., Orleans, C.T., Spring, B., Trudeau, K.J., & Whitlock, E.P. (2003). Evidence-based behavioral medicine: What is it and how do we achieve it? *Annals of Behavioral Medicine*, 26, 161–171.

Davidson. L., & Strauss, J.S. (1992). Sense of self in recovery from severe mental illness. *British Journal of Medical Psychology*, 65, 31–45.

Deegan, G. (2003). Discovering recovery. *Psychiatric Rehabilitation Journal*, 26, 368–376.

DeSisto, M., Harding, C., McCormick, R., Ashikaga, T., & Brooks, G. (1995a). The Maine and Vermont three-decade studies of serious mental illness I. Matched comparison of cross-sectional outcome. *British Journal of Psychiatry*, 167, 331–338.

DeSisto, M., Harding, C., McCormick, R., Ashikaga, T., & Brooks, G. (1995b). The Maine and Vermont three-decade studies of serious mental illness II. Longitudinal course comparisons. *British Journal of Psychiatry*, 167, 338–342.

Dixon, L., & Goldman, H. (2004). Forty years of progress in community mental health: The role of evidence-based practices. *Administration and Policy in Mental Health*, 31, 381–392.

Drake, R., Goldman, H., Leff, H., Lehman, A., Dixon, L., Mueser, K., & Torrey, W. (2001). Implementing evidence-based practices in routine mental health service settings. *Psychiatric Services*, 52, 179–182.

Drake, R.E., Rosenberg, S.D., Teague, G.B., Bartels, S.J., & Torrey, W.C. (2003). Fundamental principles of evidence-based medicine applied to mental health care. *Psychiatric Clinics of North America. Special Evidence-based Practices in Mental Health Care*, 26, 811–820.

Engel, G.L. (1980). The clinical application of the biopsychosocial model. *American Journal of Psychiatry*, 137, 535–544.

Essock, S., Goldman, H., Van Tosh, L., Anthony, W., Appell, C., Bond, G., Dixon, L., Dunakin, L., Ganju, V., Gorman, P., Ralph, R., Rapp, S., Teague, G., & Drake, R. (2003) Evidence-based practices: setting the context and responding to concerns. *Psychiatric Clinics of North America*, 26, 919–938.

Freedman, A.M. (1995). The biopsychosocial paradigm and the future of psychiatry. *Comprehensive Psychiatry*, 36, 397–406.

Frese, F., Stanley, J., Kress, K., & Vogel-Scibilia, S. (2001). Integrating evidence-based practices and the recovery model. *Psychiatric Services*, 52, 1462–1468.

Harding, C., Brooks, G., Ashikaga, T., Strauss, J., & Brier, A. (1987). The Vermont longitudinal study of persons with severe mental illness, I. Methodology, study sample, and overall status 32 years later. *American Journal of Psychiatry*, 144, 718–726.

Harrison, G., Hopper, K., Craig, T., Laska, E., Siegel, C., Wanderling, J., Dube, K.C., Ganev, K., Giel, R., an der Heiden, W., Holmberg, S.K., Janca, A., Lee, P.W., Leon, C.A., Malhotra, S., Marsella, A.J., Nakane, Y., Sartorius, N., Shen, Y., Skoda, C., Thara, R., Tsirkin, S.J., Varma, V.K., Walsh, D., & Wiersma, D. (2001). Recovery from psychotic illness: A 15- and 25-year international follow-up study. *British Journal of Psychiatry*, 178, 506–517.

Liberati, A., & Vineis, P. (2004). Introduction to the symposium: What evidence based medicine is and what it is not. *Journal of Medical Ethics*, 30, 120–121.

Liberman, R.P., Hilty, D.M., Drake, R.E., & Tsang, H.W. (2001). Requirements for multidisciplinary teamwork in psychiatric rehabilitation. *Psychiatric Services*, 52, 1331–1342.

Lloyd, C., King, R., Bassett, H., Sandland, S., & Savige, G. (2001). Patient, client or consumer? A survey of preferred terms. *Australasian Psychiatry*, 321–324.

Lloyd, C., Bassett, H., & King, R. (2004). Occupational therapy and evidence-based practice in mental health. *British Journal of Occupational Therapy*, 67, 83–88.

McGuire-Snieckus, R., McCabe, R., & Priebe, S. (2003). Patient, client or service user? A survey of patient preferences of dress and address of six mental health professions. *Psychiatric Bulletin*, 27, 305–308.

Pilgrim, D. (2002). The biopsychosocial model in Anglo-American psychiatry: Past, present and future? *Journal of Mental Health*, 11, 585–594.

Resnick, S., Rosenheck, & Lehman, A. (2004). An exploratory analysis of correlates of recovery. *Psychiatric Services*, 55, 540–547.

Sackett, D.L., Rosenberg, W.M.C., Muir-Gray, J.A., Haynes, R.B., & Richardson, W.S. (1996). Evidence-based medicine: What it is and what it isn't. *British Medical Journal*, 312, 71–72.

Schiff, A. (2004). Recovery and mental illness: Analysis and personal reflections. *Psychiatric Rehabilitation Journal*, 27, 212–218.

Tanenbaum, S. (2003). Evidence-based practice in mental health: Practical weaknesses meet political strengths. *Journal of Evaluation in Clinical Practice*, 9, 287–301.

Trinder, L. (Ed.) with Reynolds S. (2000). *Evidence-based practice: A critical appraisal*. Oxford: Blackwell Science.

Turner-Crowson, J., & Wallcraft, J. (2002). The recovery vision for mental health services and research: A British perspective. *Psychiatric Rehabilitation Journal*, 25, 245–254.

Chapter 2

MAJOR MENTAL ILLNESS AND ITS IMPACT

Tom Meehan

Overview of chapter

This chapter reviews the major mental health conditions and discusses the disability associated with such conditions. Consideration is given to diagnostic systems, especially ICD-10 and characteristics of schizophrenia and severe affective disorder are identified. Factors that impact on recovery are examined and a case for the provision of rehabilitation programmes for people with severe disability is established. The focus is on severe mental illness (schizophrenia and more severe forms of mood disorder). These conditions often compromise people's ability to live independent and productive lives and account for the bulk of people who need psychosocial rehabilitation interventions.

The burden of mental illness

Although mental illness is responsible for little more than one percent of deaths, it accounts for almost 11% of disease burden worldwide. Traditional approaches to the assessment of the disease burden used mortality (i.e. years lost through premature death) as the primary method of calculation. However, more recent approaches recognise the impact of disability associated with a given disease (i.e. years lived with a disability) and this is now considered in the assessment of burden. Together these two elements of burden are termed 'Disability Adjusted Life Years Lost' or DALYs (Murray & Lopes, 1996). Thus, one DALY represents one lost year of healthy life. Once the mortality and disability aspects of illness are combined into a single score, the magnitude of the burden associated with mental disorders becomes apparent. Five of the ten leading causes of disability worldwide in 2000 were psychiatric conditions: unipolar depression, alcohol use, bipolar affective disorder, schizophrenia and obsessive–compulsive disorder (World Health Organization, 2002). By itself, unipolar depression was responsible for one in every ten years of life lived with a disability worldwide. Murray & Lopes (1996) suggest that by 2020, depression will follow ischaemic heart disease as the second greatest cause of disease burden. The relatively high burden associated with depression stems from a combination of its high prevalence, high impact on functioning, and early age of onset (Ustun et al., 2004).

Treatment environment and service utilisation

Up to the early 1950s, mental health care was carried out primarily in large institutions. These institutions were usually located on the edges of urban areas or out of public view in the country. Admission to the 'asylum' generally resulted in a life sentence, with little or no prospect of discharge. Although the institutions claimed total responsibility for the lives of those admitted, they provided little by way of therapy or rehabilitation. The majority of state institutions lacked medical supervision and provided nothing more than custodial care for the insane.

By the late 1950s, powerful social, medical, legal and economic factors turned the tide away from care in institutions to care in the community. It was postulated that community treatment would promote independence and result in secondary gains such as reintegration into a daily routine, preservation of the family unit and minimal disruptions to employment (Durham, 1989). In Australia, the number of long-stay beds at stand-alone hospitals decreased from 300 per 100 000 inhabitants in 1960 to 40 per 100 000 in 1990 (Whiteford, 1994). This decline in bed numbers has continued and a recent estimate suggests that there are now approximately 15 beds per 100 000 located in stand-alone psychiatric hospitals (Department of Health and Aging, 2003).

Although psychiatric hospitals were significantly reduced in size, the financial resources required to maintain them continued to escalate. Tension developed between psychiatric hospitals and the 'new' community services which competed for limited resources. Moreover, people with serious mental illness, particularly those with schizophrenia, showed little interest in keeping appointments and were frequently lost to the system. Large numbers of mentally ill people received no treatment and among those who did, the treatment they received was frequently inappropriate or inadequate (Kessler et al., 2005a).

It was recognised that improving outcomes for people with mental illness required more than the provision of mental health services (Whiteford, 1994). Effective and cooperative links between mental health, primary health care, e.g. general practitioners (GPs), and non-health sectors (such as housing, disability services, vocational and rehabilitation services, etc.), were seen as crucial. A recent review of service delivery in Australia highlighted the increasing role of GPs in the treatment of mental health conditions (Australian Institute of Health and Welfare, 2005). Of those presenting to GPs with mental health problems, affective disorders were the most frequently treated condition (Table 2.1). As expected, schizophrenia was the most common condition treated by community mental health services. Taken together, these two disorders account for approximately 40% of all mental health conditions treated by GPs and 70% of those treated by community mental health services.

Table 2.1 Mental health related problems managed by general practitioners and community based mental health services in Australia (2003–2004)

Disorder	General practice (%)	Community mental health services (%)
Mood (affective) disorders	33	24
Schizophrenia and related psychotic disorders	6	46
Neurotic, stress related somatoform disorders	23	9
Disorders due to psychoactive substance use	10	3
Behavioural syndromes associated with physiological disturbances/physical factors	16	1
Other conditions	12	17

Australian Institute of Health and Welfare, 2005.

Although schizophrenia has a lower prevalence than most other mental health conditions (less than 1% of the population), people with schizophrenia utilise approximately 40% of all mental health services. In contrast, major depressive disorder with a prevalence rate of around 6% accounts for 30% of service utilisation (Australian Institute of Health and Welfare, 2005).

Classification of mental illness

Mental illness and mental disorder are terms commonly used to describe conditions that interfere with thought, emotion and/or behaviour. Mental illness is a general term used to describe a broad range of mental health problems including mental disorders. Mental disorder implies that a clinically recognisable set of symptoms and behaviours is present. Mental illness can also be classified as 'psychotic' or 'non-psychotic'. People experiencing a psychotic (major) illness lose contact with reality and symptoms such as hallucinations and delusions are accepted as being real (e.g. the schizophrenias, major depression, bipolar disorder). Non-psychotic conditions on the other hand are less severe in the sense that the sufferer experiences less distortion of reality – hallucinations and delusions are absent. Anxiety states and obsessive–compulsive disorder (OCD) are examples of neurotic/non-psychotic conditions.

Other ways of classifying mental health problems employ internationally recognised classification systems such as the Diagnostic and Statistical Manual (DSM) of the American Psychiatric Association (APA, 1994) or the International Classification of Diseases (ICD) promoted by the World Health Organization (1992). ICD is currently used in approximately 100 countries around the world, and by the World Health Organization, which compiles international statistics on mortality and morbidity. While DSM continues to be the primary classification and diagnostic tool for psychiatric conditions in North America, ICD has become the coding system of choice in the UK (Hart, 2004) and more recently in Australia (Janca et al., 2001).

Symptoms and consequential disability in severe and chronic forms of mental illness

The symptoms of most mental disorders are clearly described in medical and nursing texts and therefore will not be discussed in detail here. In this text we are concerned with severe disorders that produce major and chronic functional impairment requiring psychosocial rehabilitation. Thus, a brief overview of the schizophrenias and the mood disorders will be provided to facilitate understanding of symptom patterns and their impact on functioning.

Schizophrenia and related disorders

Schizophrenia is the term frequently used to describe a range of related disorders with overlapping symptoms (e.g. schizophreniform disorder, schizoaffective disorder). The original name for the illness, 'dementia praecox', arose from the progressive deterioration in cognitive functioning (i.e. dementia) that accompanied the illness. The 'schism' between what is reality in one's outer world and what is reality in one's inner world gave rise to the term schizophrenia ('split mind'). Schizophrenia has a number of subtypes, which are diagnosed on the basis of the most prominent symptoms present at the time of assessment.

Three phases of the illness have been identified, which include prodrome, active phase and residual phase. The *prodrome* is a period during which some signs and symptoms are evident but not of the intensity to warrant a diagnosis. The prodrome may be brief, with acute symptoms developing over weeks, or insidious, where symptoms develop over months or years (protracted prodrome). In 75% of cases, first admission is preceded by a prodromal phase of around five years with a psychotic 'prophase' of approximately one year (Hafner & der Heiden, 1997). The prodrome is followed by *active phase* symptoms, which are dominated by delusions, hallucinations, disorganised speech, bizarre behaviour and blunted affect. Once the active phase settles, the illness enters the *residual phase*. The features of this phase include social and occupational impairments, and abnormalities of cognition, emotion and communication. Rehabilitation efforts are usually introduced in the residual phase to offset the disability associated with the illness.

It is suggested that most of the impairment found in individuals with psychotic disorders results from alterations in neural functioning during prodrome (Larsen & Opsjordsmoen, 1996). This has shifted the focus of treatment to early identification and treatment of symptoms in people presenting with psychosis, especially first episode psychosis (McGorry et al., 2000). Untreated psychosis appears to have a noxious effect on the brain, leading to deterioration in cognition and social functioning over time (Addington et al., 2004).

Mood disorders

Depending on inclusion criteria, it is estimated that at least one in every ten individuals will suffer from depression during their lifetime (Kessler et al., 2005b). Like schizophrenia, depression is a general term used to describe a collection of conditions related to mood or affect (i.e. affective disorders). Major depression and bipolar affective disorder are two of the more serious conditions in this group.

Major depression

The lifetime prevalence of major (unipolar) depression is around 20% for women and 10% for men (Waraich et al., 2004). The gender difference is consistent across cultures and across countries. It is estimated that up to 60% of people will experience more than one episode and up to 20% of people will continue to be depressed 12 months post-diagnosis (Sargeant et al., 1990). Major depression among adolescents is frequently associated with antisocial behaviour and substance abuse, which makes diagnosis difficult. Anxiety is also found in about 70% of people with depression and is one of the most common psychiatric conditions (Goldberg, 1998). This is in keeping with the early theory put forward by Seligman (1973) which suggested that anxiety is the initial response to a stressful situation. This is slowly replaced by depression in people who feel unable to control the situation.

The essential features of major depression include a feeling of being down or sad, loss of pleasure or interest in activities, loss of energy, feelings of worthlessness or guilt, inability to concentrate, changes in appetite and weight loss/gain. These symptoms usually impact on the individuals' social and occupational functioning (Goldberg, 1998). In severe cases, psychotic symptoms such as hypochondriacal delusions are usually present, e.g. individuals may complain of having no intestines and therefore are unable to eat food. The most serious consequence of depression is suicide and about 15% of people with major depression will commit suicide (Patton et al., 1997). Depression and less severe 'dysthamia' are associated with increased utilisation of services and higher social morbidity.

Bipolar disorder

Bipolar disorder is the term now used for what used to be called manic depressive psychosis. People with this form of depression alternate between severe depression (described above) and excitement/elation, hence the term 'bipolar'. Normal mood is experienced in the period between episodes. Mania usually occurs prior to age 40 years and rarely after this. Onset is usually sudden and in the absence of treatment, symptoms usually persist for up to 6 months. During episodes of mania, thought processes are usually incoherent and the person may experience delusions, usually of the grandiose type. There is a decreased need for sleep, and pressure of speech, flight of ideas (moving quickly from one idea to another) may also be present. Excessive involvement in pleasurable activities with negative consequences is a major problem. Disinhibited behaviour and impaired judgement may result in unsound financial decisions, legal problems and damaged reputations. People with bipolar disorder are less likely to work (Zwerling et al., 2002) and tend to be over-represented in the lowest income strata (Kessler et al., 1997). A recent Australian study found that people with bipolar disorder were more disabled than subjects with major depression in terms of days out of role (Mitchell et al., 2004). In hypomania, a less severe form of mania, thought processes remain intact and major symptoms such as delusions are not present. Many people enjoy this hypomanic state as they tend to be more productive and may be reluctant to seek/adhere to treatment for this reason.

Impact of symptoms on client functioning

The symptoms of most psychiatric conditions cause a degree of distress but the impact is circumscribed and the person suffering the disorder leads a 'normal' life. This is true of many of the common anxiety disorders such as obsessive–compulsive disorder (OCD) and panic disorder. However, the symptoms of conditions such as schizophrenia and the major mood disorders can have a significant impact on individual functioning. The symptoms of these conditions are frequently unrelenting, may be extremely distressing, and may impair basic cognitive functions such as attention and concentration.

In conditions such as schizophrenia, symptoms are frequently classified as either 'positive' or 'negative'. This is an important dichotomy for treatment staff. The positive symptoms (hallucinations, delusions and disorders of thought) are usually the focus of clinical intervention and to a large extent, respond to antipsychotic medications. Negative symptoms (lack of motivation, blunted emotions, loss of drive, social withdrawal and inattention) are major determinants of disability (Carpenter, 1996) but unlike positive symptoms, they respond poorly to conventional antipsychotic medications. Indeed, it has been suggested that neuroleptic medications may exacerbate negative symptoms and give rise to the so called 'neuroleptic induced deficit syndrome' (NIDS), which includes apathy, slowing of thought processes and diminished capacity to experience pleasure. Emerging evidence suggests that atypical antipsychotics may be more effective in combating negative symptoms (Velligan et al., 2003).

Secondary disability and handicap

Primary psychopathology associated with psychotic conditions such as schizophrenia and bipolar disorder tends to plateau and even cease following the active phase of the illness. However, the 'secondary' effects (e.g. isolation, self-neglect, withdrawal, etc.) continue to accumulate, and these tend to become the focus of rehabilitation efforts. Extrapyramidal side effects are a common cause of secondary negative symptoms. Individuals experiencing akinesia, for example, may present with decreased speech and decreased motivation. Positive symptoms (e.g. paranoid ideas about being watched) can also lead to secondary symptoms such as isolation. Some of the more prominent secondary symptoms are summarised in Table 2.2.

Although all of the secondary symptoms listed above are likely to impact on recovery, factors such as stigma, residual symptoms, self-neglect and loss of social supports are likely to present major barriers to recovery.

Table 2.2 Secondary symptoms and impact on client

Secondary symptom	Impact on client
Stigma	Isolation, loneliness, low self-esteem
Residual positive symptoms	Isolation, anxiety, distress
Self-neglect	Unable to care for oneself
Lack of insight	Loss of skills, withdrawal, neglect
Socialisation into patient role	Loss of hope, withdrawal
Inability to make and keep friends	Isolation, loneliness
Side effects of medications	Blunting of emotions

Stigma

Despite efforts to combat stigma, the negative effects of stigma continue to have a major impact on the individual and their recovery. Link and Phelan (2001) identified a number of mechanisms through which this can occur:

- Once identified as being mentally ill, society may continue to reject the person even when the symptoms have subsided.
- The trauma associated with past rejection may continue to impact on the present functioning of the individual.
- While the symptoms of the illness may have subsided, the individual may go on to internalise the rejection. The negative impact of this can continue even in the absence of the original rejection.

Residual symptoms

Although many of the symptoms of the illness respond to clinical interventions such as medications and, in the case of depression and anxiety, psychological treatments, some individuals continue to experience persistent symptoms. These uncontrolled symptoms, combined with the side effects of the medications, reinforce the perception that people with mental illness are different. Symptoms such as difficulty in thinking and delayed responding may be interpreted as dullness or low intelligence, and the symptoms of depression as laziness. While more recent medications tend to have a lower side effect profile (see Chapter 7), any visible indication of illness can hinder community acceptance and impede recovery.

Self-neglect

Although most clinicians can recognise and describe the features of an individual who self-neglects, the concept of self-neglect remains poorly understood among health professionals. Lauder and colleagues (2002) define self-neglect as 'the failure to engage in those self-care actions necessary to maintain a socially acceptable standard of personal and household hygiene' (p. 331). While there is insufficient evidence to support the existence of a discrete self-neglect syndrome, self-neglecting behaviour appears to be associated with mental illness. Cooney and Hamid (1995) suggest that up to 50% of all severe self-neglect cases have a mental illness.

The treatment of self-neglect poses a major challenge for the client and carers. Self-neglect can range from mild problems with hygiene to severe neglect that places the individual at risk of disease and even death. In cases of severe neglect, the need for intervention is rarely questioned. In less severe cases the need for intervention is widely debated among clinical staff and carers. There are those who believe that people with mental illness have rights and the freedom to live as they choose, even if this involves elements of self-neglect. There are also those who hold the view that self-neglect is a manifestation of deviant behaviour and that statutory control mechanisms are justified to compel unwilling individuals to acceptable community norms. Clearly, intervention is required when the behaviour places the client at risk. As noted by Lauder (1999), the level and type of intervention from staff will depend on whether the individual 'cannot clean, will not clean, finds it difficult to clean or does not see the need for cleaning'.

Inability to make/keep friends – social isolation

The relationship between having a mental illness and social isolation is well established. Many people who develop psychotic disorders such as schizophrenia exhibit subtle abnormalities in attention and cognitive functioning in early childhood (Cornblatt & Keilp, 1994). These abnormalities tend to persist into adulthood and impact on the individual's ability to develop social roles. Thus, social isolation is usually well established prior to the onset of the illness. This raises the question of whether social isolation is a cause or a consequence of mental illness. The positive symptoms of schizophrenia, for example, can interfere with the individual's ability to cope with the demands of interpersonal interaction and the decoding of social communication. Consequently, many people with mental illness living in the community continue to live in an isolated 'mental health world' where the only people that visit them are paid to do so (i.e. mental health staff).

Recovery patterns

Views on the outcomes of mental disorders have changed radically in recent years. Findings from a number of studies over the past 40 years indicate that up to 70% of people demonstrate significant improvement in their condition (Table 2.3). Studies in both the United States and Europe involving more than 1300 people with schizophrenia found that 46% to 68% of people either improved or recovered significantly over the long term (Harding et al., 1992). Hegarty and colleagues (1994) conducted a meta-analysis of the available outcome studies and concluded that 50% of people with schizophrenia will improve and up to 20% will recover.

Taken together, these studies suggest that symptoms and functioning can improve even in individuals discharged from the 'back-wards' of psychiatric institutions (Davidson & McGlasham, 1997). These findings challenge the belief that

Table 2.3 Outcome of follow-up studies of people with schizophrenia

Authors	Country	Year published	No. of patients in study	Follow-up period (years)	Recovered or improved significantly (%)
Tsuang et al.	USA	1979	186	35	46
Harding et al.	USA	1987	269	32	68
DeSisto et al.	USA	1995	99	35	49
Mason et al.	UK	1996	58	13	44

conditions such as schizophrenia follow a course of progressive deterioration. However, despite these positive indications, a degree of caution is required when considering the outcomes of conditions such as schizophrenia. Geddes and colleagues (2000) found that despite the introduction of atypical antipsychotics, progress in the treatment of conditions such as schizophrenia is modest at best. A recent review found that less than 15% of people met criteria for 'recovery' at 5 years after a first episode of psychosis (Robinson et al., 2004).

The variation in the proportion of clients rated as being improved or recovered is likely to stem from the way in which recovery is defined. Some studies used standardised rating scales to assess outcomes, while others employed more subjective assessments such as 'improved' or 'recovered'. Differences in the level of treatment/ rehabilitation provided during the study period may also influence outcomes. For example, the clients followed up by Harding et al. (1987) were receiving intensive rehabilitation, which may have contributed to the better outcome reported.

In contrast to schizophrenia, which is likely to show some improvement over time, the course of recurrent mood disorders tends to have two outcomes: full recovery with no further episodes (approximately 50% of cases) or episodic recurrence with a trend towards increasing frequency of episodes with the passage of time (Kessing et al., 2004). Most people manage ordinary lives that are interrupted from time to time by periods of incapacity. However, this does not imply that the impact of the illness is less severe. The emerging view from follow-up studies is that individuals with acute bipolar disorder frequently respond slowly to modern treatments and continue to experience high levels of symptoms and disability. In people with bipolar disorder, depression appears to be strongly associated with ongoing disability and excess mortality through suicide (Thase & Sachs, 2000). While the course of affective disorders can be improved through the use of medication, non-compliance with treatment is a common problem, particularly in those with bipolar disorder.

Factors associated with better outcomes

As outlined previously, there is growing evidence to support a more optimistic outcome for people with serious mental illness. However, there is considerable variation in outcome – even among individuals who present with the same clinical profile.

Table 2.4 Factors associated with good prognosis

Absence of family history of mental illness
A normal personality/functioning prior to the onset of illness
Acute onset with rapid recovery
Period between onset of symptoms and treatment less than 6 months
Presence of participating stressors
Presence of affective symptoms
Good response to treatment/medications
Onset of first episode after age 30
Absence of coexisting conditions such as substance abuse
Cultural variation – living in a developing country
Female gender

Notwithstanding this, a number of factors associated with better outcomes for people with psychotic conditions have been isolated from the literature and are summarised in Table 2.4.

Absence of family history of mental illness

Recent twin studies confirm that psychotic conditions such as bipolar disorder and schizophrenia have a high genetic loading. For example, 12% of those born to one parent and 46% born to both parents with schizophrenia go on to develop the illness (Jones & Cannon, 1998). Similarly, up to 20% of relatives of people with depressive disorder are likely to have a depressive or bipolar disorder (Kelsoe, 1999). Indeed, there is evidence to suggest that the degree of psychotic symptoms experienced in bipolar disorder is consistent in families. Schurhoff and colleagues (2003) demonstrated an equal proneness to delusions in first-degree relatives of people with schizophrenia and bipolar depression. This seems to suggest that people with schizophrenia or bipolar disorder are likely to have similar psychotic features and to the same severity as other first-degree relatives with the illness.

Intact personality prior to onset of illness

Teachers and family members frequently report abnormal behaviour and symptom manifestations in people with psychosis well before the onset of overt positive symptoms. These may present as diminished social drive, decreased emotional response, suspicion, withdrawal, short attention span, delayed developmental milestones and poor motor coordination (McGorry et al., 2000). Cognitive impairment and poor scholastic development have also been found to be associated with poor prognosis. Social behaviour disturbances such as lack of responsiveness and emotional expression have been identified in children who later go on to develop schizophrenia (Buchanan & Carpenter, 2005). It has also been demonstrated that people with schizophrenia tend to be attracted to low status jobs and have rapid job turnover prior to first admission (Hafner & der Heiden, 1997).

Age of onset

Early onset psychosis (before age 21 years) appears to be related to more severe symptoms and an overall poorer outcome (Hafner & der Heiden, 1997). There are gender differences in presentation in that males with late onset (40+ years) tend to experience milder symptomatology and have better outcomes than males with early onset. The opposite is true for females, who appear to have more severe problems when diagnosed later in life. It has been suggested that the female hormone, oestrogen, may be protective in early onset cases (Seeman & Lang, 1990). Closer to menopause the diminishing effects of the hormone results in more severe symptoms. Although women develop schizophrenia on average 3–4 years later than men, patients of either gender with a high genetic load tend to develop the illness at a much younger age.

Response to treatment

While treatment often fails to bring about complete and permanent remission, it can have substantial positive impact on the course of major disorders such as schizophrenia and depression. Hogarty (1993) analysed the reports from a number of studies and noted that medication on its own was able to reduce the rate of relapse in people with schizophrenia from 67% to 39%. Medications reduce symptoms, increase the likelihood of clinical stability and reduce the risk of relapse. Prognosis has been found to be better for those with good initial response to medication (Breier et al., 1991). Medications appear to have greater efficacy in patients experiencing first episode psychosis than during subsequent episodes (Kane, 1989). Moreover, lower doses of antipsychotic medications are required to achieve the desired effect during first episode. While medication is an important factor in recovery, poor medication compliance among people with psychotic disorders is common and tends to hamper its effectiveness and lead to poorer outcomes.

Onset of symptoms

The onset of florid psychotic symptoms is typically abrupt (i.e. with a brief prodrome) in about 50% of people and insidious (protracted prodrome) in the remainder. An insidious onset is characterised by gradual increase and symptoms that are less florid. While there may be suspicions that a disorder such as schizophrenia is present, it may be very difficult in practice to elicit sufficient symptoms to warrant a formal diagnosis. Individuals with insidious type onset are likely to have poor long-term prognosis (Harding, 1988).

Short duration of untreated psychosis

Recent research suggests that the prognosis of psychotic disorders may be related to 'duration of untreated psychosis' (DUP), in that long DUP has been associated with higher levels of positive symptoms and poor social functioning (Addington et al., 2004; McGorry et al., 2000). Carpenter and Strauss (1991) suggest that psychopathology tends to be worse early in the illness and then stabilises with late course improvement rather than progressive deterioration. This emerging research is responsible for the emphasis on early detection and intervention. While it is important to treat symptoms early, there is, as yet, little evidence that early intervention programmes will improve outcomes (Craig et al., 2000). Indeed, it is often difficult to recognise early prodromal symptoms. The social withdrawal and reluctance to disclose internal conflicts, which accompany the early stages of psychosis, make diagnosis difficult (Peralta et al., 2005). It also raises issues for early intervention and whether one should commence treatment for psychotic conditions (i.e. powerful antipsychotic medications) in the absence of a definitive diagnosis. These are matters of current debate and considerable practical importance and are examined in more detail in Chapter 13.

Substance abuse

People with mental illness may turn to illicit drugs to cope with the emotional pain and symptoms associated with their illness. Substance abuse is now the most predictive factor for relapse in schizophrenia (Linzen et al., 1994). Cannabis remains one of the most commonly abused drugs due to its availability and the relatively low cost. Consumed on its own, or in combination with alcohol (which is frequently the case), cannabis use in people with psychotic disorders significantly increases relapse rates and the need for hospitalisation (Linzen et al., 1994). Substance abuse is most common among individuals with schizophrenia who are male, young and who have depressive symptoms (Rakfeldt & McGlashan, 1996). Indeed, substance abuse is so common in conditions such as schizophrenia that it is now considered a normal part of the illness (Drake et al., 2004). The presence of dual diagnosis usually complicates attempts to treat the initial condition. Neither mental health services nor substance abuse services provide the comprehensive treatment required by these individuals (see Chapter 12).

Cultural variation

One of the most unexpected findings from studies conducted in the 1970s was that individuals living in developing countries had better outcomes than their colleagues in the developed world. In a study of people with schizophrenia in Sri Lanka, Waxler (1979) speculated that factors such as more tolerant and supportive family networks, choice between western and native treatment options and externalisation of causative factors (less stigma) may contribute to better outcomes. Treatment systems in these developing countries promote rapid return to normality so that individuals can become self-sustaining. This seems to suggest that social and cultural factors have a greater impact on the course of schizophrenia than disease factors.

Gender

There is evidence that being female is associated with better recovery from schizophrenia (Seeman & Lang, 1990). The gender difference is evident in the first years of treatment and persists through the entire period of the illness (Moriarty et al., 2001). Males have earlier onset, more negative symptoms and poorer social functioning (Usall et al., 2002). Possible reasons for the better prognosis among females may include a better response to antipsychotic medication, in that oestrogen may alter the action of dopamine. Moreover, it is likely that the 'deficit' form of schizophrenia (the subtype that results in greater disability) is predominantly a male disease (Buchanan & Carpenter, 2005).

Conclusions

A number of conclusions can be drawn from this review of major mental health conditions:

- Mental illness has a major impact not only on the individual who is directly affected, but on the whole community through Disability Life Years Lost.
- It is clear that the course of severe disorders such as schizophrenia is not straightforward and there is considerable variation in outcomes, even among people with the same diagnosis.
- While the majority of people with serious mental illness can achieve improvement in their condition, complete recovery is difficult to achieve. However, the long-term picture for recovery from schizophrenia is more positive than commonly thought.
- Symptoms are only part of the problem – secondary disabilities and handicaps can have a major impact on recovery.
- Many people will be challenged by relapse and ongoing exacerbations of their condition and will experience both negative and positive outcomes.
- There needs to be a separation of positive and negative symptoms – treating positive symptoms does not imply that negative symptoms will dissipate. Thus, a combination of pharmacological and psychosocial interventions is required.
- Early identification and treatment of mental health conditions offer the best prospects of recovery.
- Substance use is a major factor in relapse.
- Identifying how major mental health conditions produce impairment and building strategies to offset this may offer the best prospects for the immediate future.

References

Addington J, Van Mastrigt, Addington D. (2004). Duration of untreated psychosis: impact on 2-year outcome. *Psychological Medicine, 34*, 277–284.

American Psychiatric Association. (1994). *Diagnostic and statistical manual of mental disorders* (4th ed.). Washington, DC: American Psychiatric Association.

Australian Institute of Health & Welfare (AIHW). (2005). *Mental health services in Australia 2002–2003.* Canberra: AIHW (Report No. 6).

Breier, M.D., Schreiber, J.L., Dyer, J., & Pickar, D., (1991). National Institute of Mental Health longitudinal study of chronic schizophrenia. *Archives of General Psychiatry, 48,* 239–246.

Buchanan, R., & Carpenter, W. (2005). Concept of schizophrenia. In: B. Sadock & V. Sadock (Eds.), *Kaplan and Sadock's comprehensive textbook of psychiatry* (pp. 1329–1344). Philadelphia: Lippincott Williams & Wilkins.

Carpenter, W. Jr. (1996). Maintenance therapy of persons with schizophrenia. *Journal of Clinical Psychiatry, 57,* (Suppl. 9), 10–18.

Carpenter, W.T., & Strauss, J.S. (1991). The prediction of outcome in schizophrenia, IV: Eleven-year follow-up of the Washington IPSS cohort. *Journal of Nervous Mental Disorder, 179,* 517–525.

Cooney, C., & Hamid, D. (1995). Review: Diogenes syndrome. *Age and Ageing, 24,* 451–453.

Cornblatt, B., & Keilp, J. (1994). Impaired attention, genetics and the pathophysiology of schizophrenia. *Schizophrenia Bulletin, 20,* 3–46.

Craig, T., Bromet, E., Fennig, S., Tanenberg-Karant, M., Lavelle, J., & Galambos, N. (2000). Is there an association between duration of untreated psychosis and 24-month clinical outcome in a first-admission series? *American Journal of Psychiatry, 157,* 60–66.

Davidson, L., & McGlasham, T. (1997). The varied outcomes of schizophrenia. *Canadian Journal of Psychiatry, 42,* 34–43.

Department of Health and Aging. (2003). *National mental health report. Summary of changes in Australia's mental health services under the national Mental Health Strategy 1993–2002.* Canberra: Commonwealth of Australia.

DeSisto, M., Hardong, C.M., McCormick, R., Ashinkaga, R., & Brooks, G. (1995). The Maine and Vermont three-decade studies of serious mental illness: Longitudinal course comparisons. *British Journal of Psychiatry, 167,* 338–342.

Drake, R., Mueser, K., Brunette, M., & McHugo, G. (2004). A review of treatments for people with severe mental illnesses and co-occurring substance use disorders. *Psychiatric Rehabilitation Journal, 27,* 360–374.

Durham, M. (1989). The impact of deinstitutionalization on the current treatment of the mentally ill. *International Journal of Law in Psychiatry, 12,* 117–131.

Geddes, J., Freemantle, N., Harrison, P., & Bebbington, P. (2000). Atypical antipsychotics in the treatment of schizophrenia: Systematic overview and meta-regression analysis. *British Medical Journal, 321,* 1371–1376.

Goldberg, R. (1998). *The care of the psychiatric patient.* St Louis: Mosby.

Hafner, H., & der Heiden, W. (1997) Epidemiology of schizophrenia. *The Canadian Journal of Psychiatry, 42,* 139–149.

Harding, C., Brooks, G., Ashikaga, T., Strauss, J., & Brier, A. (1987). The Vermont longitudinal study of persons with severe mental illness, I. Methodology, study sample, and overall status 32 years later. *American Journal of Psychiatry, 144,* 718–726.

Harding, C. (1988). Course types in schizophrenia: An analysis of European and American studies. *Schizophrenia Bulletin, 14,* 633–643.

Harding, C., Zubin, J., & Strauss, J. (1992). Chronicity in schizophrenia: Revisited. *British Journal of Psychiatry, 161,* (Suppl. 18), 27–37.

Hart, D. (2004). Common mental health problems. In S. Kirby, Hard, D., Cross, D., Mitchell, G. (Ed.), *Mental health nursing: competencies for practice* (pp. 79–106). Hampshire: Palgrave MacMillan.

Hegarty, J., Baldessarini, R., & Tohen, M. (1994). One hundred years of schizophrenia: A meta-analysis of the outcome literature. *American Journal of Psychiatry*, *151*, 1409–1416.

Hogarty, G. (1993). Prevention of relapse in chronic schizophrenic patients. *The Journal of Clinical Psychiatry*, *54*, (Suppl. 3), 18–23.

Janca, A., Ahern, K., & Rock, D. (2001). Introducing ICD-10 into psychiatric coding practice: A Western Australian experience. *Australian and New Zealand Journal of Public Health*, *25*, 376–377.

Jones, P., & Cannon, M. (1998). The new epidemiology of schizophrenia. *Psychiatric Clinics of North America*, *12*, 1–25.

Kane, J. (1989). The current status of neuroleptics. *Journal of Clinical Psychiatry*, *50*, 322–328.

Kelsoe, J. (1999). Mood disorders: Genetics. In B. Sadock & V. Sadock (Eds.), *Kaplan and Sadock's comprehensive textbook of psychiatry* (pp. 1582–1594). Philadelphia: Lippincott Williams & Wilkins.

Kessing, L., Hansen, M., & Anderson, P. (2004). Course of illness in depressive and bipolar disorders. Naturalistic study, 1994–1999. *British Journal of Psychiatry*, *185*, 372–377.

Kessler, R., Rubinow, D., Holmes, C., Abelson, J., & Zhao, S. (1997). The epidemiology of DSM-III-R bipolar I disorder in a general population survey. *Psychological Medicine*, *27*, 1079–1089.

Kessler, R., Delmer, O., Frank, R., Olfson, M., Pincus, H., Walters, E., Wang, P., Wells, K., & Zaslavsky, A. (2005a). Prevalence and treatment of mental disorders, 1990 to 2003. *New England Journal of Medicine*, *352*, 2515–2523.

Kessler, R., Chiu, W., Demler, O., & Walters, E. (2005b). Prevalence, severity, and comorbidity of 12-month DSM-IV disorders in the National Comorbidity Survey Replication. *Archives of General Psychiatry*, *62*, 617–627.

Larsen, T., & Opsjordsmoen, S. (1996). Early detection and treatment of schizophrenia: conceptual and ethical considerations. *Psychiatry*, *59*, 371–380.

Lauder, W. (1999). Constructions of self-neglect: a multiple case study design. *Nursing Inquiry*, *6*, 48–57.

Lauder, W., Anderson, I., & Barclay, A. (2002). Sociological and psychological theories of self-neglect. *Journal of Advanced Nursing*, *40*, 331–338.

Link, B., & Phelan, J. (2001). Conceptualizing stigma. *Annual Review of Sociology*, *27*, 363–385.

Linzen, D., Dingemans, P., & Lenior, M. (1994). Cannabis abuse and the course of recent-onset schizophrenic disorders. *Archives of General Psychiatry*, *51*, 273–279.

Mason, P., Harrison, G., Glazebrook, C., Croudace, T., & Medley, I. (1996). The course of schizophrenia over 13 years: A report from the international study on schizophrenia (ISoS) coordinated by the World Health Organization. *British Journal of Psychiatry*, *169*, 580–586.

McGorry, P., Krstev, H., & Harrigan, S. (2000). Early detection and treatment delay: implications for outcomes in early psychosis. *Current Opinion in Psychiatry*, *13*, 37–43.

Mitchell, P.B., Slade, T., & Andrews, G. (2004). Twelve-month prevalence and disability of DSM-IV bipolar disorder in an Australian general population survey. *Psychological Medicine*, *34*, 777–785.

Moriarty, P., Lieber, D., Bennett, A., White, L., Parrella, M., Harvey, P., & Davis, K. (2001). Gender differences in poor outcome patients with lifelong schizophrenia. *Schizophrenia Bulletin, 27*, 103–113.

Murray, C., & Lopes, A. (1996). *The global burden of disease (summary)*. Harvard: World Health Organization.

Patton, G., Harris, R., & Carlin, J. (1997). Adolescent suicide behaviour: A population based study of risk. *Psychological Medicine, 27*, 715–724.

Peralta, V., Cruesta, M., Martinez-Larrea, A., Serrano, J., & Langarica, M. (2005). Duration of untreated psychotic illness: The role of premorbid social support networks. *Social Psychiatry and Psychiatric Epidemiology, 40*, 345–349.

Rakfeldt, J., & McGlashan T. (1996). Onset, course, and outcome of schizophrenia. *Current Opinion in Psychiatry, 9*, 73–76.

Robinson, D., Woerner, M., McMeniman, M., Mendelowitz, A., & Bilder, R. (2004). Symptomatic and functional recovery from first episode of schizophrenia or schizoaffective disorder. *American Journal of Psychiatry, 161*, 473–479.

Sargeant, J., Bruce, M., Florio, L., & Weissman, M. (1990). Factors associated with 1-year outcome of major depression in the community. *Archives of General Psychiatry, 47*, 519–526.

Schurhoff, F., Szoke, A., Meary, A., Bellivier, F., Pauls, D., & Leboyer, M. (2003). Familial aggregation of delusional proneness in schizophrenia and bipolar pedigrees. *American Journal of Psychiatry, 160*, 1313–1319.

Seeman, M., & Lang, M. (1990). The role of oestrogens in schizophrenia: Gender differences. *Schizophrenia Bulletin, 16*, 185–194.

Seligman, M. (1973). Fall into hopelessness. *Psychology Today, 7*, 43–44.

Thase, M., & Sachs, G. (2000). Bipolar depression: Pharmacotherapy and related therapeutic strategies. *Biological Psychiatry, 48*, 558–572.

Tsuang, T., Woolson, R., Fleming, J. (1979). Long-term outcome of major psychoses. *Archives of General Psychiatry, 39*, 1295–1301.

Usall, J., Haro, J., Ochoa, S., Marquez, M., & Araya, S. (2002). Influence of gender on social outcome in schizophrenia. *Acta Psychiatrica Scandinavica, 106*, 337–342.

Ustun, T.B., Ayuso-Mateos, J.L., Chatterji, S., Mathers, C., & Murray, C.J.L. (2004). Global burden of depressive disorders in the year 2000. *British Journal of Psychiatry, 184*, 386–392.

Velligan, D., Prihoda, T., Sui, D., Ritch, J., Maples, N., & Miller, A. (2003). The effectiveness of quetiapine versus conventional antipsychotics in improving cognitive and functional outcomes in standard treatment. *Journal of Clinical Psychiatry, 64*, 524–531.

Waraich, P., Goldner, E., Somers, J., & Hsu, L. (2004). Prevalence and incidence studies of mood disorders: A systematic review of the literature. *Canadian Journal of Psychiatry, 49*, 124–138.

Waxler, N. (1979). 'Is outcome for schizophrenia better in non-industrial countries? The case of Sri Lanka'. *Journal of Nervous and Mental Disease, 3*, 144–158.

Whiteford, H. (1994). Intersectoral policy reform is critical to the National Mental Health Strategy. *Australian Journal of Public Health, 18*, 342–344.

World Health Organization. (1992). *ICD-10 classification of behavioural and mental disorders: clinical descriptions and diagnostic guidelines*. Geneva: WHO.

World Health Organization. (2002). *World Health Report 2002. Reducing the risks, promoting healthy life*. Geneva: WHO.

Zwerling, C., Whitten, P., Sprince, N., Davis, C., Wallace, R., Blanck, P., & Heeringa, S. (2002). Workforce participation by persons with disabilities: The National Health Interview Survey Disability Supplement, 1994 to 1995. *Journal of Occupational and Environmental Medicine, 44*, 358–364.

Chapter 3
LIVED EXPERIENCE PERSPECTIVES

Helen Glover

'My recovery did not come to me in a person, a drug or a programme. It came dressed in ordinariness. When I look back, it was the ordinary things that were significant; those relationships you formed, the ad hoc conversations you had, the meeting of people who influenced you by their challenges, courage and determination, and the everyday tasks you just had to do. I did not know this was my "recovery journey" – that language came to me much later. I did not have a thought-out plan of how to get better. I just kept on having a go and not accepting that this was all there was to life. I suppose somewhere deep within me I knew being mentally ill was not all of me – that it did not have to be permanent. I suppose this is what HOPE is.' (HG)

Overview of chapter

For people experiencing mental illness, recovery involves not only dealing with the challenges presented by the symptoms, but negotiating a service environment that often encourages passivity and struggling with a personal identity that is shaped by community perceptions and responses to mental illness. This chapter explores recovery from the perspective of the lived experience of people engaged in the work. It draws on the personal experience of the author and on personal accounts provided by people she has worked alongside. The narratives used in this chapter are either examples from her personal experience or stories told by people she has worked with. It also presents some of the philosophy and learned wisdom from the 'recovery' body of knowledge as informed by lived experience. The chapter is designed to assist rehabilitation practitioners and others to develop greater sensitivity to this lived experience so as to promote more collaborative and genuinely therapeutic relationships with clients engaged in the process of recovery.

Knowledge bases that inform 'recovery'

Within the field of recovery in mental health it is acknowledged that there are a number of knowledge bases that need to be considered to ensure the services are indeed delivered from a recovery orientation (Trainor et al., 2004). Traditionally within mental health care only professional knowledge has informed practice and service delivery, drawn from areas of medicine, psychology, social work, nursing, occupational therapy, and speech pathology.

Within a recovery oriented framework, additional knowledge needs to be utilised. The recovery body of knowledge is informed and influenced primarily by those that have struggled and triumphed over mental illness/distress. This 'lived experience/expert knowledge' has started to inform and challenge professional knowledge bases (Deegan, 1988; Faulkner & Thomas, 2002; Mental Health Foundation, 1997, 2000; Onken et al., 2002). One of the great risks to this lived experience informed knowledge base is that of professional colonisation. When people without a lived experience speak about recovery and recovery based practice in professional and academic forums there will always be a risk that the spirit and language of recovery will have been lost to the dominant professional paradigm. This key tension always needs to be considered when discussing recovery, and recovery based practice.

When the term 'lived experience' is used, it serves to acknowledge the whole experience of overcoming and coming through the experience of illness/distress, including the experience of external and internal stigma, numerous losses and the sense of disengagement and marginalisation. Having a 'lived experience/expertise' encompasses more than just experiencing a mental illness/distress; it implies that a person is able to draw on and make sense of their own experiences, and those of others, in order that they can be informative and helpful to a broader base. This knowledge base is neither new nor owned by any particular person/s. It is constantly being formed and informed by those that have gone before and those that still struggle with the experience of distress.

Both professional and lived experience bodies of knowledge equally inform recovery based knowledge. The ability to draw on both knowledge bases helps refine and deepen the quality of knowledge of what helps and what hinders individual recovery processes. Simultaneously drawing on both knowledge bases also creates the desired tensions within a recovery oriented environment and reduces the risks of professional colonisation. Environments need to be created that actively support an individual's recovery journey and do not stand in the way of that effort. Productive change for an individual or a system of care cannot occur without the creation of these tensions.

The professional knowledge has been dominant for many years and has been supported to create and sustain such dominance. The lived experience knowledge may not yet share the same rigour, yet it has an important role in validating the uniqueness and personal aspects of individual recovery narratives. Within a recovery oriented environment, one without the other remains incomplete. A synthesising and rebalancing of both knowledge bases will inform the development and sustenance of recovery oriented environments (Figure 3.1).

A summary of some of the main points of difference between the professional (clinical) and lived experience perspectives of recovery can be found in Table 3.1.

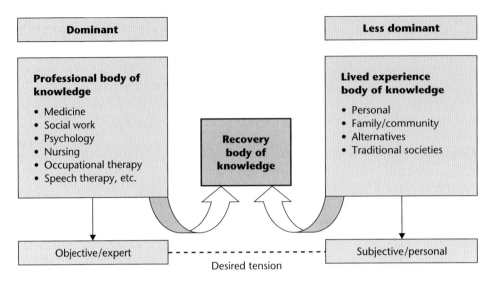

Figure 3.1 Recovery body of knowledge.

Lived experience construct of recovery

As indicated in Chapter 1, the word 'recovery' is possibly not the most useful term to capture what people with a lived experience understand. Traditionally, and especially within the medical field, the term recovery is usually linked with understanding of cure, with no longer having symptoms, and that people have returned to their previous level of functioning. The 'lived experience' understanding of recovery embraces a number of elements that extend the concept of recovery beyond cure and a person regaining premorbid functioning.

The challenge in quantifying and defining recovery from a 'lived experience' perspective is that any one definition cannot embrace the uniqueness and focus of each individual's recovery process. People who have recovered have talked about commonalities within the recovery journey. Recovery as understood from a 'lived experience' perspective highlights the differences from the traditional understanding of the word recovery. The discussion of recovery provided here is designed to elaborate and extend some of the recovery concepts introduced in Chapter 1. The *re* of recovery means to go back. This is not helpful to the understanding of 'recovery' from a lived experience perspective. Recovery from a lived experience perspective acknowledges a forward movement where the journey contributes positively to a person's sense of self and quality of life. It is not so much returning to what you had, but using the experiences and challenges that a mental illness invites, to continue forward in the recovery process.

Recovery is what people overcoming the experience of mental illness and its associated treatment do. Recovery acknowledges there is no set time or way to recover and it is usual that the most unlikely event will be a turning point in someone's life and not the planned treatment or intervention. Recovery happens in the ordinary

Table 3.1 Clinical versus lived experience understanding of the term recovery

Clinical understanding of the term recovery	Lived experience understanding of the term recovery
Recovery means returning to premorbid level of functioning	Recovery means a forward movement often thriving beyond premorbid functioning
External application of treatment is valued as central to the recovery process	Internal knowledge is named as valuable in the recovery process. Requires active involvement
Recovery primarily involves the effort of others	Recovery requires active involvement of the person
Recovery focuses on treatment and treatment programmes as to making the change in people	Recovery focuses on participating in the *ordinariness* of life and in meaningful relationships as contributing significantly to recovery
Letting go of roles and responsibilities may be promoted in recovery processes	Maintaining roles and responsibilities is an important consideration within recovery processes
Spirituality and creating meaning is not important in the recovery process	Developing meaning and purpose and utilising spirituality is seen as an important aspect in recovery
Recovery infers that a person *no longer experiences active symptoms*	Being 'in recovery' may mean *re-experiencing symptoms* from time to time yet in a way that does not impede a person's quality of life or sense of self
Crisis is seen as a *failure or relapse*	Crisis is seen as an *active recovery space* where a person can learn and thrive
Recovery is seen as an end point in the destination	Recovery acknowledges the importance of the process and that the process is ongoing
Predetermined nature of the recovering process	*Unique and individual* process of recovery
Recovery is seen as a *linear process* where someone is improving every day	Recovery values its *non-linear* nature where the ups and downs contribute to richness of the recovery process
The experience of recovering from a mental illness *detracts* from their quality of life	The experience of recovering from a mental illness *contributes* positively to the quality of life

and not the exceptional. Treatment programmes or clinical interventions are usually not named by those with a 'lived experience' as the most significant contributors to their recovery. In many written and verbal recovery narratives, repeated themes emerge, such as, but not limited to:

Helpful factors

- The presence of hope
- Utilising self-determination

- Making discoveries and meaning
- Taking and being in control
- Taking personal responsibility
- Remaining connected to friends, family, roles and responsibilities
- Being actively involved in treatment and life
- Able to make choices
- Appreciating recovery as an ongoing and non-linear journey
- The uniqueness and individual nature of recovery
- The role of ordinariness in recovering
- Utilising turning points and adverse situations

Hindering factors

- Relationships based on power, control and coercion
- Lack of ability to make choices
- Limited treatment options
- Decisions made without the person or on behalf of the person
- Overcoming treatment/professional/societal and self stigma
- Stimulating and iatrogenic treatment environments

Recovery is constantly active

It is not uncommon to hear from others, whether they be professionals or significant others, that a person is not ready to recover. Comments such as these presume a number of myths:

- *That there is a beginning and an end to a recovery process.* Recovery is an ongoing process that does not have a distinct beginning or end. Recovery acknowledges that everyone is on part of the journey.
- *That a person has to be ready before recovery can begin.* Recovery is active all the time, not just when outsiders can recognise the potential for a 'good life'.
- *Other people or treatment determine a person's recovery.* It is acknowledged by many that recovery is an internal process. External supports alone cannot artificially manufacture a recovery space for an individual.
- *That a person's recovery cannot be supported in difficult times.* Times of crisis and adversity are potentially rich recovery spaces. 'Outsiders' can support a person to draw on their resilience and to focus on people's previous abilities of overcoming distress, and resist the urge to over intervene and take recovery opportunities away. This does not imply abandoning a person in distress, but supporting a person to manage their distress.
- *That service delivery is different for people who appear not able to recover.* It is not unusual for people to be provided a service that simply maintains the status quo. It is not until a person has the capacity to demonstrate their readiness for recovery that services respond accordingly. Services need to be provided at all times 'as though' recovery is a reality.

- *That people need to recover in a set time.* Comments such as 'not ready' serve to justify a need to see a set improvement within a set timeframe. 'Not ready' assumes that a person's recovery is determined by others and communicates messages of personal failure.

Impacts of a mental illness

It is not just the experience of overcoming symptoms of a mental illness that is a challenge for people recovering. Unfortunately, many people's experiences of recovery are compounded by numerous environmental and treatment impacts. Institutionalising practices, treatment and services are constantly named as being retraumatising or contributing to a person's identity of illness and disability. Stigma from society, family, professionals, and ultimately self-stigma significantly contribute to the internalisation of distress.

People's relationships with friends and family are often severed or change significantly. It is not unusual to hear people talk about their paid workers as being the closest supports they have in their lives. Sometimes the expectations others have for people's recovery are lowered and people are often provided with opportunities that are unstimulating or overprotected. This usually leads to the loss of roles and responsibilities once held, and the loss of ability to earn income. Consequently the challenge of recovery is exponentially increased in the face of such impoverished resources. The effects of these impediments and obstacles in many people's lives remain a heavy burden and require a constant effort to overcome. Many recovery narratives focus on the effort of overcoming the pain caused by adverse treatment and environmental factors as the main obstacles in recovery and not just the symptoms per se.

A common saying by people who have found a recovery space is, '*I got over the illness but I am still getting over the treatment.*'

Hard work – the effort of recovering

'*I thought for a long time that all I had to do was turn up for my appointments to get better. I didn't know or appreciate that I had to do the work of getting better and that others couldn't do it for me. I expected others to find the answers and even got angry when what they offered wasn't working.*' (HG)

The work for an individual recovering cannot be underestimated. People who are more aware of themselves in their recovery processes talk about the immense personal effort that it takes to gain and maintain a recovery space. States of recovery cannot be manufactured by another, no matter how much they desire them for the people they care for. Recovering from a mental illness requires a commitment to wellness, a commitment to see a life beyond the impact of mental illness. Many people reflect on the journey of recovery as having richly contributed to their quality of life rather than detracting from it (Tooth et al., 2003). Often the struggle and triumph of recovery gives rise to new meaning and hope.

A framework that supports individual recovery processes

Recovery is a unique and individual process. There is not a flawless recipe or manual to follow for people that ensures recovery. Table 3.2 is one construct of understanding the work of recovery. It embraces some of the commonalities and elements of the work involved in moving from a non-recovery space to a recovery space.

Many testimonies of recovery from a mental illness highlight the importance of turning points as the catalyst for promoting a forward movement in a person's recovery journey and ultimately contributing to the evidence of hope. (Tooth et al., 2003; Topor, 2001) These turning points come in all shapes and forms: some are prompted externally, others internally; some are sudden and some build their momentum slowly. What is important to remember is that turning points are significant to the person alone and are most often not related to any planned treatment intervention or outcome.

From despair to hope

Individual work involves the ability:

● To hold hope
● To believe that mental illness is not a permanent state
● To believe that mental illness need not control or decide my future
● To reach out to people who can be a 'holder of hope' when I cannot hold my own hope
● To know that I am entitled to my dreams and aspirations

Hope plays a central role in mental health recovery, just as it does in recovery from any major illness or trauma. Hope is a repeated theme named in most recovery

Table 3.2 The work of recovering

Non-recovery work		Recovery work
1. Feeling hopeless/despair	to	Holding hope
2. A passive sense of self	to	Engaging an active sense of self
3. Others in control	to	Being in personal control
4. Others understanding	to	Developing discovery and meaning
5. Being disconnected	to	Maintaining connection

narratives. In undertaking the work of hope people move from places of hopelessness or despair to being able to hold and sustain their own hope. People draw on a range of things to hold their hope. People talk about their sense of spirituality, resilience, core beliefs and values, their hopes and dreams, the importance of their family and friends, and the focus on roles and responsibilities beyond illness in order to maintain hope. Hope asks a person to invest in their own future rather than maintaining a focus on the present, and to believe that they deserve to recover. Narratives of people who experience a mental illness talk about the damage to their recovery when other people or systems of care dash their hope. Ultimately, environments of hopelessness and despair contribute to people internalising the lack of hope for their future.

Personal stories of the work of hope

Tanya had come to stay in the crisis house. She had been living in a supported accommodation environment. Tanya had been a recipient of care for many years. The next morning, Tanya came downstairs with her washing and handed it to a Recovery Guide. 'When will it be back?', she asked. The Recovery Guide gently placed the washing in her arms and said, 'When it is done'. Tanya became very distressed. 'I can't do my washing; I have a mental illness', cried Tanya. It probably had been quite some time since Tanya had had the opportunity to do her own washing.

The Recovery Guide held the space and said, 'I can see that asking you to do your washing has caused you distress and I am sorry people have taken away your basic right of doing your own washing. I would like to support you to do your washing, but I am not going to do it for you, as I don't think your current mental health crisis has anything to do with your inability to do your washing.'

Tanya heard something different – an invitation to reclaim what was lost may years before. It would have been a lot easier for the Recovery Guide to do Tanya's washing, but in doing it she knew that her actions would contribute to Tanya's knowledge of her inability rather than ability. (Tanya aged 27: personal communication)

From passive to active sense of self

Individual work involves the ability:

- To appreciate the parts of me that are actively contributing to my wellness
- To make active choices to meet my self-identified needs
- To know that I have some mastery over my illness
- To engage the well parts of me despite feelings of being overwhelmed with distress
- To contribute my wisdom of what helps and what doesn't help – based on my own experience

Recovering from a mental illness or any major adversity is an internal process. It cannot be owned, started or completed by anyone but the person whose journey it is. Many people, whether they are family, friends or mental health professionals often so desperately want a person to experience recovery that they are tempted to do the work for the person. Unfortunately this only serves to increase the person's sense of passivity. It also serves to tell people that there is nothing about them that is needed in their recovery and it is the external supports alone that are making any difference in their lives.

Why is it that some people seem to thrive when faced with a mental illness whilst others surrender? There are many answers to this question, but one that people with a lived experience talk about is the aspect of the 'internal active self'. Many lived experience narratives are filled with examples of determination, stubbornness, resilience, and active decision making. (Deegan, 1996, 1999, 2002; Leete, 1989; Lovejoy, 1984; Mead & Copeland, 2000; Tooth et al., 2003). The following statements are taken from people who have shared their stories of recovery with the author.

Self-determination

'It was my self-determination – sheer bloody-mindedness not to let the illness win.' (JS)

Stubbornness

'My stubbornness will probably kill me but it also is the one thing that keeps me alive.' (TM)

Fight

'You don't wish it on your worst enemy but you ultimately have two choices to lie down and take it or to fight.' (SR)

Resilience

'I have had other difficulties so I knew that I could get through this as well.' (FD)

Active choice

'I started to see that the nurses and doctors could maintain me but I had to have an active role in this too if I was going to get better – after all it was my life.' (LP)

Humour

'I need to find the humour in it . . . if I can't find the humour it is all too sad, depressing and this becomes overwhelming . . .' (GT)

From 'others in control' to being in personal control

Individual work involves the ability:

- To believe that I am in control of aspects of my life and that not all of me is 'totally out of control'
- To take more and more control in my day-to-day life and the choices and actions that I take
- To actively negotiate with people the support I need to regain control

> 'Feeling out of control is one of the most frightening and debilitating experiences anyone can have. It can feel like you lose control of what seems everything. It slips so easily like a child on a slippery slide. Before long the noise in your head is unrelenting. Doing basic things like cooking, cleaning and shopping feel insurmountable. Staying still, and not going out seems the only active thing you can do to stem the slide. It takes time to learn that this feeling of being out of control is not total, nor permanent. People that come into your life to "do everything for you in the name of help" risk reinforcing my knowledge of inability, dependency and lack of control. There is a fine yet essential balance between being supported to regain control and supported to remain in others' control.' (KJ)

It is common for a person who experiences a mental illness to be told and given strong messages of their inability to be in control, usually by others taking responsibility or control for many aspects of their lives. Paradoxically it is doubtful that anyone that has gained a sense of recovery has done so without regaining a sense of personal control. Personal responsibility is not a word that sits comfortably with most people let alone people who experience a mental illness. Even when people are unwell they are unlikely to be totally out of control. There will aspects of control that they will still have over their life. Regaining a sense of control and responsibility is one of the repeated tenets of many lived experience narratives of recovery (Deegan, 1996, 1999, 2002; Mead & Copeland, 2000, Faulkner & Layzell, 2000; Tooth et al., 2003).

This does not deny that from time to time people may require intensive support to remain in, or regain, a sense of personal control. There will be circumstances when others have taken over the responsibility for decisions and actions in the course of acute experiences of mental illness/distress. This support from others, if it is to assist personal recovery, must acknowledge and amplify opportunities for regaining personal control and not simply be acts of others taking control alone.

By the very nature of receiving mental health support it is usual that a power imbalance exists between the helper and those being helped. Helpers are privileged with power for numerous reasons. They have many advantages that contribute to a power imbalance, such as being:

- Employed and educated
- Responsible for determining treatment and the power to enact relevant legislation to enforce treatment

- In control of the time, space and content of the therapeutic encounter
- Able to refuse a person access to treatment or limit treatment

It is difficult to mitigate and ameliorate all the power imbalances within mental health systems of care (Playle & Keeley, 1998). Within a recovery framework, it is important that workers be constantly vigilant to the potential misuse of power and control in the name of treatment. Opportunities need to be taken that amplify and support a person's sense of personal power. It is not uncommon for treatment decisions to be made without the person's full involvement and communicated to them retrospectively. It is also not uncommon for people not to know the sort of treatment they are receiving, the names of medications, or even how the treatment should be making a difference in their lives. People quickly learn that in order to keep privileges, to remain out of hospital, or to get out of hospital, a certain amount of compliance is expected.

The word compliance is frequently used in both clinical discussions and in the mental health literature. Unfortunately the seeking of compliance has very little to do with recovery. It implies a passive relationship with treatment rather than a collaborative relationship. It speaks more about the control and power that others have, ultimately meaning the person changes their behaviour, actions and thoughts to what others want. Seeking compliance alone risks a person becoming more passive in their life and treatment decisions.

'You are my most non-compliant patient but my most recovered.' (Personal communication to author)

From alienation to discovery

Individual work involves:

- The work of discovering more and more about the impact of mental illness on my life and how I can create meaning from this
- The ability to refine the things that work to help me stay well, to achieve the things that are important to me and do less of the things that work at cross purposes
- The discovery that I can still find a purpose for my life despite experiencing a mental illness/distress

It is common to hear from people who have discovered a recovery space that the experience of recovering from a mental illness has contributed far more to their lives than it has taken away. Comments like these reinforce the belief that people can thrive from adversity rather than surrender to it. People talk about the 'Ahah' moments that were significant turning points in their recovery journey. It is these moments when something makes sense or has significant meaning to them. People talk about appreciating something about themselves or their situation that they didn't know previously. No longer is someone else holding all the meaning or understanding of his or her illness or distress.

Without a person being able to create personal meaning and understanding it is also unlikely that their recovery will progress. It is not unusual for clinicians to give a person the label of 'insightless' when they hold a different understanding of their distress to the dominant professional understanding. The understanding another person provides may hold merit but until it is internalised by the person it remains meaningless.

Assessment of a person is traditionally seen as a one-way process. It is much more vital that a person is supported to make their own discoveries and understandings of situations rather than simply being assessed and labelled. Assessment and labelling in isolation only serve to increase a sense of alienation. The importance of people reclaiming their own recovery process involves discovering and doing more of what works and less of what does not. The wellness tools that can support an individual's recovery process are numerous. It is important that an individual is able to discover their own wellness tools in their recovery process, rather than simply having them prescribed.

When any wellness tool is prescribed by another, e.g. '*I think you should do some meditation/take this medication/go to this group/get a job/lose weight*', etc., it is probably safe to say that it has been externally generated and at risk of not being utilised by the person.

From disconnectedness to connectedness

Individual work involves the ability:

- To remain connected and regain connection to my life roles, responsibilities and relationships
- To receive and contribute support, not based on my experience of illness/distress
- To transcend the role of 'a patient' despite experiencing distress and needing support
- To overcome my 'stigmatising self-doubts' in order to reclaim the 'citizen space' with dignity

The experience of disconnection is common for many people who experience a mental illness. There are many aspects of society that contribute to the feelings of disconnectedness. The effects of societal, professional, family and self-stigma all contribute to the isolation that people feel. In addition many specialised mental health programmes are focused on a person's participation in their community being strongly connected with their identity with illness. This serves to reinforce messages that people have a need to remain marginalised and not participate in community life as a full citizen.

Feelings of disconnection are amplified with the loss or change to roles and responsibilities once held. Very quickly, many people who access services are seen just as service recipients. The use of language that refers to people as 'consumers' or 'service users' is prolific and only serves to strengthen the impression that the identity of the person is a function of their relationship to mental health services.

A major effort for a person in their recovery is that of re-establishing their place in society and their community. People talk about the importance and the effort in re-establishing relationships that are not contingent on their illness, and establishing roles and responsibilities and interests that provide opportunities to move beyond being solely a recipient of services to being able to also contribute to society. People appreciate that their identity is not just that of 'a mental illness', but that they have diverse roles such as mother, daughter, son, uncle, worker, friend, tax payer, sportsman, avid reader, music lover, etc.

The work of connectedness involves a transition from dependence to interdependence. Often a person's knowledge of their recovery is reinforced when they mutually contribute to relationships and their community.

Some mental health workers have been named as having a pivotal role in helping people to reclaim a sense of connectedness. People describe the nature of facilitating relationships as important in their recovery processes and can clearly articulate the qualities of those who 'were just doing their job' as opposed to more valued workers who related to the person not through their identity of illness (Tooth et al., 2003; Topor, 2001).

People with a 'lived experience' of recovery talk about helpful workers in terms of being the ones that inferred: 'I was more than an illness'; 'Gave a damn'; 'Saw something in me that others didn't'; 'Encouraged me to fight – to not give up'; 'Went the distance with me'; 'Did things beyond their call of duty'.

Laura's story of connectedness

'I used to go to the peer run resource centre every day. It was an important part of my life. I had a role and identity when I was there that was comfortable. It had taken a fair amount of courage and effort to start to get out of the house five years ago but now I needed to push myself once again. It was safe within the confines of peers but I needed to test my wellness in the general community.

With fear and trepidation I took my first baby steps out of the cocoon of "the world of mental illness". I was amazed that no one could tell of my mental illness . . . My participation had nothing to do with my mental illness – it had a lot to do with my interest for play reading. The people I have met through this group have become great friends. It seems such a long way from the days when I would only ever socialise or do anything with people that had a mental illness.

I still need some help from time to time but it is not all consuming now – it has a balance about it that makes me know that I am not just a 'mental illness.' (Laura, aged 32 – personal communication)

A word on the elements of recovery

There are many possible personal constructions of understanding the experience of recovering from a mental illness, not just the framework discussed above. Not everyone who is actively working on their recovery will name these elements as they have been written. It would also be unusual for a person to wake and say, 'today I am going to do some work on hope/personal responsibility/connectedness, etc.' It is usually retrospectively that a person is aware that they have taken a few more steps along the journey. A person may be aware of the importance of these elements and may act and make choices to support a move further towards their 'recovery space' or actively not make choices that take them further away from their recovery space. It is important to appreciate that although the elements appear discrete pieces of work, they are constantly active and interrelate with each other.

Whose responsibility is recovery? – the role of the 'other'

Recovery should not, and cannot, be the business of services and clinicians. The work of recovering or overcoming mental illness/distress can only be the work of the individual. Despite the other person willing recovery for a person, the role of the other is to:

- Believe in the ability of the person to recover
- Work 'as though' that recovery is always a reality
- Provide environments that are supportive of individual recovery efforts, and
- Not stand in the way of an individual's recovery process

References

Deegan, P.E. (1988). Recovery: The lived experience of rehabilitation. *Psychosocial Rehabilitation Journal*, *11*, 11–19.

Deegan, P.E. (1996). Coping with recovery as a journey of the heart. *Psychiatric Rehabilitation Journal*, *19*, 91–97.

Deegan, P.E. (1999). Seasons of recovery. In: P. Ridgway (Ed.), *The recovery papers* (pp. 1–42). Lawrence, Kansas: School of Social Work, University of Kansas.

Deegan, P.E. (2002). Reclaiming your power during medication appointments with your psychiatrist. http://www.power2u.org/articles/selfhelp/reclaim.html

Faulkner, A. & Layzell, S. (2000). *Strategies for living: a report of user-led research into people's strategies for living with mental distress*. London: Mental Health Foundation.

Faulkner, A., & Thomas, P. (2002). User-led research and evidence-based medicine. *British Journal of Psychiatry*, *180*, 1–3.

Leete, E. (1989). How I perceived and manage my illness. *Schizophrenia Bulletin*, *15*, 197–200.

Lovejoy, M. (1984). 'Recovery from schizophrenia: A personal odyssey.' *Hospital and Community Psychiatry*, *35*, 809–812.

Mead, S., & Copeland, M.E. (2000). What recovery means to us. *Community Mental Health Journal*, *36*, 315–328.

Mental Health Foundation (1997). *Knowing our own minds*. London: Mental Health Foundation.

Onken, S., Dumont, J., Ridgway, P., Dornan, D., & Ralph, R. (2002). *Mental health recovery: What helps and what hinders?* New York: NASMHPD Office of Technical Assistance.

Playle, J.F. & Keeley, P. (1998). Non compliance and professional power. *Journal of Advanced Nursing, 27:2* (1), 304–311.

Thomas, P., & Bracken, P. (2004). Critical psychiatry in practice. *Advances in Psychiatric Treatment, 10,* 361–370.

Topor, A. (2001). Managing the contradiction – recovery from severe mental disorders. Stockholm: Department of Social Work, Stockholm University.

Tooth, B., Kalyanasundaram, V., Glover, H., & Momenzadah, S. (2003). Factors consumers identify as important to recovery from schizophrenia. *Australasian Psychiatry, 11,* 70–77.

Trainor, J., Pomeroy, E., & Pape, B. (2004). *A framework for support* (3rd ed.). Toronto: Canadian Mental Health Association.

Chapter 4

THE FRAMEWORK FOR PSYCHOSOCIAL REHABILITATION: BRINGING IT INTO FOCUS

Lindsay G. Oades and Frank P. Deane

Overview of chapter

This chapter builds on the key concepts and definitions in Chapter 1 to provide the practitioner with a framework to understand and evaluate psychosocial rehabilitation in mental health. A key challenge in psychosocial rehabilitation is to clearly define, operationalise and measure what we mean by psychosocial rehabilitation. To address this, the current chapter provides a definition of psychosocial rehabilitation that is relevant to five areas of intervention foci. A framework of psychosocial rehabilitation is presented using the metaphor of a lens to assist clarification of the complexities of psychosocial rehabilitation. Within each lens, principles are presented and indicators of good practice are described and this yields a list of thirty-six criteria to evaluate psychosocial rehabilitation programmes. Possible future directions of psychosocial rehabilitation are considered, including the challenges from the recovery and positive psychology movements as well as opportunities from contemporary approaches in self-help and self-management of chronic health conditions.

Introduction

Psychosocial rehabilitation, also referred to as 'psychiatric rehabilitation' (Anthony, 1998) or 'rehabilitation in mental health' (NSW Health Department, 2002) has been a politically and scientifically suspect endeavour for some years. This has been particularly due to multiple definitions and poorly operationalised concepts (Anthony et al., 1982; Cnaan et al., 1988). It is difficult to claim that psychosocial rehabilitation is effective, if researchers and practitioners apply the term differently. Anthony (1998) referred to the 'black box' of psychiatric rehabilitation, stating that from a process point of view we know what the inputs are and what the outputs are, but what happens in between has been ill defined. This chapter provides a definition of psychosocial rehabilitation consistent to that provided in Chapter 1, but goes one step further by prescribing five domains of psychosocial rehabilitation. The definition is as follows:

Psychosocial rehabilitation is a purposeful interpersonal process that involves a person with a mental illness making subjective and objective progress towards at least one of the following aims:

- Self-management of the mental illness and overall health
- Meaningful occupation
- Increased and improved social interaction and community inclusion
- Management of a changed sense-of-self and emotions from living with a long-term mental illness, and
- Improved living conditions

Psychosocial rehabilitation involves professional or peer support services that provide interventions consistent with these five aims. There are many strategies for providing psychosocial rehabilitation services to meet these aims and it is equally important for services to be able to describe comprehensively the range of specific service characteristics that meet these needs (e.g. philosophy, staffing, organisational structures, types of interventions provided, etc.).

The definition of psychosocial rehabilitation above complements recovery, as described in Chapter 1, which can be viewed as a personal rather than interpersonal process. Recovery may or may not involve these five areas, but is likely to involve the management of a changed sense-of-self and emotions related to living with a long-term mental illness. The metaphor of a lens is useful to clarify and understand the topography of psychosocial rehabilitation. A lens can zoom in to characteristics of an individual's chemistry or zoom out to communities and society. A lens can be well focused or out of focus. A lens can take stills, snapshots such as measurement of outcomes, or ongoing films, such as understanding the recovery process. Different lenses will emphasise different aspects of the topography, for example emphasising the empirical, the ethical, the economic or the conceptual. A lens can have different filters, for example highlighting deficits or strengths. A lens can capture a myriad of brilliant colours (e.g. quality of relationships) or just black and white (e.g. hospitalised or not). Moreover, a lens can be held by different people (e.g. family, consumer, clinician) from many different vantage points (e.g. control, care) and is portable.

A framework for psychosocial rehabilitation in mental health

The framework employs the definition of psychosocial rehabilitation described, and includes the following ten lenses:

- Recovery lens
- Ethical lens
- Empirical lens
- Conceptual lens
- Environmental lens

- Empowerment lens
- Economic lens
- Service lens
- Cultural and linguistic lens, and
- Relationship lens

Table 4.1 provides a description of the appropriate scope of these lenses, the relevant principle to focus psychosocial rehabilitation, and examples of indicators of what good practice might look like when this principle is followed.

The recovery lens

The recovery movement has had increasing influence on policy, practice and recently research. The scope of the recovery lens is the day-to-day experience of someone with a mental illness. As Resnick et al. (2005) asserted, traditionally recovery was narrowly defined as an outcome at a discrete point in time after an illness when one's health has been entirely regained (Corrigan et al., 1999). These authors refer to the 'expanded usage' of the term recovery as a process representing the belief that all individuals, even those with severe psychiatric disabilities, can develop hope for the future, participate in meaningful activities, exercise self-determination, and live in a society without stigma and discrimination. Hence, depending on whether the traditional usage or expanded usage of the term recovery is employed, one may be discussing an advocacy movement (Copeland, 1997, 2004; Ellis & King, 2003), symptom resolution (Harding et al., 1987; Strauss et al., 1985), returned functioning (Fitzpatrick, 2002), an outcome, a process – which may involve phases or stages (Andresen et al., 2003; Pettie & Triolo, 1999; Spaniol et al., 2002), a lived experience (Deegan, 1988), a service vision (Anthony, 1993; Jacobson & Curtis, 2000; Lyons, 2003), an attitude or life orientation (Resnick et al., 2005), and in some ways a socially negotiated acceptable way of discussing mental health service practice. In many ways, the commonalities appear to be that recovery is:

- Subjective
- Positive and progressive
- Involves personal ownership and choice, and
- Is a process rather than an event

Liberman & Kopelowicz (2005) distinguished the *process* of recovery (e.g. awareness, hope) from recovery as an *outcome* (e.g. symptom reduction, employment). However, they highlighted, 'It is not easy to separate process from outcome in delineating recovery . . .' (p. 106). Despite this concern, they proposed a preliminary definition of recovery based on 10 proposed criteria (e.g. remission of symptoms and signs, independent living without supervision, cordial family relations). Ralph (2005) agreed with the difficulty in separating process and outcome in recovery by suggesting they are on the same continuum. She described more verbal and visual models of recovery driven by personal accounts by consumers.

Table 4.1 A framework for psychosocial rehabilitation

Lens	Appropriate scope	Principle in focus	Examples of visible indicators in practice
Recovery	Day-to-day experience of someone with a mental illness	Provision of psychosocial rehabilitation should be guided by a recovery and goal directed philosophy that emphasises personal choice, hope, meaning and responsibility for managing health and wellbeing	• Documented evidence of collaborative goal striving • Measures of practitioner attitudes towards client goals and recovery • Audit of practitioner written and verbal language will reveal terms consistent with a recovery orientation • Demonstrated staff training in recovery and goal-based practice
Ethical	Rights and values	Values underpinning the approach to psychosocial rehabilitation should be stated explicitly	• Documented and visible statements (e.g. policy documents) of values at level of each module • Value clarification exercises with practitioners will reveal values similar to those documented above
Empirical	Scientific evidence available	Managers and practitioners should (a) be guided by evidence from similar practice settings, (b) have documented procedures and measures of fidelity, and (c) generate their own evidence of the effectiveness of the intervention	• Practitioner evidence-based guidelines available within unit • Documentation of procedures for modules and what constitutes fidelity to programme • Active research and evaluation programme within practice unit • Demonstrated evidence of practitioner exposure to concepts and examples of evidence-based practice relevant to (a) modules, and (b) local practice setting and resources
Conceptual	Theories, models and concepts used to understand or construct mental illness and its effects	Each component of psychosocial rehabilitation should be clearly defined, measurable and modular-easily bundled with other components to make a whole	• Observable modularised programmes that are tailored to different individual needs • All practitioners should be able to articulate spontaneously the conceptual basis underpinning each practice module, e.g. biopsychosocial model, behavioural theory, working alliance, self-determination theory
Environmental	Amount and quality of social and physical resources available	Social and physical resources should be actively accessed or improved in terms of carers, occupation, housing and general community inclusion	• Carer involvement in psychosocial rehabilitation and access to respite • Clients will be able to articulate relevant range of services and resources in their accessible area • Evidence of proactive organisational partnership with community organisations, e.g. approaching local employers to develop employment programmes • Direct linkage to case management services

Economic	Financial and social cost of long-term mental illness and associated interventions	Psychosocial interventions should consider (a) cost effectiveness of intervention, and (b) financial impact on client	• Cost-effectiveness studies at level of program module individually and in combination with reference to established health economic units e.g., QALY, days out of role • Meaningful opportunities for paid employment • Subsidies for medical and allied health treatments
Empowerment	The disempowering effects of mental illness and systems that have historically maintained power differentials	All aspects of the process of psychosocial rehabilitation should seek to empower clients and their carers	• Legislation protecting against discrimination against those people with a mental illness • Evidence of advocacy for those people with a mental illness • Clients involved (supported, paid and trained) in selection, policy, evaluation, research, service provision and advocacy relating to psychosocial rehabilitation
Service	Psychosocial rehabilitation (by definition) includes five key domains: (1) Self-management of the mental illness and overall health (2) Meaningful occupation (3) Increased and improved social interaction and community inclusion (4) Management of a changed sense-of-self and emotions from living with a long-term mental illness (5) Improved living conditions	Psychosocial rehabilitation services should offer evidence-based, modularised and portable interventions in a manner consistent with all other principles	• Rigorous quality and client satisfaction reviews • Programmes targeting self-management skills including (a) medication, (b) physical health, e.g. exercise, diet, (c) stress and coping skills, (d) symptom management, (e) drug and alcohol use • Programme based on Assertive Community Treatment • Programmes involving (a) supported employment, (b) education • Programmes involving (a) social skills, (b) normalising inclusion within community, (c) family psychoeducation • Programmes with strong subjective focus targeting issues to deal with changed sense-of-self and coping emotionally with long-term illness • Programme linked with housing and accommodation support with provision of client choice
Diversity	How ethnic, cultural, gender, age and linguistic differences impact on the construction and alleviation of distress caused by mental illness and its impact	Psychosocial rehabilitation should be responsive to the diverse range of experiences of mental illness relating to ethnicity, culture, gender and language	• Availability of interpreters in service provision • Examples of diversity in practitioner selection to match needs of client groups • Workforce development specific to range of relevant diversity issues, e.g., culture bound stigma
Relationship	The relationships between key stakeholders within the psychosocial rehabilitation process	Psychosocial rehabilitation, which is by definition an interpersonal process, should make explicit reference to and seek to maintain a strong working alliance between clients, carers, practitioners and their organisations	• Documented evidence of memoranda of understandings or strategic alliance between associated organisations • Evidence of face-to-face contact and joint operational level initiatives between organisations • Evidence of practitioner training in developing and maintaining effective working alliance • Measures of working alliance between practitioner and client within service evaluation

Within this model, stages of recovery are specified (e.g. awakening, wellbeing, empowerment) along with changes that may occur in various domains (e.g. cognitive, spiritual). Hence, to return to the lens metaphor, recovery definitions can have a lens that is more outside, looking in (Liberman & Kopelowicz, 2005) or more inside, looking out (Ralph, 2005).

The provision of psychosocial rehabilitation should be guided by a recovery and goal directed philosophy that emphasises personal choice, hope, meaning and responsibility for managing health and wellbeing. Goal orientation is especially fruitful in conceptualising and measuring recovery (Austin & Vancouver, 1996; Sheldon & Elliot, 1998). Recovery is the process of working towards various life goals in parallel, together with the thoughts, feelings and emotions associated with the chosen paths towards these goals. When we use the recovery lens, goals and recovery are inextricably linked (Ades, 2003; Lecomte et al., 2005).

Table 4.1 illustrates four indicators of good psychosocial rehabilitation practice using the recovery lens. An audit of a psychosocial rehabilitation service should find documented evidence of collaborative goal striving (Oades et al., 2000). The audit should yield evidence that the service measures practitioner attitudes towards client goals and recovery, and when possible uses training and/or selection to improve these attitudes. An audit of practitioner written and verbal language will evaluate the extent to which usage is consistent with a recovery orientation, e.g. use of terms such as 'hope', 'meaning', 'autonomy'. A fourth indicator of recovery oriented practice is demonstrated evidence of staff training in recovery and goal based practice (Oades et al., 2005b).

The ethical lens

The ethical lens includes all aspects of the rights, responsibilities and values relevant to practitioners and clients of psychosocial rehabilitation services (Rudnick, 2002). The ethical lens is often closely linked to legislative issues related to mental illness. A key principle is that values underpinning the approach to psychosocial rehabilitation are stated explicitly. A good psychosocial rehabilitation service has documented and visible statements (e.g. policy documents) of values relating to each module of service provided. Value clarification exercises with practitioners can be used to reveal and clarify whether values of practitioners are congruent with those stated as part of good psychosocial rehabilitation practice, e.g. autonomy of client (Prilletensky et al., 1996). Allott et al. (2002) referred to values based practice, placing values as central to mental health, rather than hidden.

The empirical lens

The empirical lens examines the scientific evidence concerning the effectiveness of psychosocial rehabilitation (Barton, 1999). With the recent growth of the evidence based practice movement, this has become a very important lens for psychosocial rehabilitation. Corrigan and Ralph (2005) summarised those evidence based psychosocial rehabilitation interventions identified by consensus groups (p. 8):

- Assertive community treatment
- Family psycho-education
- Illness self-management skills
- Integrated treatments for mental illness and substance abuse
- Supported employment, and
- Targeted psychopharmacology

However, there is debate about the extent that such interventions reflect consumers' priorities regarding recovery. There are also reasons to be cautious about direct extrapolation from research findings to clinical practice. These include possible differences between study samples and actual service users, difficulties implanting practice protocols, inflation of research findings as a result of allegiance and placebo effects and cost–benefit considerations (Lloyd, King, & Bassett, 2002).

To help meet such challenges managers and practitioners should:

- Be guided by evidence from similar practice settings (Corrigan et al., 2001)
- Have documented procedures and measures of fidelity (Bond et al., 2000), and
- Generate their own evidence of the effectiveness of the intervention

In a good psychosocial rehabilitation practice, several indicators will be evident including:

- Practitioner evidence-based guidelines available within unit
- Documentation of procedures for modules and what constitutes fidelity to programme
- An active research and evaluation programme within the practice unit, and
- Demonstrated evidence of practitioner exposure to concepts and examples of evidence-based practice relevant to modules, and local practice, setting and resources

The conceptual lens

The conceptual lens examines the theories, models and concepts used to understand or construct mental illness and its effects. While there are many concepts relevant to mental health (Farhall et al., 2002), concepts used in psychosocial rehabilitation should be those that assist with contemporary issues such as the need for evidence, the need to integrate recovery and goal constructs and the need to better recognise the interpersonal nature of psychosocial rehabilitation.

To meet these needs, each component of psychosocial rehabilitation should be clearly defined, measurable and modular. Modularity refers to the ability of the component to 'fit together' with another module to make a meaningful whole. That is, the module can be used by itself or added meaningfully to another module. However, each module should be clearly defined, measured and have its own procedures and criteria that specify relevant measures of fidelity. There are two key advantages to this approach. Firstly, a service can increase or decrease its service offerings dependent upon resources. Secondly, the effectiveness of each module can be evaluated in isolation or in combination.

In a good psychosocial rehabilitation practice there will be:

- Observable modularised programmes that are tailored to different individual needs, and
- Practitioners that can spontaneously articulate the conceptual basis underpinning each practice module, e.g. biopsychosocial model (Pilgrim, 2002), behavioural theory, working alliance, self-determination theory. That is, the practitioners will understand the concepts that guide their practice.

The environmental lens

This is one of the broadest lenses within this framework and includes the amount and quality of social and physical resources available to a person who has mental illness. These resources include carers, occupational resources, housing, resources that assist general community inclusion and the mental health system. A good psychosocial rehabilitation practice will involve actively accessing and seeking to improve these resources. Hence, it is not just changing the key (person) to fit the lock (environment); it may be changing or finding a new environment (lock). A detailed description of the issues related to carers, occupation, housing and community inclusion is beyond the scope of this chapter. These issues are also covered in other chapters (e.g. Chapters 8, 10, 11). Given the definition of psychosocial rehabilitation, each of the other lenses should be directed at teaching these four aspects of the environment. That is, for a person with mental illness to manage their own mental illness and general health, they will also need to manage their environment.

In a good psychosocial rehabilitation practice the following should be seen through the environment lens:

- Carer involvement in psychosocial rehabilitation and access to respite
- Clients able to access a range of relevant services and resources
- Proactive organisational partnership with community organisations, e.g. approaching local employers to develop employment programmes, and
- Effective communication protocols or direct integration with clinical case management services

The economic lens

The economic lens examines the financial and social cost of long-term mental illness and associated interventions. Psychosocial rehabilitation interventions should consider cost effectiveness of intervention (Hargreaves et al., 1998) and the financial impact of the mental illness and the psychosocial rehabilitation intervention on the client. Through the economic lens, in a good psychosocial rehabilitation practice you will observe:

- Cost-effectiveness studies at level of both individual programme components and total programme with reference to established health economic units, e.g. QALY, days out of role
- Opportunities for meaningful and paid employment, and
- Subsidies for medical and allied health treatments required

The empowerment lens

The empowerment lens examines power, and particularly the disempowering effects of mental illness and systems that have historically maintained power differentials. Empowerment has become an increasingly popular term in mental health, explicitly recognising power within the relationships, practices and systems of mental health (Chamberlin, 1997; Clark & Krupa, 2002; Ochocka et al., 1999; Wilson, 1996). When considering good psychosocial rehabilitation practice from an empowerment perspective, legislation protecting against the discrimination of people with a mental illness would be expected. Moreover, one should see evidence of advocacy for those people with a mental illness. The clients should be involved, supported, paid and trained in selection, policy, evaluation, research, service provision and advocacy relating to psychosocial rehabilitation (Linhorst & Eckert, 2002; Oades et al., 2005a, b).

The service lens

At the beginning of this chapter, we indicated that psychosocial rehabilitation has five aims:

- Self-management of the mental illness and overall health
- Meaningful occupation
- Increased and improved social interaction and community inclusion
- Management of a changed sense-of-self and emotions from living with a long-term mental illness, and
- Improved living conditions

Interventions or service modules should be designed to address each of these aims. Psychosocial rehabilitation services should offer evidence-based, modularised and portable interventions in a manner consistent with the other principles set out in this chapter. Looking through the service lens one should observe rigorous quality and client satisfaction reviews in a manner equivalent to successful private service organisations.

In terms of the five main aims, for self-management skills services might target:

(1) Medication
(2) Physical health, e.g. exercise, diet

(3) Stress and coping
(4) Symptom management, and
(5) Drug and alcohol use

Moreover, given the evidence, there should be a programme based on Assertive Community Treatment. To address occupation goals, services such as supported employment (Drake et al., 1996) and education could be provided. In terms of social environment, you should see programmes involving social skills, normalising inclusion within community, and family psychoeducation. Consistent with the recovery lens you will also see programmes with a strong subjective focus, targeting issues to deal with changed sense-of-self and coping emotionally with long-term illness. Finally, consistent with the fifth aim of psychosocial rehabilitation you will see programmes linked with housing and accommodation support with provision of client choice.

The diversity lens

The diversity lens examines how ethnic, cultural, gender, age and linguistic differences impact on the construction and alleviation of distress caused by mental illness and its impact (Jablensky et al., 1992). Psychosocial rehabilitation should be responsive to the diverse range of experiences of mental illness relating to ethnicity, culture, gender and language. Looking through the diversity lens for good practice in psychosocial rehabilitation you should see:

- Availability of interpreters in service provision
- Examples of diversity in practitioner selection to match needs of client groups, e.g. different services for different age groups, and
- Workforce development specific to a range of relevant diversity issues, e.g. culture bound stigma

The relationship lens

Given that psychosocial rehabilitation is defined as an interpersonal process, the relationship lens is particularly important. This lens examines the relationships between key stakeholders within the psychosocial rehabilitation process. Psychosocial rehabilitation should make explicit reference to and seek to maintain a strong working alliance between clients, carers, practitioners and their organisations (Howgego et al., 2003; Martin et al., 2000). Chapter 6 covers many of the issues involved in development of a positive therapeutic relationship with a client. However, at an organisational level, good practice could involve documented evidence of memoranda of understanding or strategic alliance organisations associated with the environment of the person with a mental illness. Moreover there will be evidence of face-to-face contact and joint operational level initiatives between these organisations. Staff development includes practitioner training in developing and maintaining an effective working alliance with clients (Deane et al., 2005; Gehrs

& Goering, 1994). There may also be measures of working alliance between practitioner and client within service evaluation.

Does the use of different lenses result in conflicting perspectives?

At times, recovery based approaches and evidence based approaches have been viewed as polar opposites (Frese et al., 2001). To some extent this may reflect differences in positivist versus constructivist views of recovery (see Loveland et al., 2005 for discussion). These concerns probably also reflect differing use of the term recovery from a defined end state more consistent with traditional medical models of illness to a highly individual process derived from consumer experiences. However, if one examines the empirically guided positive psychology movement and its emphasis on hope, strengths, goals, values and self-determination (Seligman & Csikszentmihalyi, 2000; Sheldon et al., 2003), it is entirely congruent with recovery and strengths based approaches (Björkman et al., 2002). One possible future direction for psychosocial rehabilitation is to link its conceptual framework more closely with those of positive psychology. In this way, at a conceptual level it will be more consistent with consumer views of recovery and also draws on a well established evidence base. Similarly self-help and self-management of chronic conditions (Holman et al., 2000) may provide a means of reconciling recovery and evidence-based perspectives. The self-help emphasis on autonomy and ownership is entirely consistent with the recovery movement, while at the same time having an empirical basis.

Conclusion

This chapter provided a proscriptive definition of psychosocial rehabilitation with reference to five aims. The metaphor of a lens was used to examine the complexity of psychosocial rehabilitation, and 10 principles of good psychosocial rehabilitation were described and 36 indicators were specified. It was argued that the 'goal' construct is useful in further elaborating our understanding of recovery from mental illness, and practices to assist this recovery. To meet the challenge of the recovery and evidence-based practice movements it is suggested that psychosocial rehabilitation practitioners further employ ideas from the positive psychology movement, the self-help literatures and the self-management of chronic illness in physical health.

References

Ades, A. (2003). *Mapping the journey: Goal setting. Psychosocial rehabilitation*. Vol. 5. VicServ, State of Victoria: New Paradigm Press.

Allott, P., Loganathan, L., & Fulford, K.W.M. (2002). Discovering hope for recovery. *Canadian Journal of Community Mental Health*, 21, 13–33.

Andresen, R., Oades, L.G., & Caputi, P. (2003). The experience of recovery from schizophrenia: Towards an empirically validated stage model. *Australian and New Zealand Journal of Psychiatry*, 37, 586–594.

Anthony, W.A. (1993). Recovery from mental illness: The guiding vision of the mental health service system in the 1990s. *Psychosocial Rehabilitation Journal*, 16, 12–23.

Anthony, W.A. (1998). Psychiatric rehabilitation technology: Operationalizing the 'black box' of the psychiatric rehabilitation process. *New Directions for Mental Health Services*, 79. Boston: Jossey Bass.

Anthony, W.A., Cohen, M.R., & Farkas, M.D. (1982). A psychiatric rehabilitation program: Can I recognize one if I see one? *Community Mental Health Journal*, 18, 83–96.

Austin, J.T., & Vancouver, J.B. (1996). Goal constructs in psychology: Structure, process and content. *Psychological Bulletin*, 120, 338–375.

Barton, R. (1999). Psychosocial rehabilitation services in community support systems: A review of outcomes and policy recommendations. *Psychiatric Services*, 50, 525–534.

Björkman, T., Hansson, L., & Sandlund, M. (2002). Outcome of case management based on the strengths model compared to standard care. A randomised controlled trial. *Social Psychiatry and Psychiatric Epidemiology*, 37, 147–152.

Bond, G.R., Evans, L., Salyers, M.P., Williams, J., & Hea-Won, K. (2000). Measurement of fidelity in psychiatric rehabilitation. *Mental Health Services Research*, 2, 75–87.

Chamberlin, J. (1997). A working definition of empowerment. *Psychiatric Rehabilitation Journal*, 20, 43–46.

Clark, C.C., & Krupa, T. (2002). Reflections on empowerment in community mental health: Giving shape to an elusive idea. *Psychiatric Rehabilitation Journal*, 25, 341–349.

Cnaan, R., Blankertz, L., Messinger, K., & Gardner, J. (1988). Psychosocial rehabilitation: Toward a definition. *Journal of Psychosocial Rehabilitation*, 11, 61–77.

Copeland, M.E. (1997). *Wellness recovery action plan*. Dummerston, VT: Peach Press.

Copeland, M.E. (2004). Self-determination in mental health recovery: Taking back our lives. In: J. Jonikas & J. Cook (Eds.), *UIC NRTC's national self-determination and psychiatric disability invitational conference: Conference papers* (pp. 68–82). Chicago, IL: UIC National Research and Training Center on Psychiatric Disability.

Corrigan, P.W., & Ralph, R.O. (2005). Introduction: Recovery as a consumer vision and research paradigm. In: R.O. Ralph and P.W. Corrigan (Eds.), *Recovery in mental illness: Broadening our understanding of wellness* (pp. 3–17). Washington, D.C.: APA.

Corrigan, P.W., Giffort, D., Rashid, F., Leary, M., & Okeke, I. (1999). Recovery as a psychological construct. *Community Mental Health Journal*, 35, 231–239.

Corrigan, P.W., Steiner, L., McCracken, S., Blaser, B., & Barr, M. (2001). Strategies for disseminating evidence-based practices to staff who treat people with serious mental illness. *Psychiatric Services*, 52, 1598–1606.

Deane, F.P., Oades, L.G., King, R., Crowe, T., Lloyd, C., & Clarke, S. (2005). Working alliance and recovery from chronic and recurring mental disorders (CRMD). Poster presented at the Society for Psychotherapy Research conference, Montreal, Canada.

Deegan, P.E. (1988). Recovery: The lived experience of rehabilitation. *Psychosocial Rehabilitation Journal*, 11, 11–19.

Drake, R.E., McHugo, G.J., Becker, D.R., Anthony, W.A., & Clark, R.E. (1996). The New Hampshire study of supported employment for people with severe mental illness. *Journal of Consulting and Clinical Psychology*, 64, 391–399.

Ellis, G., & King, R. (2003). Recovery focused interventions: Perceptions of mental health clients and their case managers. *Australian e-Journal for the Advancement of Mental Health* 2. www.auseinet.com/journal/vol2iss2/ellis.pdf

Farhall, J., Fossey, E., Keble-Devlin, B., Meadows, G., Roberts, S., & Singh, B. (2002). Conceptual models in mental health practice. In: Meadows, G. & Singh, B. (Eds.), *Mental health in Australia: Collaborative community practice* (pp. 19–41). Melbourne: Oxford University Press.

Fitzpatrick, C. (2002). A new word in serious mental illness: Recovery. *Behavioural Healthcare Tomorrow*, *11*, 16–21, 33, 44.

Frese, F.J., Stanley, J., Kress, K., & Vogel-Scibilia, S. (2001). Integrating evidence-based practice and the recovery model. *Psychiatric Services*, *52*, 1462–1468.

Gehrs, M., & Goering, P. (1994). The relationship between the working alliance and rehabilitation outcomes of schizophrenia. *Psychosocial Rehabilitation Journal*, *18*, 43–54.

Harding, C.M., Brooks, G.W., Ashikaga, T., Strauss, J.S., & Brier, A. (1987). The Vermont longitudinal study of persons with severe mental illness: I. Methodology, study sample, and overall status 32 years later. *American Journal of Psychiatry*, *144*, 727–735.

Hargreaves, W.A., Shumway, M., Hu, T., & Cuffel, B. (1998). *Cost-outcome methods for mental health*. San Diego: Academic Press.

Holman, H., Sobel, D., Laurent, D., Gonzalez, V., Minor, M., & Lorig, K. (2000). *Living a healthy life with chronic conditions: Self-management of heart disease, arthritis, diabetes, asthma, bronchitis, emphysema and others* (2nd ed.). Boulder: Bull Publishing.

Howgego, I.M., Yellowlees, P., Owen, C., Meldrum, L., & Dark, F. (2003). The therapeutic alliance: The key to effective patient outcome? A descriptive overview of the evidence in community mental health case management. *Australian and New Zealand Journal of Psychiatry*, *37*, 169–183.

Jablensky, A., Sartorius, N., Ernberg, G., Anker, M., Korten, A., Cooper, J.E., Day, R., & Bertelsen, A. (1992). Schizophrenia: Manifestations, incidence and course in different cultures. A World Health Organization ten-country study. *Psychological Medicine Monograph Supplement*, *20*. Cambridge: Cambridge University Press.

Jacobson, N., & Curtis, L. (2000). Recovery as policy in mental health services: Strategies emerging from the states. *Psychiatric Rehabilitation Journal*, *23*, 333–341.

Lecomte, T., Wallace, C.J., Perreault, M. & Caron, J. (2005). Consumers' goals in psychiatric rehabilitation and their concordance with existing services. *Psychiatric Services*, *56*, 209–211.

Liberman, R.P., & Kopelowicz, A. (2005). Recovery from schizophrenia: A criterion-based definition. In: R.O. Ralph and P.W. Corrigan (Eds.), *Recovery in mental illness: Broadening our understanding of wellness* (pp. 101–129). Washington, D.C.: APA.

Linhorst, D.M., & Eckert, A. (2002). Involving people with severe mental illness in evaluation and performance improvement. *Evaluation and the Health Professions*, *25*, 284–301.

Lloyd, C., King, R., & Bassett, H. (2002). Evidence-based practice in occupational therapy – why the jury is still out. *New Zealand Journal of Occupational Therapy*, *49*, 10–14.

Loveland, D., Randall, K.W., & Corrigan, P.W. (2005). Research methods for exploring and assessing recovery. In: R.O. Ralph and P.W. Corrigan (Eds.), *Recovery in mental illness: Broadening our understanding of wellness* (pp. 19–59). Washington, D.C.: APA.

Lyons, K. (2003). *Recovery. Background paper: A guide for the future*. Brisbane: Queensland Health.

Martin, D.J., Gaske, J.P., & Davis, M.K. (2000). Relation of the therapeutic alliance with outcome and other variables: A meta-analytic review. *Journal of Consulting and Clinical Psychology*, *68*, 438–450.

NSW Health Department (2002). *Framework for rehabilitation in mental health*. Mental health implementation group. Sydney: NSW Government Action Plan.

Oades, L.G., Caputi, P., Morland, K., & Bruseker, P. (2000). Collaborative Goal Index: A new technology to track goal striving and attainment in psychosocial rehabilitation. *Conference Proceedings at the World Association for Psychosocial Rehabilitation, VIIth World Congress*. Paris, France.

Oades, L.G., Deane, F.P., Crowe, T.P., Lambert, W.G., Kavanagh, D., & Lloyd, C. (2005a). Collaborative Recovery: An integrative model for working with individuals that experience chronic or recurring mental illness. *Australasian Psychiatry, 13*, 279–284.

Oades, L.G., Viney, L.L., Malins, G., Strang, J., & Eman, Y. (2005b). Consumer evaluation of mental health services: The process and products. *New Paradigm: The Australian Journal of Psychosocial Rehabilitation, March*. Melbourne: VicServ.

Ochocka, J., Neslon, G., & Lord, J. (1999). Organizational change towards the empowerment-community integration paradigm in community mental health. *Canadian Journal of Community Mental Health, 18*, 59–72.

Pettie, D., & Triolo, A.M. (1999). Illness as evolution: The search for identity and meaning in the recovery process. *Psychiatric Rehabilitation Journal, 22*, 255–262.

Pilgrim, D. (2002). The biopsychosocial model in Anglo-American psychiatry: Past, present and future? *Journal of Mental Health, 11*, 585–594.

Prilletensky, I., Rossiter, A., & Walsh-Bowers, R. (1996). Preventing harm and promoting ethical discourse in helping professional: Conceptual, research, analytical and action frameworks. *Ethics and Behaviour, 6*, 287–304.

Ralph, R.O. (2005). Verbal definitions and visual models of recovery: Focus on the recovery model. In: R.O. Ralph and P.W. Corrigan (Eds.), *Recovery in mental illness: Broadening our understanding of wellness* (pp. 131–145). Washington, D.C.: APA.

Resnick, S.G., Fontana, A., Lehman, A.F., & Rosenheck, R.A. (2005). An empirical conceptualization of the recovery orientation. *Schizophrenia Research, 75*, 119–128.

Rudnick, A. (2002). The goals of psychiatric rehabilitation: An ethical analysis. *Psychiatric Rehabilitation Journal, 25*, 310–313.

Seligman, E.P., & Csikszentmihalyi, M. (2000). Positive psychology. An introduction. *American Psychologist, 55*, 5–14.

Sheldon, K.M., & Elliot, A.J. (1998). Not all goals are personal: Comparing autonomous and controlled reasons as predictors of effort and attainment. *Personality and Social Psychology Bulletin, 24*, 546–557.

Sheldon, K.M., Williams, G., & Joiner, T. (2003). *Self-determination theory in the clinic: Motivating physical and mental health*. New Haven: Yale University Press.

Spaniol, L., Wewiorski, N., Gagne, C., & Anthony, W.A. (2002). The process of recovery from schizophrenia. *International Review of Psychiatry, 14*, 327–336.

Strauss, J.S., Hafez, H., Lieberman, P., & Harding, C.M. (1985). The course of psychiatric disorder, III: Longitudinal principles. *American Journal of Psychiatry, 142*, 289–296.

Wilson, S. (1996). Consumer empowerment in the mental health field. *Canadian Journal of Community Mental Health, 15*, 69–85.

Chapter 5

BUILDING AND MAINTAINING A RECOVERY FOCUSED THERAPEUTIC RELATIONSHIP

Frank P. Deane and Trevor P. Crowe

Overview of chapter

In this chapter we review the evidence for the importance of therapeutic relationship and particularly therapeutic or working alliance in facilitating recovery processes for individuals with mental illness. Most of the existing empirical evidence comes from psychotherapy research related to the treatment of non-psychotic disorders. However, there is growing evidence that therapeutic alliance may also be an important predictor of treatment outcome for people with serious mental illness, including those diagnosed with psychotic disorders.

Consumer perspectives on the therapeutic relationship

In describing their own experiences and meaning of recovery, Mead & Copeland (2000) commented on the nature of the therapeutic relationship with health care professionals. They highlighted the need to 'discard the kinds of paternalistic relationship some of us have experienced in the past' and argued that 'a truly supportive therapeutic relationship begins with honesty and a willingness to take a critical look at assumptions learned during training' (p. 320). In describing guidelines for recovery-oriented services they listed a number of issues, which relate closely to therapeutic relationship. To paraphrase a few (p. 327):

- Treat the person as a fully competent equal
- Never scold, threaten, punish, patronise, judge or condescend to the person
- Focus on how the person feels, what the person is experiencing
- Accept that a person's life path is up to them
- Listen to the person . . . making sure their goals are truly theirs and not yours

As will be seen in this chapter, a number of these suggestions relate directly to therapeutic relationship and alliance. Key themes repeated in both the recovery and therapeutic relationship literature are: listening, understanding others' experiences, acceptance, non-judgmental stance, honesty, hopefulness and collaboration regarding goals.

Components of therapeutic relationship

Rogers (1957) argued that the relationship between client and therapist was itself therapeutic and was more important than factors such as specific interventions based on a particular theoretical orientation. Rogers suggested that a therapist required the personal qualities of accurate empathy, non-possessive warmth and unconditional acceptance, and genuineness to establish a quality therapeutic relationship, which would in turn facilitate positive change.

Accurate empathy

Whilst there is some debate regarding the meaning of accurate empathy, it is essentially a cognitive and affective state that involves engaging with the client's affect or cognition and reflecting this back to them from moment to moment (Duan & Hill, 1996). It has been defined as 'an emotional response resulting from the recognition of another's emotional state or condition, one that is very similar or identical to what the other individual is perceived to experience' (Eisenberg et al., 1997, p. 73). This involves a mental health practitioner being able to step outside of her or his own view of the world to imagine or understand the client's experience and then to accurately reflect this back. This reflection could be a verbal statement or affective (emotional) response.

Understanding another's experience is a difficult process, and trying to grasp the experiences of individuals who are having psychotic experiences is even more challenging because their symptoms are outside the scope of most practitioners' experience. Practitioners can draw on similar personal experiences to get a sense of a client's view, but they should be cautious not to presume that their experiences and reactions are the same as those of their clients. Similarly, you cannot simply imagine yourself being in the same situation as a client because your reaction to the same circumstances may be quite different.

Accurate empathy involves listening carefully to what clients say, how they say it, and being aware of non-verbal information that might also help understand their experience. It also involves reflecting back what you think the client is experiencing. It is equally important to listen to the cues the client provides about whether you have accurately understood what she or he is experiencing.

Non-possessive warmth and unconditional acceptance

Non-possessive warmth refers to caring, respect, support and valuing the client. The non-possessive nature refers to caring without attempting to control the other person (Todd & Bohart, 1994). 'Being non-possessive in therapy means acknowledging clients' autonomy, accepting their choices, and not imposing one's will on them' (Todd & Bohart, 1994, p. 222). You can see from this definition that the emphasis on autonomy and choice is highly consistent with recovery-oriented perspectives. Unconditional acceptance refers to that ability to listen and respond to others without being judgmental or disapproving. This does not necessarily imply that a practitioner will approve of all a client says or does.

Genuineness

Genuineness refers to the ability of a mental health worker to be honest, open and authentic in their interactions with clients. 'Genuine people are congruent. This means that their outer actions are congruent with some facet of their inner thoughts and feelings' (Todd & Bohart, 1994, p. 226). Genuineness is reflected in consistency between how a person acts and how they think and feel.

Whilst empathy, warmth, acceptance and genuineness are widely accepted as key therapist characteristics for a good therapeutic relationship, the client–therapist partnership involves reciprocity and these additional factors are captured in the broader term *therapeutic alliance*.

Therapeutic alliance

There is some variation in definitions of the therapeutic alliance construct but Gaston (1990) suggested the following characteristics are common:

- Client's positive affective relationship with the therapist
- Client's capacity to work purposefully in therapy
- Therapist's empathic understanding and involvement
- Client–therapist agreement on the goals and tasks of therapy

Bordin (1979) described the 'therapeutic working alliance' as comprised of:

- Mutual understanding and agreement about goals
- Agreement on the necessary tasks to move toward these goals, and
- Establishment of a bond between the partners involved in the work (typically health care provider and client)

Tasks are distinguished from goals in that they 'refer to the specific activities that the partnership will engage in to instigate or facilitate change' (Bordin, 1994, p. 16). Tasks represent proposals for client action (e.g. homework, such as client recording behaviour or practising relaxation). Bordin (1994) further highlighted that negotiation, particularly around goals and tasks, is integral to building alliance.

The bond in the partnership is consistent with the core therapeutic relationship issues described by Rogers (1957), and Bordin (1994) described this as 'expressed and felt in terms of liking, trusting, respect for each other, and a sense of common commitment and shared understanding in the activity' (p. 16). The bond provides 'therapeutic leverage'. This is important because therapeutic change makes significant demands on the client's personal resources and can be a source of strain in the therapeutic relationship.

Therapeutic alliance and treatment outcomes

There is now a substantial body of evidence to support the role of therapeutic alliance factors in treatment outcome. However, relatively little of this research has been with clients with severe mental illness. For example, a meta-analytic review of 79 studies over an 18-year span found a minority of studies (23%) included more severely disordered clients (i.e. psychotic or with severe personality disorders) (Martin et al., 2000). The meta-analysis revealed a moderate relationship between therapeutic alliance and outcome, with an overall weighted correlation of 0.22. No other moderator variables influenced the alliance–outcome relationship, which is consistent with the hypothesis that the alliance is therapeutic in and of itself and regardless of other psychological interventions (Martin et al., 2000).

Research into the role and impact of therapeutic alliance in working with individuals with chronic and recurring psychotic mental illnesses such as schizophrenia is very limited (e.g. Gehrs & Goering, 1994). In a study of clients with non-chronic schizophrenia it was found that the alliance predicted medication adherence, and was negatively related to psychopathology, frequency of positive symptoms, and treatment dropout. Alliance also predicted improved social functioning, and illness acceptance, and accounted for more outcome variance than social class, intelligence, insight, baseline symptom level, optimism, motivation to change, and level of pre-morbid functioning (Frank & Gunderson, 1990).

A descriptive review that focused on studies of alliance–outcome in community psychiatry and case management located five studies assessing the relationship in these contexts (Howgego et al., 2003). Most of the clients in these studies had severe mental health problems such as schizophrenia, but again diagnosis was not directly analysed in any of the studies. The authors concluded there was 'minimal' but 'encouraging' evidence that stronger case manager–client therapeutic relationships resulted in improved outcomes. In two of the studies a relationship between alliance measures and medication compliance was found. The authors suggested that this population may require a longer time period to develop a positive alliance and that the social or relationship competence of clients may influence the formation of the alliance (a point which is elaborated further below). A major contextual issue for the development of alliance for individuals with psychosis is the extent to which they are voluntarily seeking help or are coerced as a result of involuntary court ordered treatment (Howgego et al., 2003). Although encouraging, clearly more research is needed and the authors of the review indicated they are conducting a prospective longitudinal study to address this need.

Subsequent to this review Lustig et al. (2002) found that significantly stronger working alliance was reported by clients who were employed compared with unemployed clients, and that working alliance was significantly positively correlated with both current job satisfaction and positive expectations of future employ-ment prospects. The authors argued that 'rehabilitation counsellors may be able to improve outcomes by facilitating a strong working alliance with their clients' (Lustig et al., 2002, p. 30).

Other studies assessing the role of therapeutic alliance on outcome with people who have psychotic disorders are being conducted in Australia both in relation to medication adherence (Byrne et al., 2004) and in relation to recovery oriented treatment approaches (Oades et al., 2005). An important component of the 'collaborative recovery' approach to treatment of Oades et al. is a strong emphasis on therapeutic bond in the context of a recovery philosophy. In addition, they highlighted the importance of collaborative goal planning and task assignment to promote both relationship and goal attainment. The 'systematic' administration of homework (tasks) offers the opportunity for strengthening the relationship and improving homework adherence, which should lead to improved goal attainment.

Practical considerations

Practitioner attitudes

Instillation of hope and enhancement of meaning of life are core components of recovery-oriented models (Andresen et al., 2003; Anthony, 2000). The values, atti-tudes and beliefs of practitioners are likely to have a direct effect on the therapeutic relationship and alliance, particularly in the context of working in a manner con-sistent with recovery principles. Regrettably, there is evidence that professionals often have low expectations concerning recovery of people with severe mental ill-ness and may not anticipate developing a therapeutic alliance with such clients (Mirabi et al., 1985; Packer et al., 1994).

Whilst these are older studies and attitudes may well have changed, it remains important for practitioners to reflect on their attitudes toward people with schizo-phrenia or other psychotic disorders. To what extent do these attitudes interfere with their capacity to develop positive therapeutic alliance? As a practitioner you should ask yourself the question, 'Am I hopeful for the clients I work with?' A key facet of recovery described by consumers is that 'There is hope. A vision of hope that includes *no limits*' (Mead & Copeland, 2000, p. 317).

Increasing empathy

Another major threat to therapeutic alliance is a lack of empathy for the experiences of those with psychosis (Chadwick et al., 1996). A lack of empathy was found to be related to less involvement by staff, and increases in belittling comments (Fox, 2000).

Empathy training can lead to increased empathic communication and positive effects on clients (Nerdrum & Ronnestad, 2003). The empathy exercises for psychosis have included listening to audiotaped 'voices' and discussion of unusual feelings or perceptions that staff participants may have experienced, such as perceptual disturbances associated with sleep deprivation from shift work (McLeod et al., 2002). Other strategies to increase empathy include effortful attempts to simply imagine another perspective (Davis et al., 2004), and the use of movies (Shapiro & Rucker, 2004). Practitioners should review and address their own attitudes, hopefulness and empathy for clients as an essential precursor to developing a positive therapeutic alliance with their clients. Self-directed reflection can be supplemented with clinical supervision in this preparation process.

Engagement

Initial engagement can occur in a number of contexts, but often takes place during the assessment phase. Chapter 4 has outlined assessment, the development of a rehabilitation plan and the importance of good therapeutic alliance in this process. It is important to be aware that the development of positive alliance during assessment is related to subsequent alliance early in treatment and reductions in early treatment termination (Ackerman et al., 2000).

Where possible, initial meetings should be conducted in an environment where the client feels safe (Nelson, 1997). For most people familiar surroundings feel safer than unfamiliar surroundings, so consideration should be given to meeting the person in familiar surroundings. Health practitioners should also consider surroundings where they feel safe and comfortable.

Listening non-judgmentally and carefully to a client's story is the best approach to take in the early stages. Avoid confrontation during the engagement stage. For individuals who may be particularly hostile or paranoid, keeping initial interactions on non-controversial subjects until rapport has been established is likely to help avoid premature disengagement. There may be opportunities for brief informal contacts prior to more formal and structured sessions. This might involve introductions at a drop-in centre, supported residence or work setting. The opportunity to just 'say hello' in a low demand situation and non-threatening environment often helps increase comfort levels prior to more formal working sessions.

The assessment process and development of therapeutic alliance are inextricably intertwined (see also Chapter 6). Meaningful assessment will be severely hampered or impossible without a positive therapeutic relationship, and the assessment process itself is an important vehicle for strengthening the therapeutic alliance. For example, in assessing need and establishing goals and tasks collaboratively, therapeutic alliance is essential.

A key part of establishing a 'working' therapeutic alliance is getting agreement about the expectations of therapy. The roles of client and practitioner need to be clarified and agreed. Typically, this involves emphasising the collaborative nature of the therapeutic relationship; the client accepting some responsibility for his or her own wellness, and being an active participant in treatment by identifying goals and accepting the need to complete negotiated tasks to achieve these goals (i.e. homework activities). Bordin (1994) emphasised that negotiation around goals and tasks was 'an integral part of alliance building' (p. 15).

When clients have had a long history of mental health service use, there is likely to be a range of prior experiences that may have an impact on the development of a therapeutic relationship. Specifically, clients may have had negative prior experiences in prior treatment contexts. Some clients believe that therapy is not helpful or that they are not capable of change. These clients may have had practitioner–patient relationships that they experienced as coercive, belittling, uncaring, unfriendly, disrespectful, paternalistic, critical or judgmental. Those who have experienced delusions may simply worry that they will not be believed or may be very suspicious. The risk of having experienced these kinds of events or feelings may be particularly high in circumstances where a client has been assessed or treated as an involuntary patient.

Maintenance of therapeutic alliance during treatment

Balancing therapeutic alliance and specific treatment tasks

Assessment of need and negotiation of goals are important opportunities for building alliance, but it is possible to move too quickly to specific therapeutic tasks. Thus, a balance between the development and maintenance of relationship and specific therapeutic tasks needs to be maintained. Similarly, excessive focus on therapeutic technique might be experienced as an imposition on the client or a failure to meet his/her immediate needs. Kivlighan & Tarrant (2001) found that when therapy specific behaviours were offered too early by therapists in group therapy, there was a negative impact on client engagement which was in turn related to client outcome. These findings suggest the need to balance the use of specific therapeutic techniques in relation to the strength of the therapeutic alliance.

Relationship patterns

Clients' and workers' ways of relating and capacity to develop relationships vary from individual to individual. Hersoug et al. (2002) found that the quality of both current and past interpersonal relationships was associated with working alliance ratings. They concluded that the client's relationship style or pattern impacts on the expectations regarding the therapeutic relationship, and consequently the strength of the working alliance, for both the client and therapist. It has been found that clients who have an interpersonal style described as 'under-involved' tended to have poorer alliance and treatment outcomes (Hardy et al., 2001). A difficult client relational style is more likely to elicit negative responses from the therapist (Klee et al., 1990). Similarly the therapist's relationship style can elicit positive or negative responses from the client. For example, a paternalistic relating style might be met with a submissive or resistant response from the client.

Characteristics of some individuals with psychosis can also elicit particular responses from practitioners that will affect the nature of the relationship interaction. For example, Stark et al. (1992) found gender differences in practitioners, suggesting that male practitioners were inclined to reduce their therapeutic commitment with clients with disturbances of ego function, attention, or perception. Female practitioners felt rejected by clients with delusions and with formal thought disorders. Stark (1994) and Stark & Siol (1994) found that, when working with high relapse risk clients, male practitioners reacted like 'underinvolved fathers' with distance, helplessness, and feelings of insufficiency, whereas female practitioners showed emotional closeness and solicitude, like 'overinvolved mothers'. Both types of response may be counter productive and it is important for practitioners to be aware of such relationship patterns with a view to improving alliance.

'Expressed emotion' has been extensively researched in studies of families providing care for someone with severe mental illness (see Chapter 8) and there is reason to believe that it is a construct of relevance to the therapeutic relationship between staff and clients. High expressed emotion (especially critical, negative and hostile attitudes towards clients) has been found to be present in approximately one quarter of staff working with people with severe long term psychiatric impairment (Van Humbeeck et al., 2001). When expressed emotion is high, clients are more likely to leave a care environment (Ball et al., 1992) and clients interviewed by high expressed emotion workers are less likely to volunteer statements of self-affirmation (Moore & Kuipers, 1992).

Overcoming strains or 'ruptures' in the therapeutic alliance

What are alliance ruptures?

Alliance 'ruptures' consist of an impairment or negative fluctuation in the quality of the alliance between the practitioner and the client. Safran & Muran (1996) suggested that alliance ruptures are characteristically common, interactional phenomena, a function of both client and practitioner contributions, and vary in intensity, duration and frequency depending on the particular practitioner–client dyad. Ruptures are typically identified as one of two categories:

(1) Confrontational – where the client may express negative thoughts and feelings toward the practitioner, and/or terminate therapy prematurely
(2) Withdrawal – where the client engages in avoidance behaviours or may exhibit uncharacteristic compliance or agreeableness (Safran et al., 1990; Safran & Muran, 1996).

These categories reflect seven subtle themes or markers: the overt expression of negative sentiments; indirect communication of negative sentiments or hostility (may be non-verbal or passive–aggressive); disagreement about the goals or tasks of therapy; uncharacteristic or sudden compliance; avoidance manoeuvres; self-esteem-enhancing operations; and non-responsiveness to interactions (Safran et al., 1990).

Morrison et al. (2004) highlighted that 'Disagreement between patient and therapist about relevant goals may be the first point of confrontation in therapy'

(p. 111). The establishment of a strong bond may provide some buffering effects in negotiating these areas of disagreement.

Resolving alliance ruptures

Safran et al. (1990) suggested six strategies to resolve alliance ruptures:

- Talking directly about what is currently happening in the therapeutic relationship (metacommunication)
- Awareness and an understanding of alliance rupture markers and a frame of reference that is sensitive to fluctuations in relationship dynamics
- Awareness of one's own feelings
- Accepting appropriate responsibility for the rupture
- Attempting to empathise with the client's experience, and
- Maintaining the stance of the participant observer (i.e. being able to reflect on the dynamics of the interaction as opposed to spontaneously reacting to the interactions)

Safran et al. (1990) suggested that early detection of alliance ruptures by the practitioner is critical to successful therapy. They also suggested that the resolution of alliance ruptures can be potent change events. The successful resolution of disagreement and associated loss of bond in the relationship can help clients recognise that: (i) fluctuations in relationship quality are normal, can be tolerated and can be repaired, and (ii) they have the skills or capacity to be able to resolve these interpersonal issues (i.e. problem solve, negotiate, tolerate anxiety or annoyance, etc.). Foreman & Marmar (1985) found that if practitioners dealt with clients' problematic feelings towards the practitioner, therapy outcome improved. They also found that, in unimproved cases, problematic feelings were avoided or ignored by the practitioner.

For some clients, being able to reflect on and talk directly about the therapeutic relationship may be difficult, foreign, threatening and/or anxiety provoking. However, practitioners are strongly encouraged to reflect on their therapeutic relationship with a client and to consider components such as emotional climate, power and reciprocity in the relationship. If clients appear to withdraw or express negative thoughts or feelings toward the therapist or therapy, these are cues to consider what is going on in the relationship. To start, gentle clarification and questioning that does not necessarily directly focus on the relationship might be needed. For example, making an observation about the changes in the interaction during the sessions (e.g. 'you seem less talkative during our meetings lately'), clarifying what thoughts or feelings are being experienced, and whether there are other things going on in the person's life that might be having an impact on the relationship. Other sequential invitations may also help assess how the client is feeling about the therapeutic relationship, such as how they feel treatment is going and what other things might help, and then whether there are specific things about the way the two of them work together that might be improved.

Text box 5.1   Case study: Sam

> Sam is a young man who was referred following hospitalisation. He was experiencing paranoid delusions and persistent auditory hallucinations and was initially, very distrustful of his practitioner. The presence of suspiciousness made initial engagement difficult but the practitioner did several things early in the relationship to help develop alliance with Sam. The practitioner provided transport for Sam to help him get to various appointments. On the first visit he noticed an old car sitting in the garage, and knowing Sam had an interest in restoring the vehicle he engaged him in a conversation about it. This interaction took about 15 min but Sam was clearly very enthusiastic about the possibilities for the vehicle. The practitioner actually knew a lot about motor vehicles, knew this car was in very bad shape, and also realised that it was not economically a very wise decision to restore it because a second hand vehicle of the same make and model could be purchased at a fraction of the price it would take to restore it. However, the practitioner recognised this as an opportunity to allow Sam to open up and be positive about something in an informal setting.

Several issues are raised by the interaction between Sam and his rehabilitation practitioner. Does the practitioner's silence regarding the poor shape of the car and his belief that it is not wise to restore it constitute a lack of genuineness and honesty in the relationship? In this case, the practitioner recognised that what was important to the client was not how much it would cost to restore the car, but the potential and satisfaction in doing the work. The practitioner showed accurate empathy by listening carefully to what Sam said and how he said it, and was aware of non-verbal information (such as stroking the car hood) that helped him understand this car was very important to Sam. Clarifying what is personally meaningful to the client and reflecting this back to the client is often the first step in helping the client feel the practitioner is really with him/her, and that a working partnership may be possible. Later, Sam did raise concerns about the cost of restoration and the practitioner gave his opinion about relative merits of restoration versus purchasing another second hand vehicle. Even so, Sam still decided that despite the higher cost he wanted to fix the car up. Consistent with the core elements of positive therapeutic alliance, the practitioner acknowledged the client's autonomy and accepted his choice.

The consistency of the practitioner's contacts with Sam over time and the ongoing support for Sam's goals further strengthened the therapeutic alliance. However, after about 4 months of relatively steady progress, the practitioner noticed that on several occasions when he went to collect Sam to attend the local clubhouse, Sam was not yet out of bed. In addition, Sam appeared to be reluctant and slow getting ready. Initially, the practitioner put Sam's quietness on the drive to the clubhouse down to him being rushed and getting up late. However, on the third occasion it occurred to him that this may represent something else that was bothering Sam.

The practitioner knew that Sam had again been having some conflict with his parents, who complained about him keeping them awake at night. He asked an open question about how he was getting along with his folks. Sam mumbled something about how they and 'everyone' were on his case about watching TV at night. After some gentle probing it became clear that Sam was not only angry at his parents 'nagging', but also resented something his practitioner had said regarding staying awake at night. This had occurred during a family conference when the parents tried to problem solve with the practitioner and Sam about ways to reduce the noise at night. Sam had felt the practitioner had taken his parents' side and felt the practitioner did not understand how restless he was at night.

This represented a 'strain' or 'rupture' in the therapeutic alliance. Sam's 'lateness' getting out of bed may have been in part due to staying up through the night, but it also seemed to involve passive avoidance (of practitioner and treatment) and he clearly stated he was unhappy with something that had occurred in the relationship. The rupture was able to be resolved by the practitioner empathising with Sam's feelings of rejection, accepting that his comments could have been seen as 'taking sides', clarifying that his comments were aimed at helping to resolve some of the difficulties Sam was experiencing around conflict with his parents, but also taking Sam's distress regarding restlessness at night as more of a focus of the problem. The practitioner also praised Sam for sharing his feelings about what had happened and reinforced his ability to talk about it openly.

Conclusion

It has been suggested that 'bond' is not just an ingredient supplied by the practitioner and responded to by the client. Development of a good working alliance is a process that is on the one hand as simple as caring about another person and at the same time as infinitely diverse and complicated as any relationship between two people. Whether alliance primarily facilitates other interventions or is an active ingredient itself likely depends on the needs and disposition of the client. Stiles & Shapiro (1994) suggested that a linear relationship between the so-called active ingredients of therapy and treatment outcomes is unlikely as the therapeutic relationship is typically characterised by constant adjustments and the 'responsiveness' of the practitioner and client to each other; the implication being that psychotherapy clients who are capable of establishing a good alliance will also be able to utilise certain interventions (e.g. interpretations) reasonably effectively. Clients who are less capable of forming a strong alliance may respond better to supportive interventions. This might suggest that more supportive and perhaps structured interventions should be favoured with clients where there have been difficulties in forming a strong alliance.

An alliance might be formed by the practitioner and client by finding 'common ground' or engaging in relatively non-threatening or recreational activities. However, the therapeutic relationship should be more than a friendship. The practitioner should be looking for opportunities to engage the client in conversations about nurturing his/her recovery vision and hope, his/her personal recovery goals and what activities or tasks may be helpful in relation to working towards attaining these goals.

Our experience has been that if practitioners are attentive to the issues previously described, if they are collaborative, optimistic and consistent yet responsive in their work with clients, they will develop a quality therapeutic alliance that may assist with facilitating recovery. In addition, they will open the opportunity to enjoy, learn and grow from the experience of genuinely connecting with another person.

References

Ackerman, S.J., Hilsenroth, M.J., Baity, M.R., & Blagys, M.D. (2000). Interaction of therapeutic process and alliance during psychological assessment. *Journal of Personality Assessment, 75*, 82–109.

Andresen, R., Oades, L.G., & Caputi, P. (2003). The experience of recovery from schizophrenia: Towards an empirically validated stage model. *Australian and New Zealand Journal of Psychiatry, 37*, 586–594.

Anthony, W.A. (2000). A recovery-oriented service system: Setting some system level standards. *Psychiatric Rehabilitation Journal, 24*, 159–168.

Ball, R.A., Moore, E., & Kuipers, L. (1992). Expressed emotion in community care staff. A comparison of patient outcome in a nine month follow-up of two hostels. *Social Psychiatry and Psychiatric Epidemiology, 27*, 35–39.

Bordin, E.S. (1979). The generalizability of the psychoanalytic concept of the working alliance. *Psychotherapy: Theory, Research and Practice, 16*, 252–260.

Bordin, E.S. (1994). Theory and research on the therapeutic working alliance: New directions. In: A.O. Horvath & L.S. Greenberg (Eds.), *The working alliance: theory, research, and practice* (pp. 13–37). New York: Wiley.

Byrne, M., Deane, F.P., Lambert, G., & Coombs, T. (2004). Enhancing medication adherence: Clinician outcomes from the 'Medication Alliance' training program. *Australian and New Zealand Journal of Psychiatry, 38*, 246–253.

Chadwick, P., Birchwood, M., & Trower, P. (1996). *Cognitive therapy for delusions, voices, and paranoia.* West Sussex, England: Wiley.

Davis, M.H., Soderlund, T., Cole, J., Gadol, E., Kute, M., Meyers, M., & Weihing, J. (2004). Cognitions associated with attempts to empathize: How do we imagine the perspective of another? *Personality and Social Psychology Bulletin, 30*, 1625–1635.

Duan, C., & Hill, C.E. (1996). The current state of empathy research. *Journal of Counseling Psychology, 43*, 261–274.

Eisenberg, N., Murphy, B.C., & Shepard, S. (1997). The development of empathic empathy. In: W. Ickes (Ed.), *Empathic accuracy* (pp. 73–116). New York: Guilford Press.

Foreman, S.A., & Marmar, C.R. (1985). Therapist actions that address initially poor therapeutic alliances in psychotherapy. *American Journal of Psychiatry, 142*, 922–926.

Fox, V. (2000). Empathy: The wonder quality of mental health treatment. *Psychiatric Rehabilitation Journal, 23*, 292–293.

Frank, A.F., & Gunderson, J.G. (1990). The role of therapeutic alliance in the treatment of schizophrenia: Relationship to course and outcome. *Archives of General Psychiatry, 47*, 228–236.

Gaston, L. (1990). The concept of the alliance and its role in psychotherapy: Theoretical and empirical considerations. *Psychotherapy, 27*, 143–153.

Gehrs, M., & Goering, P. (1994). The relationship between the working alliance and rehabilitation outcomes of schizophrenia. *Psychosocial Rehabilitation Journal, 18*, 43–54.

Hardy, G.E., Cahill, J., Shapiro, D.A., Barkham, M., Rees, A., & Macaskill, N. (2001). Client interpersonal and cognitive styles as predictors of response to time-limited cognitive therapy for depression. *Journal of Consulting and Clinical Psychology, 69*, 841–845.

Hersoug, A.G., Monsen, J.T., Havik, O.E., & Hoglend, P. (2002). Quality of early working alliance in psychotherapy: Diagnoses, relationship and intrapsychic variables as predictors. *Psychotherapy & Psychosomatics, 71,* 18–27.

Howgego, I.M., Yellowlees, P., Owen, C., Meldrum, L., & Dark, F. (2003). The therapeutic alliance: The key to effective patient outcome? A descriptive review of the evidence in community mental health case management. *Australian and New Zealand Journal of Psychiatry, 37,* 169–183.

Kivlighan, D.M. Jr., & Tarrant, J.M. (2001). Does group climate mediate the group leadership–group member outcome relationship?: A test of Yalom's hypotheses about leadership priorities. *Group Dynamics, 5,* 220–234.

Klee, M.R., Abeles, N., & Muller, R.T. (1990). Therapeutic alliance: Early indicators, course, and outcome. *Psychotherapy, 27,* 166–174.

Lustig, D.C., Strauser, D.R., Rice, N.W., & Rucker, T.F. (2002). The relationship between working alliance and rehabilitation outcomes. *Rehabilitation Counseling Bulletin, 46,* 25–33.

Martin, D.J., Garske, J.P., & Davis, M.K. (2000). Relation of the therapeutic alliance with outcome and other variables: A meta-analytic review. *Journal of Consulting and Clinical Psychology, 68,* 438–450.

McLeod, H., Deane, F.P., & Hogbin, B. (2002). Changing staff attitudes and empathy for working with people with psychosis. *Behavioural and Cognitive Psychotherapy, 30,* 459–470.

Mead, S., & Copeland, M.E. (2000). What recovery means to us: Consumers' perspectives. *Community Mental Health Journal, 36,* 315–328.

Mirabi, M., Weinman, M.L., Magnetti, S.M., & Keppler, K.N. (1985). Professional attitudes toward the chronic mentally ill. *Hospital and Community Psychiatry, 36,* 404–405.

Moore, E., & Kuipers, L. (1992). Behavioural correlates of expressed emotion in staff–patient interactions. *Social Psychiatry and Psychiatric Epidemiology, 27,* 298–303.

Morrison, A.P., Renton, J.C., Dunn, H., Williams, S., & Bental, R.P. (2004). *Cognitive therapy for psychosis: A formulation-based approach.* New York: Brunner–Routledge.

Nelson, H. (1997). *Cognitive behavioural therapy with schizophrenia: A practice manual.* Cheltenham, UK: Stanley Thornes Publishers.

Nerdrum, P., & Ronnestad, M.H. (2003). Changes in therapists' conceptualization and practice of therapy following empathy training. *Clinical Supervisor, 22,* 37–61.

Oades, L.G., Deane, F.P., Crowe, T.P., Lambert, W.G., Kavanagh, D., & Lloyd, C. (2005). Collaborative recovery: An integrative model for working with individuals that experience chronic and recurring mental illness. *Australasian Psychiatry, 13,* 279–284.

Packer, S., Prendergast, P., Wasylenki, D., Toner, B., & Ali, A. (1994). Psychiatric residents' attitudes toward patients with chronic mental illness. *Hospital and Community Psychiatry, 45,* 1117–1121.

Rogers, C.R. (1957). The necessary and sufficient conditions of therapeutic personality change. *Journal of Consulting Psychology, 21,* 95–103.

Safran, J.D., & Muran, J.C. (1996). The resolution of ruptures in the therapeutic alliance. *Journal of Consulting and Clinical Psychology, 64,* 447–458.

Safran, J.D., Crocker, P., McMain, S., & Murray, P. (1990). Therapeutic alliance rupture as a therapy event for empirical investigation. *Psychotherapy, 27,* 154–165.

Shapiro, J., & Rucker, L. (2004). The Don Quixote Effect: Why going to the movies can help develop empathy and altruism in medical students and residents. *Families, Systems, & Health, 22,* 445–452.

Stark, F.M. (1994). The therapist–patient relationship with schizophrenic patients. *Behaviour Change, 11*, 234–241.

Stark, F.M., Lewandowski, L., & Buchkremer, G. (1992). Therapist–patient relationship as a predictor of the course of schizophrenic illness. *European Psychiatrist, 7*, 161–169.

Stark, F.M., & Siol, T. (1994). Expressed emotion in the therapeutic relationship with schizophrenic patients. *European Psychiatrist, 9*, 299–303.

Stiles, W.B., & Shapiro, D.A. (1994). Disabuse of the drug metaphor: Psychotherapy process–outcome correlations. *Journal of Consulting and Clinical Psychology, 62*, 942–948.

Todd, J., & Bohart, A.C. (1994). *Foundations of clinical and counselling psychology* (2nd ed.). New York: Harper Collins.

Van Humbeeck, G., Van Audenhove, C., Pieters, G., De Hert, M., Storms, G., Vertommen, H., Peuskens, J., & Heyrman, J. (2001). Expressed emotion in staff–patient relationships: the professionals' and residents' perspectives. *Social Psychiatry and Psychiatric Epidemiology, 36*, 486–492.

Chapter 6

INDIVIDUAL ASSESSMENT AND THE DEVELOPMENT OF A COLLABORATIVE REHABILITATION PLAN

Robert King

Overview of chapter

This chapter takes the general principles of psychosocial rehabilitation, introduced in Chapter 4, and explores their application in individual assessment as the starting point for the development of a collaborative rehabilitation plan. Assessment is a process by which the practitioner and client get to know each other and develop the shared information base that enables them to work together towards the recovery of the client. It is a highly complex process, which has both an information gathering and alliance developing function. The chapter sets out reasons why a focus on client strengths and recovery style, and client perceptions and priorities, is as important as identifying objective disability, impairment and handicap. The chapter provides guidance with respect both to effective interpersonal communication during the assessment process and to the use of standardised instruments to enhance the reliability of assessment and provide an objective means of evaluating progress in rehabilitation. A basic rehabilitation plan template is provided and a case study illustrates assessment and rehabilitation planning in practice.

Assessment of needs

The biopsychosocial model is well established in contemporary mental health practice, notwithstanding the continuing appeal of a simpler biomedical model (Pilgrim, 2002). The biopsychosocial model asserts that both the understanding and treatment of mental illness requires that the impact of biological, psychological and social systems be taken into account. At the level of assessment of the individual, the biopsychosocial model provides the framework for assessment of needs. The challenge for the health professional is to discover the needs, and especially the unmet needs, of the client so as to develop an approach to rehabilitation that addresses these needs. An approach to meeting this challenge is set out in some detail below and some standardised tools to assist with assessment of needs are also discussed below.

Focus on need and assessment of need shifts the emphasis from exclusive concern with narrow clinical questions to broader questions about the subjective experience and quality of life of the client. This reflects the recognition that diagnostic category alone is an inadequate indicator of the kinds of service a person is likely to need (Wing et al., 1992). It also reflects the finding that a lower quality of life is related to the number of unmet needs experienced by a person with mental illness (Hansson et al., 2003).

Early approaches to assessment treated needs as objective phenomena that the health professional could ascertain by using a systematic and structured enquiry (Brewin et al., 1987). Subsequent research identified discrepancies between the needs identified by health professionals and needs that clients identified, including evidence that health professionals tended to recognise fewer unmet needs (Slade et al., 1998) and that health professionals and clients often prioritised different needs (Ellis & King, 2003; Hansson et al., 2001; Lasalvia et al., 2000). The result has been a developing focus on client perceived needs as being of at least equal importance to clinician identified needs (Marshall et al., 1995). When assessment of needs is collaborative and practitioners are aware of client perceptions, the level of agreement between client and practitioner is much higher (Macpherson et al., 2003).

Text box 6.1 What the evidence shows

- Quality of life for people with mental illness is related to the extent to which their rehabilitation needs are met (Hansson et al., 2003)
- Clients often report different needs and priorities from those identified by practitioners (Lasalvia et al., 2000; Hansson et al., 2001; Ellis & King, 2003)
- Collaborative assessment of need and focus on client perceptions promotes practitioner/client agreement as to needs (Macpherson et al., 2003)
- Diagnosis is not a reliable guide to client service needs (Wing et al., 1992)
- Focus on client strengths has a positive impact on rehabilitation (Rapp & Wintersteen, 1989; Stannard, 1999; Björkman et al., 2002; Barry et al., 2003)
- Congruence with client coping style is relevant to rehabilitation planning (McGlashan, 1987; Beutler et al., 2001)
- Using standardised measures in needs assessment assists in identifying unmet needs (Lockwood & Marshall, 1999)

Strengths approach to assessment

Attention to client strengths is an important antidote to the risk that a focus on needs alone might add to the sense of inadequacy and general demoralisation that frequently accompanies mental illness. While identifying needs may lead to hope that the needs will be met, it can also construct a simplistic narrative that identifies the client as being needy and helpless. By contrast, finding out about client strengths can serve both as a reminder to the client of his or her capacities and a useful guide to the personal resources that the client might bring to the recovery process.

There is also evidence that a strengths approach can improve clinical and psychosocial outcomes. Rapp & Wintersteen (1989) reported that clients of a strengths approach set more goals than clients of standard case management. Stannard (1999) found that clients of staff trained in a strengths approach to case management had overall quality of life and better outcomes with respect to educational and vocational outcomes compared with clients of staff using standard case management. Björkman et al. (2002) found that a strengths approach resulted in reduced needs for care compared with a standard approach. Barry et al. (2003) found that a strengths approach to assertive case management was associated with reduced clinical symptoms after two years compared with standard assertive case management.

Standardised measures in assessment for psychosocial rehabilitation

Standardised measures are tools, usually taking the form of a questionnaire, that are administered in a standard manner and yield scores that give quantitative expression to current functioning. Some measures are self-report, meaning that the client completes the questionnaire and other measures are externally rated, meaning that another person, usually the practitioner, completes the questionnaire about the client.

There are several advantages of standardised measures:

- They are systematic and structured. This means that important issues or areas for assessment will not be accidentally overlooked.
- Scores can be compared over time. This enables both client and practitioner to see what kind of progress is being made.
- Scores can be compared with normative samples. This enables practitioner and client to see whether impairments are greater or less than those of other similar groups of people. (Any discussion of comparative impairment with clients should be handled with considerable sensitivity and is not recommended as standard practice as it has the potential to be demoralising.)
- Service scores can be compared over time. This enables a service to determine the extent to which, overall, clients are progressing with their recovery.

There are also limitations with standardised measures:

- They are impersonal and have the potential to be alienating if they are not used in the context of a positive therapeutic relationship.
- They are inflexible and may not measure characteristics that are of central importance to the rehabilitation process.
- Some measures have weak psychometric properties (see below), which means they must be interpreted with considerable caution.

- Some measures can only be used effectively if the practitioner has had substantial specialist training.

Standardised measures should only be used if they have acceptable psychometric properties. This is a complex and technical topic that is beyond the scope of this book, but essentially means that they must be reliable (consistent in their measurement), valid (actually measure what they claim to measure) and sensitive to change (significant progress in recovery must be reflected in score changes). Further discussion of standardised measures and their properties can be found in Chapter 14.

There are two broad categories of standardised measure. On the one hand, there are measures that are concerned primarily with the systematic evaluation of individual functioning across one or more dimensions. On the other hand, there are measures that are concerned primarily with the evaluation of individual needs. There is some overlap between the two categories because there is a tendency for people with lower levels of functioning to have higher levels of needs. However, they are not interchangeable and selection of measure will depend on the primary purpose of its use.

Standardised measures of *functioning* with acceptable psychometric properties that are suitable for use in rehabilitation settings and do not require extensive training include:

- Behaviour and Symptom Identification Scale (BASIS): Eisen et al. (1986)
- Health of the Nations Outcome Scale (HoNOS): Wing et al. (1998)
- Life Skills Profile (LSP): Rosen et al. (1989)
- Role Functioning Scale (RFS): Goodman et al. (1993)
- Mental Health Inventory (MHI): Veit & Ware (1983)

The BASIS and MHI are consumer rated, whereas the other measures are clinician rated.

The general utility of these scales was investigated by Stedman et al. (2000), who found that all measures were regarded favourably by both clinicians and consumers. The HoNOS is a particularly useful general index of functioning that can be used not only as a part of an assessment process but also as a means of tracking recovery. Gallagher & Teesson (2000) found HoNOS to be sensitive to change and Parker et al. (2002) found HoNOS was more sensitive to global change than LSP, and was therefore a better general measure if the aim of measurement was to evaluate global improvement.

Standardised measures of *need* with acceptable psychometric properties that are suitable for use in rehabilitation settings and do not require extensive training include:

- Camberwell Assessment of Needs (CAN): Phelan et al. (1995); short form CANSAS
- Cardinal Needs Schedule (CNS): Marshall et al. (1995) (developed from the MRC Needs for Care Assessment of Brewin et al., 1987)

- Salford Needs Assessment Schedule for Adolescents (S.NASA): Kroll et al. (1999)
- Perceived Needs for Care Questionnaire (PNCQ): Meadows et al. (2000)

There is some preliminary evidence that the use of a standardised measure of need has a positive impact on health outcomes, resulting in greater attention to unmet needs than is the case when needs are assessed informally (Lockwood & Marshall, 1999).

What is assessed?

The psychosocial assessment should be systematic and comprehensive. The kinds of information that are likely to be important are discussed below.

Nature of the mental illness (diagnosis, symptom profile, onset, course)

This information is essential for developing realistic expectations and time frames and also for developing the relapse prevention components of recovery plans. Mental illness can be quite variable and the health professional needs to keep an open mind as to the course of recovery. However, it is reasonable to expect that disorders such as schizophrenia, once established, will have an ongoing impact and rehabilitation will need to take this into account. Bipolar disorders are likely to include periods of more or less full recovery interrupted by periods of acute disturbance, which need to be taken into account when developing a recovery plan. Depression, especially in its more severe forms may insidiously return after a period of full recovery and, unlike bipolar symptoms, the return of depression may be difficult to detect until well established. Personality disorders and substance use disorders are complicating factors that may have a major impact on the recovery process and it is important to be fully aware of the presence of such disorders. Refer to Chapter 2 for a more detailed discussion of psychopathology, impairment, disability and handicap.

Functional impact of the illness (the kinds of things the person is now unable to do as a result of illness)

Mental illness typically impacts most severely and directly on complex and socially demanding activities such as work and maintenance of family and social relationships. However, mental illness can also affect motivation and morale such that even though a person might be able to do something, she or he has no desire or interest. As a result, basic household management and personal hygiene may be adversely affected by mental illness. Finally, mental illness can impact on pleasure and concentration so that simple recreational activities such as watching television can be affected.

Current functional capacities (the things the person can do despite the illness)

No matter how severe the illness, some functional capacities will remain. In many cases there will be a large spectrum of functional capacities. A person who has become demoralised by mental illness may feel and honestly believe that she or he is unable to do anything and may be pleasantly surprised by the functional capacities that a careful assessment identifies.

Pre-morbid strengths (capacities and achievements characteristic of the person prior to the onset of the illness)

Identifying pre-morbid strengths serves two important purposes. First, it identifies aspects of the client that may not be prominent in the context of the illness, and might be readily mobilised during the course of recovery. Second, the identification of pre-morbid strengths may help to counteract the demoralising process of the illness by reminding the person of past achievements or abilities. In this way, the rehabilitation assessment may contrast with the standard psychiatric assessment that often focuses on difficulties or traumas from the past.

Text box 6.2 Seven categories of strength

- Aesthetic – capacity to enjoy music art, drama, natural environment etc. (does not mean 'highbrow')
- Humour – capacity to enjoy comedy, to see the funny side, to be funny (check TV programme choice)
- Intimacy – capacity to form close, confiding supportive relationships, whether with sexual partners, family members, friends or therapists
- Spirituality – capacity to draw comfort from religious practice, faith or belief in a higher power or a deeply held value system
- Occupational skills – capacity to perform socially valued and rewarding activities at any level, now or in the past
- Recreational skills – capacity to occupy time with activity that is enjoyable or absorbing
- Creative – e.g. cooking, sewing, artistic, building, repairing, etc.

Recovery stage (where the client is at in the recovery process)

Recovery is a complex process and does not take place in an orderly linear fashion. It is common for periods of recovery to be interrupted by setbacks associated with episodes of acute illness or other life difficulties. There will be periods of consolidation when things might seem rather static and periods of rapid development. Each recovery point or stage raises specific issues and it is important for the practitioner to take into account the impact of these issues on rehabilitation planning. A schematic overview of recovery stages based loosely on Strauss et al. (1985) can be found in Figure 6.1. It is important to bear in mind that although this scheme implies some kind of sequence, the sequence can be regularly interrupted.

Figure 6.1 A schematic model of recovery from mental illness (based in part on Strauss et al., 1985).

Stage	Tasks/challenges	Issues
Acute illness/crisis	Stabilisation, symptoms, management, containment	Safety, treatment efficacy
Post-traumatic	Dealing with disruption to internal and external world	Catastrophic reaction, damage control
Stocktaking	Making assessment of extent of impact of illness on personal and social life	Personal morale, reality testing
Rebuilding (wood-shedding)	Rediscovering personal capacities	Sense of self
Reaching out	Re-engaging with the social world	Trust, support, stigma
Consolidation	Engaging in long-term projects such as relationships, careers, studies or creative activities	Faith

Recovery and coping style (the characteristic ways the person deals with the illness experience)

Every person has typical ways of dealing with difficulties. These are often divided into *externalising/sealing over* strategies, such as attributing problems to circumstances beyond the control of the person, blaming other people or agencies, putting it behind and moving on; and *internalising/integrating* strategies such as trying to work our what the person did wrong or how things could be handled differently in the future (Beutler et al., 2001; McGlashan, 1987). In the rehabilitation assessment, both kinds of strategy are seen as being potentially healthy and successful, and the aim is to develop a picture of the person's preference for one or other strategy so that the rehabilitation plan is congruent with the client's coping style.

Current social environment (quality of family supports, friendships, affiliations and other relationships)

Recovery takes place in a social context and this social context may be more important (in both positive and negative ways) than the clinical service environment. People who maintain very close and intimate relationships with the client, such as immediate family members, are likely themselves to be affected by the mental illness and may themselves need information and support. Being aware of the components of social environment and some of the characteristics of the relationship between the client and people within the social environment is essential to the rehabilitation plan.

Current treatment environment (people or agencies involved in physical and mental health care)

The rehabilitation plan must take into account the contributions being made by other individuals and agencies, and possible need to communicate with other people involved in the client's care. Duplicating or, even worse, counteracting other rehabilitation interventions is best avoided. A complex array of services can be confusing to clients, especially when key messages are inconsistent. There is also some risk that the rehabilitation practitioner becomes inadvertently involved in competition or conflict with other services.

Current physical environment (quality of housing, income, clothing, diet)

It is difficult for any person to focus on recovery from mental illness if his or her most basic needs are not being met. There will be different views as to what constitutes adequate housing, income, clothing and diet, but the key questions that must be addressed are whether they are adequate to enable the client to focus on other matters, whether they are consistent with safety and physical health, and whether they are adequate to enable the client to progress in relation to primary goals.

Recovery priorities (what the person would most like to achieve in the short and longer term)

The rehabilitation plan must reflect client priorities. Rehabilitation practitioners are susceptible to introducing their own agenda for recovery. The role of the rehabilitation practitioner is not to introduce her or his own agenda, but rather to give practical form to the client's agenda. This means clarifying priorities, helping to sort them into short term and longer term priorities, and working with priorities that at first might seem unrealistic so as to establish meaningful pathways or equivalent but more achievable priorities.

Text box 6.3   Maintaining a recovery focus: tips for practitioners

- Approach assessment as an opportunity for therapeutic engagement as well as information gathering
- Find out about client strengths as well as needs
- Seek information about client recovery style
- Identify client priorities among rehabilitation needs
- Use standardised measures to supplement the assessment interview
- Ensure the rehabilitation plan is collaborative in process and expressed in language that is meaningful to the client
- Avoid confusion of goals and strategies in the rehabilitation plan

The assessment strategy

Check how the client is feeling about the interview

Clients bring a wide spectrum of feelings to an assessment interview, ranging from optimistic hope, through apprehension to negativity and resentment. Often there will be a mix of all these feelings and, depending on the form of the interview, one or other might become more prominent. Non-verbal signals may convey a lot of information about how the client is feeling, but sometimes an effect of mental illness is to mask non-verbal information. It is a good idea to check how the client is feeling about the interview at the beginning and to remain alert for any signs of uneasiness, discomfort or negativity as the interview proceeds.

Explain the rationale for the assessment interview

Clients will often have been through many assessment interviews in the course of treatment. New assessments can seem to be repetitive and pointless. Clients may say, 'Why don't you talk to my doctor? – I have told him everything' or, 'It is all in the medical record – why don't you just read it?' The key messages to communicate in explaining the rationale for the interview are:

- This is a way of me getting to know you – and also for you to learn a bit about me, and what we can offer to help you recover from your illness.
- The things I will be asking you about are directly relevant to developing your recovery plan.
- I will be asking some of the same things you have been asked before, but you will also find that I will be wanting to learn about things that have probably not come up much in previous interviews.
- I need to hear it directly from you. I will talk with the doctor and read the medical record, but I really want to hear your perspective.

Take your time

There is no rush or urgency about psychosocial rehabilitation. It is not a crisis assessment (although the rehabilitation practitioner needs to remain alert to the possibility of crisis, which is commonplace in mental illness). The psychosocial assessment can take place over several meetings.

Think about the setting

Assessment interviews often take place in a hospital or clinic environment, but this can have limitations as well as advantages. Consider conducting the assessment across of range of settings – partly in the hospital or clinic, partly in the client's home or another environment of her or his choice, and partly in a neutral environment such as a shopping centre or park. Each setting provides an opportunity to learn about how context influences the client, as well as communicating the practitioner's willingness to venture out of her or his own comfort zone. Remember that interviews that take place out of the hospital or clinic environment present specific risks. There may be safety issues for the practitioner and the client may be more vulnerable to sexual exploitation or some other form of professional boundary violation. Consult before home visits for a second opinion about risks and consider the advantages of the presence of a third person.

Introduce assessment of current capacities and pre-morbid strengths early in the assessment process

Identifying capacities and strengths creates a positive tone to the assessment and reduces the likelihood that the relationship will take the form of the competent practitioner and the helpless client. It is important to resist the temptation to point out strengths to the client. It is not your judgement as to client strengths that is important, but rather the client's identification of his or her own capacities or strengths. The practitioner can contribute by asking for detail, and by conveying expressions of interest or surprise when the client identifies a strength. Inexperienced interviewers often fail to follow up and ask about the detail and the client might reasonably conclude that the practitioner is not really interested. A set of seven categories that can be used as a checklist is set out in Text box 6.2.

Take a flexible approach to the structure of the interview

The practitioner should retain a clear idea about what she or he wants to achieve during the assessment process, but should equally be able to move in and out of assessment areas in accordance with the flow of the interview and with sensitivity to the experience of the client. If the client seems reluctant to provide some kind of information, the practitioner can check whether it is something the client would prefer to leave for another occasion, or whether he or she wants to talk now about why it is difficult or uncomfortable.

Remember that assessment should be therapeutic

The assessment should build hope and realistic expectation of progress. The client should become clearer about priorities and goals and develop confidence in the capacity of the rehabilitation practitioner to assist with recovery. The assessment should be motivating and empowering for the client. If this is not happening, then the practitioner should review the assessment strategy and seek the advice of colleagues or supervisors. It is likely that the feelings of the client have not been accurately identified and acknowledged.

Bring closure

Although the assessment is therapeutic, the assessment phase needs to be separated from the rehabilitation phase. This is best achieved through the mutual generation of a rehabilitation plan. The production of the plan ends the assessment phase and introduces the initial phase of rehabilitation. There will be various periods of reassessment, but these will take the form of plan reviews rather than the more open-ended initial assessment.

The rehabilitation plan

Characteristics

The rehabilitation plan is a document that guides both the practitioner and the client through the recovery process. It is a working document that will be revised on a regular basis. This means that its format is suitable for development and modification. An example of a rehabilitation plan is found in the case study in Text box 6.4. Essential features of the rehabilitation plan are as follows:

- It is a collaborative document: the product of discussion and negotiation between the client and the practitioner about priorities, goals, strategies and targets.
- It is a reference document for both practitioner and client; this means that it must be written using language and style that is clear to both parties.
- It is an operational document; this means that it is not concerned with general principles or aims but rather with very specific goals, targets and strategies.
- It is central to review of recovery progress; this means that targets must be sufficiently clear and concrete to enable both the client and practitioner to tell whether or not the plan is working.

Common traps and faults in rehabilitation plans

Practitioner focus
Practitioners often have their own priorities that reflect their own organisational accountabilities and working comfort. Typically, these include the safety of the client, effective symptom management and improved personal hygiene or dress. While it is reasonable for the practitioner to have priorities and to discuss these with the client, these should not be confused with client priorities. The rehabilitation plan must reflect the recovery path mapped out by the client rather than a path mapped out by the practitioner. There is plenty of room for negotiation and the practitioner can and should point out aspects of the recovery path that appear to be unrealistic or inappropriate. However, at the end of this process the plan must reflect client priorities.

Confusing goals and strategies:
A strategy is a means of achieving a goal and is not an end in itself. It is common to find rehabilitation plans in which a number of stated goals are actually strategies. A frequent example is 'take medication regularly'. Regular compliance with medication may be a strategy for managing symptoms, but is not a goal in itself. These kinds of confusions often occur because of excessive practitioner focus – it

might, for example, be a goal for the practitioner that the client is compliant with medication.

Overly ambitious goals and targets

It is important that most goals and targets have been met by the time of review (usually at 3 months). It is better to exceed targets than to under perform. When there is a large and complex priority such as returning to work, goals, strategies and targets should be steps on the way to achieving the larger goal. For example, in discussing the process of returning to work, the client and practitioner might agree that things that need to be achieved include preparing a resume, writing job applications and handling interviews. These should be the core material of the plan. If the client obtains work during the period, then the goals have been surpassed – but if work is not obtained there are still real and important achievements.

Vagueness about targets

If a target is not specified clearly, it is impossible to know whether or not it has been met. For example, a target of 'a resume' does not have much meaning without a time frame and some specification of standard (e.g. two-page, printed).

Text box 6.4 A case study and rehabilitation plan: Sam

Sam (who we met briefly in Chapter 5) is 18 years old and has a diagnosis of schizophrenia following two admissions associated with paranoid delusions and persistent auditory hallucinations. In each case, his admissions followed angry and irrational outbursts against his parents and damage to property at home. He was referred for rehabilitation following his second discharge. On presentation, Sam was negative and antagonistic towards rehabilitation – 'you people can't help me; you only care about yourselves'. Assessment of capacities and strengths revealed that Sam has a current interest in cars and is restoring an old Nissan Skyline that his uncle gave him. Sam was a very capable student in his earlier years of schooling and was good at sport and popular with his peers. However, he did poorly in his final 2 years and was suspended on several occasions.

Sam is unclear about his illness. He says he got stressed out and blames his parents who are 'always on my back – they think I am lazy because I don't have a job'. He said he is OK now but still gets voices that interrupt him. He thinks his medication helps with the voices but he often forgets to take it and hates the thought that he is a 'psycho on drugs'. He has lost contact with a lot of friends and feels embarrassed about contacting people, after what has happened to him.

Assessment summary: Sam

Sam has a diagnosis of schizophrenia, and although onset appears to have been acute there may have been a more extended prodrome given evidence of decline in functioning during his later years of high school. It is too early to determine the course of his illness. He is currently affected both by primary or positive symptoms (auditory hallucinations) that intrude and affect his concentration, and by secondary or negative symptoms (negativity, social avoidance) that are demoralising. There is evidence of current capacity for reasonably complex visual spatial tasks (car restoration) and underlying strengths of above average intelligence and sociability.

His current recovery stage has features of the post-traumatic and stocktaking stages but he is keen to move into a rebuilding stage. His characteristic coping style is externalisation. He is not very interested in reflecting on or learning from his illness, and is inclined to blame his parents. He basically wants to get over it and move on. He lives at home with supportive, but probably overly anxious and intrusive, parents who are likely to need support and psychoeducation. He has a network of friends but has largely lost contact with them during the period of acute illness. Sam has a treating psychiatrist who prescribes antipsychotic medication but may not be fully aware of Sam's compliance problems. Sam has no single rehabilitation priority but several issues that he wants to address urgently.

Table 6.1 Rehabilitation plan

Goal	Strategy	Target
Get to trust my rehabilitation worker	I want to find out if he is for real – he says he has an interest in cars; perhaps we can start there	I really believe this person is interested in me and isn't just doing a job
Turn the voices down	Take medication as prescribed – use a blister pack to be sure I have taken them. Let my doctor know if I am getting any side effects	Voices are in the background and I can talk to people without being interrupted or distracted within one month
Get my parents off my back	My rehabilitation worker will meet with my parents and provide them with information about schizophrenia. I will think about whether I want to attend. My rehabilitation worker will give my parents information about the schizophrenia fellowship where they can talk with other parents. A yelling diary where I record daily the times and reasons my parents yell at me	Two days in a row during the next month when my parents don't yell at me (according to the yelling diary)
Get some money of my own	Meet with the Centrelink* disability officer to find out if I am entitled to any social security benefits	Make appointment now and meet next week
I really want some friends. I am sick of spending all my time at home	Work out which friend I could call up. Work out a way of explaining what has happened to me (maybe try out some approaches with my rehabilitation worker)	Pick the right person by next week. Work out how to approach the call next meeting. Call up my friend within two weeks

* Centrelink is a Commonwealth agency that coordinates all social security and family support payments in Australia.

Conclusion

Assessment is the starting point for psychosocial rehabilitation. A successful assessment establishes a rehabilitation alliance and provides the foundation for a collaborative individual rehabilitation plan. Assessment aims to identify client perceptions and priorities as well as objective indicators of client strength and disability. The complexity and importance of the assessment process means that it should not be rushed and wherever possible should take place, in part at least, in the client's own environment. The use of structured assessment instruments can enhance the reliability of assessment and facilitate the evaluation of rehabilitation outcomes. The rehabilitation plan is a logical development from the assessment process. The plan identifies the goals, strategies and targets that client and practitioner will work with during the rehabilitation process.

The rehabilitation plan is likely to be most effective when it is negotiated and collaborative, reflects client priorities and stage of client recovery, and draws on client strengths.

References

Barry, K., Zeber, J., Blow, F., & Valenstein, M. (2003). Effects of strengths model versus assertive community treatment model on participant outcomes and utilization: A two-year follow-up. *Psychiatric Rehabilitation Journal, 26*, 268–277.

Beutler, L., Brookman, L., Harwood, M., Alimohamed, S., & Malik, M. (2001). Functional impairment and coping style. *Psychotherapy: Theory, Research, Practice, Training, 38*, 437–442.

Björkman, T., Hansson, L., & Sandlund, M. (2002). Outcome of case management based on the strengths model compared to standard care. A randomised controlled trial. *Social Psychiatry and Psychiatric Epidemiology, 37*, 147–152.

Brewin, C.R., Wing, J.K., Mangen, S.P., Brugha, T.S., & MacCarthy, B. (1987). Principles and practice of measuring needs in the long-term mentally ill: The MRC needs for care assessment. *Psychological Medicine, 17*, 971–981.

Eisen, S.V., Grob, M.C., & Klein, A.A. (1986). BASIS: The development of a self-report measure for psychiatric inpatient evaluation. *The Psychiatric Hospital, 17*, 165–171.

Ellis, G., & King, R. (2003). Recovery focused interventions: Perceptions of mental health consumers and their case managers. *Australian e-Journal for the Advancement of Mental Health 2*: www.auseinet.com/journal/vol2iss2/ellis.pdf

Gallagher, J., & Teesson, M. (2000). Measuring disability, need and outcome in Australian community mental health services. *Australian and New Zealand Journal of Psychiatry, 34*, 850–855.

Goodman, S.H., Sewell, D.R., Cooley, E.L., & Leavitt, N. (1993). Assessing levels of adaptive functioning: The Role Functioning Scale. *Community Mental Health Journal, 29*, 119–131.

Hansson, L., Vinding, H.R., Mackeprang, T., Sourander, A., Werdelin, G., Bengtsson-Tops, A., Bjarnason, O., Dybbro, J., Nilsson, L., Sandlund, M., Sorgaard, K., & Middelboe, T. (2001). Comparison of key worker and patient assessment of needs in schizophrenic patients living in the community: A Nordic multicentre study. *Acta Psychiatrica Scandinavica, 103,* 45–51.

Hansson, L., Sandlund, M., Bengtsson-Tops, A., Bjarnason, O., Karlsson, H., Mackeprang, T., Merinder, L., Nilsson, L., Sorgaard, K., Vinding, H., & Middelboe, T. (2003). The relationship of needs and quality of life in persons with schizophrenia living in the community. A Nordic multi-center study. *Nordic Journal of Psychiatry, 57,* 5–11.

Kroll, L., Woodham, A., Rothwell, J., Bailey, S., Tobias, C., Harrington, R., & Marshall, M. (1999). Reliability of the Salford Needs Assessment Schedule for Adolescents. *Psychological Medicine, 29,* 891–902.

Lasalvia, A., Ruggeri, M., Mazzi, M.A., & Dall'Agnola, R.B. (2000). The perception of needs for care in staff and patients in community-based mental health services. The South-Verona Outcome Project 3. *Acta Psychiatrica Scandinavica, 102,* 366–375.

Lockwood, A., & Marshall, M. (1999). Can a standardized needs assessment be used to improve the care of people with severe mental disorders? A pilot study of 'needs feedback'. *Journal of Advanced Nursing, 30,* 1408–1415.

Marshall, M., Hogg, L.I., Gath, D.H., & Lockwood, A. (1995). The Cardinal Needs Schedule – a modified version of the MRC Needs for Care Assessment Schedule. *Psychological Medicine, 25,* 605–617.

McGlashan, T.H. (1987). Recovery style from mental illness and long-term outcome. *Journal of Nervous and Mental Disorders, 175,* 681–685.

Macpherson, R., Varah, M., Summerfield, L., Foy, C., & Slade, M. (2003). Staff and patient assessments of need in an epidemiologically representative sample of patients with psychosis – staff and patient assessments of need. *Social Psychiatry and Psychiatric Epidemiology, 38,* 662–667.

Meadows, G., Harvey, C., Fossey, E., & Burgess, P. (2000). Assessing perceived need for mental health care in a community survey: Development of the Perceived Need for Care Questionnaire (PNCQ). *Social Psychiatry and Psychiatric Epidemiology, 35,* 427–435.

Parker, G., O'Donnell, M., Hadzi-Pavlovic, D., & Proberts, M. (2002). Assessing outcome in community mental health patients: A comprehensive analysis of measures. *International Journal of Social Psychiatry, 48,* 11–19.

Phelan, M., Slade, M., Thornicroft, G., Dunn, G., Holloway, F., Wykes, T., Strathdee, G., Loftus, L., McCrone, P., & Hayward, P. (1995). The Camberwell Assessment of Need: the validity and reliability of an instrument to assess the needs of people with severe mental illness. *British Journal of Psychiatry, 167,* 589–595.

Pilgrim, D. (2002). The biopsychosocial model in Anglo-American psychiatry: Past, present and future? *Journal of Mental Health, 11,* 585–594.

Rapp, C.A., & Wintersteen, R. (1989). The Strengths model of case management: Results from twelve demonstrations. *Psychosocial Rehabilitation Journal, 13,* 23–32.

Rosen, A., Hadzi-Pavlovic, D., & Parker, G. (1989). The Life Skills Profile: A measure assessing function and disability in schizophrenia. *Schizophrenia Bulletin, 15,* 325–337.

Slade, M., Phelan, M., & Thornicroft, G. (1998). A comparison of needs assessed by staff and by an epidemiologically representative sample of patients with psychosis. *Psychological Medicine, 28,* 543–550.

Stannard, R.P. (1999). The effect of training in a Strengths model of case management on client outcomes in a community mental health center. *Community Mental Health Journal, 35,* 169–179.

Stedman, T., Yellowlees, P., Drake, S., Chant, D., Clarke, R., & Chapple, B. (2000). The perceived utility of six selected measures of consumer outcomes proposed for routine use in Australian mental health services. *Australian and New Zealand Journal of Psychiatry*, *34*, 842–849.

Strauss, J.S., Hafez, H., Lieberman, P., & Harding, C.M. (1985). The course of psychiatric disorder, III: Longitudinal principles. *American Journal of Psychiatry*, *142*, 289–296.

Veit, C.T., & Ware, J.E.J. (1983). The structure of psychological distress and well–being in general populations. *Journal of Clinical and Consulting Psychology*, *51*, 730–745.

Wing, J.K., Brewin, C.R., & Thornicroft, G. (1992). Defining mental health needs. In: G. Thornicroft, C.R. Brewin, & J.K. Wing (Eds.), *Measuring mental health needs* (pp.1–21). London: Gaskell.

Wing, J.K., Beevor, A.S., Curtis, R.H., Park, S.B., Hadden, S., & Burns, A. (1998). Health of the Nation Outcome Scales (HoNOS). Research and development. *British Journal of Psychiatry*, *172*, 11–18.

Chapter 7

INTEGRATING PSYCHOSOCIAL REHABILITATION AND PHARMACOTHERAPY

Tom Meehan, Shane McCombes and Terry Stedman

Overview of chapter

For the majority of individuals with serious mental illness, biological treatments in the form of pharmacotherapy will form an important part of their treatment. Although clients and their carers are frequently critical of the medications used in psychiatry, clients who are not stabilised on such medications usually do not obtain optimum benefit from psychosocial interventions. Indeed, the feasibility of community based care for many people with mental illness is very much dependent on effective use of psychotropic medications. While this chapter includes some discussion of the technical aspects of drug treatment, it focuses on the importance of medication in the treatment of psychiatric conditions and the application of recovery principles to the practices associated with drug treatment. This chapter concludes with a discussion of multidisciplinary involvement and opportunities to improve the quality of drug treatment. These issues will be discussed in relation to severe mental illnesses, particularly schizophrenia. The principles and practice apply equally to most other conditions encountered by a rehabilitation practitioner.

Antipsychotic medications

The modern era of pharmacotherapy began in the early 1950s with the introduction of the antipsychotic preparation chlorpromazine. This drug was found to be particularly useful in the treatment of psychotic disorders such as schizophrenia. Antipsychotics help individuals to manage acute psychosis by gradually reducing hallucinations and delusions. They also act as maintenance therapy to control symptoms and as long-term prophylactic treatment in the prevention of relapses (Carpenter & Buchanan, 1994). However, these preparations are not curative and individual response varies widely. Up to 30% of people will obtain little or no therapeutic benefit from their use (Kupfer & Sartorious, 2002; Lehman & Steinwachs, 1998).

Since the 1950s a number of antipsychotic preparations have been introduced (see Table 7.1). Although there appears to be little difference between these in terms

Table 7.1 Common typical and atypical antipsychotic medications

Typical antipsychotics	Atypical antipsychotics
Phenothiazines	Amisulpride
Chlorpromazine (Largactil)	Clozapine
Trifluoperazine (Stelazine)	Risperidone
Thioridazine (Melleril)	Olanzapine
Thioxanthene	Quetiapine
Flupenthixol (Depixol)	Ziprasidone
Butyrophenone	
Haloperidol (Haldol)	

of their mode of action and efficacy, they tend to differ in their side effects profile, dosage requirements (potency) and cost (Pratt, 2001). The 'first generation' drugs, which share actions on *dopamine* receptors, are now called 'typical' antipsychotics to differentiate them from the newer 'atypical' (or second generation) antipsychotics, which have different modes of action.

Clozapine, introduced in the late 1960s, was the first of the second generation antipsychotics. It represented a major advancement in the treatment of schizophrenia since the introduction of chlorpromazine some 15 years earlier. Despite a number of advantages over typical agents, widespread use was delayed due to the occurrence of agranulocytosis (a reduction in white blood cells) in up to 2% of those prescribed the medication (Baldessarini & Frankenburg, 1991). Strict monitoring protocols have since been introduced and these have significantly reduced the risks associated with clozapine use. The number of atypical agents available has grown over the past 10 years and atypicals have now replaced conventional medications in the treatment of psychotic conditions in Australia (Mond et al., 2003) and in the UK (Frangou & Lewis, 2000). About half of the people who were previously unresponsive to typical antipsychotics will show fair to good response to atypical preparations such as clozapine (Meltzer, 1995).

Antipsychotic medications are responsible for a range of side effects involving movement and the muscular system. The more common side effects are summarised in Table 7.2. Antipsychotics also impact on the metabolism of acetylcholine and this can lead to another group of side effects such as dry mouth, blurred vision, urinary retention, and constipation. Several atypical antipsychotic medications have been associated with increased weight gain (Allison et al., 1999; Briffa & Meehan, 1998; McIntyre et al., 2003) and the propensity to develop type II diabetes (Henderson et al., 2000).

Interestingly, clients have reported that not all side effects are unpleasant. Memory loss was considered a useful side effect by those who were trying to forget unpleasant memories of their illness, and loss of libido was welcomed in those without a partner (Svedberg et al., 2003). Therefore the client (rather than the practitioner) is the best judge of the level of distress caused by a given side effect. Clients often have to make difficult decisions concerning the trade-off between the

Table 7.2 Common motor side effects

Side effect	Brief description
Akathisia	This is a feeling of motor restlessness frequently affecting the lower limbs – the so called 'restless legs syndrome'. Treatment involves the use of an anticholinergic drug, reduction in medication or switch to an atypical agent
Acute dystonia	Dystonia usually involves the muscles of the neck and head. Signs include protrusion of the tongue (torticollis), arching of the neck to the side and/or backwards, and the upwards rotation of the eyes (oculogyric crisis). These conditions respond well to anticholinergic medications
Parkinsonian symptoms	The key signs for this condition include: rigidity of the muscles, slowed movements (often mistaken for depression), shuffling gait, and a 'pill-rolling' tremor of the hands usually accompanied by cogwheel rigidity. Again, these conditions respond to anticholinergic medications but it may be more appropriate to change to an atypical, especially in elderly patients since they are prone to falls when experiencing this condition
Tardive dyskinesia	This condition consists of involuntary movement of muscles usually around the mouth, tongue and jaw. The tongue, for example, protrudes in and out of the mouth and there may be repeated pursing of the lips. The condition usually appears following prolonged treatment with typical antipsychotics (more than 6 months – hence the word 'tardive'). While there is no known cure, the condition may improve when the drug is ceased. Risk is reduced by using the lowest dose of medication to achieve the desired effect

benefits resulting from the impact of antipsychotic medications on symptoms and disadvantages resulting from side effects. The cognitive problems commonly associated with psychotic disorders may adversely affect this decision making and rehabilitation practitioners may sometimes become strong advocates of a particular position to compensate for the client's decision-making difficulties. This may be reasonable when clients are highly impaired, but it is generally recommended that practitioners work with clients to assist them identify and weigh up the positives and negatives, rather than assume a position of advocacy.

Antidepressants

Depression impacts on the lives of millions of people around the world and its incidence appears to be on the increase (Lewinsohm et al., 1993; Murray & Lopes, 1996). Up to 20% of adults experience depressive symptoms at any given time (Kessler et al., 1994; Thase & Kupfer, 1996). Major depression and bipolar affective disorder are two of the more serious conditions in this group. Although a large number of people experience depression, many fail to seek treatment with enormous costs in terms of quality of life, productivity, and relationships (Andrews et al., 2001). This is disappointing, since a number of well constructed clinical trials support the efficacy of using antidepressant medications in the treatment of depression. Approximately 60% of people with depression will respond to anti-depressant medications. No one class of antidepressants (these are described below) appears to be more effective than another in treating depression.

In depression, two key neurotransmitters (noradrenalin and serotonin) are significantly depleted (Kaplan & Sadock, 1993). Antidepressant medications act at the synapse by either preventing the reuptake of these neurotransmitters or preventing their breakdown by monoamine oxidase (Kaplan & Sadock, 1993). Thus, drug treatments for depression help to increase the levels of one or both of these neurotransmitters in the synapses between the neurons. The commonly used antidepressants are selective serotonin reuptake inhibitors (SSRIs), tricyclics, and monoamine oxidase inhibitors (MAOIs).

SSRIs are now the most commonly used agents in the treatment of depression as they have fewer (or different) side effects than tricyclics and MAOIs (Song et al., 1993). While they are less dangerous when taken in overdose, they do have a number of side effects such as sleep disturbance, gastrointestinal problems and sexual dysfunction (Song et al., 1993). Prozac (fluoxetine) has become one of the best known preparations in this group. The tricyclic group of antidepressants acts by inhibiting the reuptake of serotonin and noradrenalin into the presynaptic neuron. While they have demonstrated their efficacy in the treatment of depression, they have a number of side effects. Overdose (common in people with depression) is very serious and can be fatal, since elevated blood concentrations cause cardiac arrhythmias and ventricular tachycardia (Kaplan & Sadock, 1993).

MAOIs are now used less frequently in the treatment of depression due to their side effect profile. These drugs act by preventing the breakdown of an enzyme that destroys noradrenalin and serotonin in the synapse (Thase et al., 1995). However, they also block the destruction of naturally occurring amines such as tyramine (found in cheese, wine, Marmite, soy products and some flu preparations). The accumula-tion of tyramine in the bloodstream can lead to a hypertensive crisis which results from extremely elevated blood pressure. Other side effects include dry mouth, blurred vision, postural hypotension, insomnia and sexual dysfunction (Thase et al., 1995).

It is clear that the use of antidepressants is on the rise. A recent review of pre-scribing patterns in Canada raised concerns about antidepressant use (Beck et al., 2005). The study found that antidepressants were commonly prescribed for anxi-ety disorders and migraine. Only one-third of those taking antidepressants had a past-year episode of major depression (Beck et al., 2005). This does not mean that antidepressants are being wrongly prescribed, as there is an established evidence base for their effectiveness with a range of anxiety disorders (Baldwin et al., 2005) and with pain (Mattia et al., 2002). However, there is some risk that the wide application of antidepressants will result in their prescription as a 'panacea', with the consequence of insufficient attention to psychosocial issues.

Mood stabilisers

Bipolar affective disorder is characterised by episodes of mania or hypomania alter-nating with episodes of depression (see Chapter 2). Up to 50% of people with moderate to severe depression will experience an episode of mania during their lifetime (Healy, 2005). Many of these people are likely to be prescribed mood stabilisers to reduce the impact of current symptoms, or as prophylaxis to prevent future episodes. The most common among this class of medications include lithium, carbamazepine and sodium valproate.

Lithium

Lithium was first isolated in the early 1950s by John Cade, a Melbourne psychiatrist. Lithium is now widely used in the treatment of mania and in the prophylactic treatment of manic depressive disorder. Although antipsychotics can also be used in the treatment of mania, lithium leads to a more specific response to mania, usually within 10 days of reaching therapeutic blood levels (Healy, 2005). Toxicity is a major problem as lithium has a narrow therapeutic window (0.6–1.1 mmol/l of blood). Therefore symptoms can occur at levels close to the therapeutic range. Early signs of toxicity include ataxia and lack of coordination.

Although lithium is one of the most effective drugs in the treatment of acute mania, a significant number of people do not respond and others find the side effects difficult to tolerate. Anticonvulsants such as carbamazepine and sodium valproate are now widely used instead of lithium for certain subgroups of people.

Carbamazepine

Carbamazepine (Tegretol) is commonly used in the treatment of epileptic disorders. However, in the late 1960s, a group of Japanese psychiatrists noticed that patients taking carbamazepine were less depressed and its potential use in the treatment of mood disorders was recognised (Harris et al., 2003). It was found to be far safer in overdose and less addictive than barbiturates, which were commonly used prior to this. Carbamazepine may be superior to lithium in the treatment of people with rapid cycling mania (usually more than four episodes in a single year) and those with dysphoric mania (Greil et al., 1997). Side effects may include drowsiness, dizziness, nausea, visual disturbances, cardiac problems and confusion (Healy, 2005).

Sodium valproate

Sodium valproate (Epilim) is another anticonvulsant that appears to be useful in the prophylactic treatment of mania. It also appears to be effective in the treatment of mania that has been non-responsive to lithium. Side effects include nausea, stomach cramps, loss of energy and weight gain. It can also impact on liver function and regular liver function tests (LFTs) are required to offset liver failure.

Value and limitations of medications in recovery from mental illness

It is clear that medications play an integral role in the treatment of mental health conditions. The efficacy of both antipsychotic and antidepressant medications has been demonstrated in numerous studies over the past 20 years. In a review of 100 well controlled studies, Lehman & Steinwachs (1998) found that antipsychotic medication significantly reduced symptoms (delusions, hallucinations and thought disorder) in up to 85% of people with schizophrenia. Antipsychotic medications can be used in the short term (minutes to hours) to relieve distress and behavioural disturbance associated with psychotic symptoms, in the medium term (days to weeks) to remove or reduce psychotic symptoms such as hallucinations, delusions or disorganisation, and in the longer term (months to years) to reduce the frequency of acute episodes. Modern medications have changed both the illness experience and treatment environment of disorders such as schizophrenia by reducing symptoms, improving clinical stability, and reducing relapse rates by up to 50% (Carpenter & Buchanan, 1994). However, it is less clear that they have brought about any significant change in recovery rates or long-term course of illness. Even with optimal treatment, fewer than 15% of people meet full criteria for remission 5 years after initial diagnosis of schizophrenia (Robinson et al., 2004).

The newer atypical medications have one clear advantage over the earlier antipsychotics. They are less likely to cause motor disturbances (akathisia, dystonia and dyskinesia) as a side effect of treatment. As a result, there is less need for anticholinergic agents, which in themselves can adversely impact on memory function (Hagan & Jones, 2005). The presence of motor disturbances associated with the typical medications was highly stigmatising and frequently prevented individuals from participating in social activities (Perlick et al., 2001). While this is a substantial benefit of recent medications, as indicated above, the atypical antipsychotics increase risk of weight gain and diabetes and thus compromise health and increase vulnerability to another source of stigma.

Atypical antipsychotics may be more effective in combating the negative symptoms observed in psychotic disorders such as schizophrenia (Kupfer & Sartorious, 2002). Both olanzapine (Kopelewicz et al., 2000) and clozapine (Moller, 1995) have been reported as having a therapeutic effect on negative symptoms. However, much of the evidence thus far has been derived from clinical experience, post-hoc analyses of controlled studies and findings from uncontrolled studies. It is possible that the improvement in negative symptoms observed with the use of atypicals is linked to the lower levels of side effects (Kane et al., 1994).

Combining pharmacological and non-pharmacological treatments

Following the introduction of antipsychotic medications in the 1950s there was concern that psychotherapy and medication might be incompatible. There was a perception that biologically based disorders should be treated with medication, psychologically based disorders with psychotherapy and social problems should be met with psychosocial interventions (Rossler & Hanker, 2003). These concerns slowly disappeared and most clients now receive a combination of treatments. Indeed, there is strong evidence to suggest that combining psychotherapy and pharmacotherapy may have advantages over either treatment alone. Hogarty & Ulrich (1998) found that the rate of relapse within 12 months for people hospitalised with a diagnosis of schizophrenia was approximately 40% when they were treated with medication alone and approximately 20% when treated with a combination of medication and psychosocial treatments. In relation to depression, Blatt and colleagues (2000) demonstrated that clients receiving cognitive behaviour therapy reported significantly greater capacity to establish and maintain interpersonal relationships and to recognise and understand the source of their depression than clients receiving antidepressant medication alone.

A number of models have been proposed for understanding interactions between pharmacological and psychosocial interventions. In relation to psychotic conditions, biological protective factors (such as medications) and social protective factors (social supports, well-functioning families and coping skills) combine to stabilise the individual. A model put forward by Marder (2000) suggested possible advantages of combining pharmacological and psychosocial strategies:

- Clients receiving an effective psychosocial treatment might require a lower dose of antipsychotic medication
- Clients who are receiving adequate medication might tolerate more intrusive and stimulating forms of psychosocial treatment than those who are unmedicated or improperly medicated
- Clients who are receiving psychosocial interventions may be more compliant with prescribed medications
- The effects of combining treatments may be more than additive, since each would enhance the effectiveness of the other
- Drugs and psychosocial treatments may affect different outcome domains (e.g. drugs may affect psychotic symptoms or relapse rates and psychosocial treatments may affect social and vocational skills

Hollon & Fawcett (1995) concluded from a summary of the literature that 'pharmacotherapy appears to provide rapid relief from acute distress, and psychotherapy appears to provide broad and enduring change, with combined treatment retaining the specific benefits of each' (p. 1957).

Using medication within a recovery framework

Although the use of antipsychotic and antidepressant medications has revolutionised the treatment of mental disorders, reliance on medication presents a number of challenges for recovery orientated practice. Individuals are often pressured to take medications and may be under a compulsory treatment order that gives them little or no input into decisions regarding their medications. Some are required to take 'depot' preparations (drug provided via intramuscular injection every 1–6 weeks), which can add to feelings of disempowerment (Walburn et al., 2001). The focus on medication as the mainstay of treatment can promote dependence on the clinician/service and undermine hope – a key element of recovery

Table 7.3 Some practical suggestions for recovery oriented prescribing

Communicate a belief in the possibility of recovery for the person

Prescribe hopefully and persist until optimal outcomes are achieved

Acknowledge differences in power between client and prescriber

Acknowledge the lack of power of the treatment relationship without the client's participation

Encourage and fully evaluate treatment proposals originating with the client

Find areas to give client's control, e.g. timing and frequency of dose

Model and expect appropriate participation in treatment planning

Encourage and support development of a personal crisis plan

(Noordsy et al., 2000). Indeed, some clients find it hard to reconcile long-term dependence on medications with personal autonomy and recovery.

Rehabilitation practitioners can work collaboratively with medical practitioners to promote a recovery orientation towards medication that emphasises participation, empowerment and choice. Even when drug treatment takes place within a compulsory treatment framework, respectful and collaborative prescribing can enhance the therapeutic alliance. Noordsy and colleagues (2000) provide guidelines for prescribing medications in a way that promote recovery based practice. These are summarised in Table 7.3.

Recovery focuses on the individual's self determination to get better and the process of taking responsibility for one's health (Anthony, 2000). These considerations must underlie all aspects of medication prescribing (assessment, prescribing and monitoring). Engaging individuals in discussions about their medications and their perceptions of the role that medications are likely to play in their recovery can assist both practitioner and client. Does the client communicate a sense that medications will be helpful in his or her recovery? Is the client willing to take ownership of his or her illness and responsibility for medication compliance? Regardless of where the clients are on their journey towards recovery, the practitioner should promote a sense of hope for the future, encourage skill development in medication use and support the consumer in establishing a life outside the illness (Svedberg et al., 2003).

Optimising compliance/adherence

Compliance with medication is the single most important factor in preventing relapse in disorders such as schizophrenia. Accumulated evidence suggests that the majority of patients with psychotic illness will experience a relapse after discontinuation of antipsychotic medications. Hogarty & Ulrich (1998) followed clients that had remained relapse-free for up to 3 years and then ceased medication. Within one year, 65% had relapsed, with most relapses occurring between 3 and 7 months after discontinuation. According to Svedberg and colleagues (2003), adherence to medication regimes is necessary to make 'ordinary life and a normal person

Table 7.4 Factors contributing to non-adherence with medication regimes

Factor	Content
Factors related to the illness	Delusional/paranoid thinking, lack of motivation, lack of insight and depressive states
Factors related to the patient	Younger age, male sex, being single, lower socioeconomic status, lack of family involvement, poor knowledge of medications
Factors related to health care system	Poor quality of care, complex dosing regimes, lack of access/control over medications
Factors related to the medications	Side effects, lack of perceived benefits, cost

more possible' (p.117). However, despite the introduction of a broader range of antipsychotics/antidepressants over the past 10 years, rates of non-compliance with medication protocols among people with mental illness remain high (Awad, 2004). Up to 60% of people with schizophrenia fail to adhere to medication regimes within 6 weeks of commencing antipsychotics (Conley & Johnson, 1991). A recent review of the literature by Awad and Voruganti (2004) identified four factors contributing to non-adherence (see Table 7.4).

One approach to overcoming relapse from non-adherence has been the replacement of the oral medications with long-acting depot preparations. Hogarty and colleagues (1994) demonstrated that clients treated with depot medications had a significantly longer time in the community prior to relapse when compared to those treated with oral medications. However, others have expressed concern about the efficacy of depot preparations (Castle et al., 2002) and client loss of control over their treatment. Injections can be experienced as embarrassing and painful (Smith et al., 1999) and can also interfere with work or travel, thus impacting on recovery (Svedberg et al., 2003). Those receiving depot preparations were motivated by the distressing memories of relapsing and losing control, and saw depot treatment as an important but uncomfortable necessity in the process of regaining control and recovering (Svedberg et al., 2003).

A related strategy involves the use of intermittent treatment protocols, which is based on the observation that the majority of clients will not develop a relapse for several months after ceasing medication (Hogarty & Ulrich, 1998). Moreover, most individuals exhibit prodromal signs of pending illness prior to relapse and careful monitoring of drug-free patients should enable treatment to be recommenced to prevent a full scale relapse (Gaebel, 1994). However, it is difficult to recognise the warning signs in most individuals and therefore treatment is frequently initiated too late. Admission rates have been found to be double in those on intermittent protocols (Gaebel, 1994). Higher doses of medication are also required to treat relapse in intermittent individuals than are required to prevent a relapse in those on continuous medication regimes. Indeed, side effects such as tardive dyskinesia are just as common in individuals on intermittent protocols.

Managing side effects

The successful management of side effects is an important factor in ensuring that individuals adhere to prescribed treatment regimens (Morrison et al., 2000). However, it is often difficult to discriminate between side effects (e.g. restlessness) and symptoms of the illness. This issue underscores the need to note a symptom baseline prior to administering medication. The use of standardised rating scales for the assessment and monitoring of medication side effects may be valuable in providing an effective, customised service to clients (Gray & Howard, 1997). Assessment schedules may increase practitioner awareness of the problems, provide a structured format for assessments, elicit data that may be used as an adjunct to clinical judgements, and provide a focus for discussion with a client on side effects. The Liverpool University Neuroleptic Side-Effect Rating Scale (LUNSERS) developed in the UK by Day and colleagues (1995) is one such assessment tool that has demonstrated utility in the monitoring of antipsychotic side effects (Morrison et al., 2000).

A recent Cochrane review (Haynes et al., 2005) suggested a number of additional strategies that have been found to significantly enhance compliance in the general population (see Text box 7.1).

Text box 7.1 Strategies for enhancing compliance with medications (adapted from Haynes et al., 2005)

- Provide information on illness and the importance of medication
- Provide clients with ample instructions (verbal, written, visual)
- Engage family in discussions about medications and dosing
- Provide telephone follow-up
- Simplify dosing (e.g. once daily dosing versus multiple daily doses)
- Tailor regime to daily habits, e.g. link medications to meals, activities, etc.
- Use of dose dispensing units – 'Dosette' boxes, etc.

It must be understood that the management of side effects and strict adherence to medication regimes will not always prevent a relapse (Ayuso-Gutierrez & del Rio Vega, 1997). The course of severe mental illness is unpredictable and a number of people will continue to experience relapses despite compliance with treatment.

The challenge for the rehabilitation practitioner is getting the right balance between validating client concerns and supporting the role of medication in relapse prevention. Rehabilitation practitioners will not usually be experts on medication but can help clients think through their concerns and can help them develop strategies to address these concerns (see Text box 7.2). Maintaining a strong alliance and respect for client autonomy is likely to reduce the risk of impulsive or oppositional cessation of medication. Even when the client is on an involuntary treatment order, concerns about medication can be discussed and reasonable solutions negotiated.

Text box 7.2   Case study ongoing: Sam

Sam, whom you met in previous chapters, has been out of hospital now for a couple of months. Recently, he has been telling Cassie, his rehabilitation practitioner, that his medications are making him tired and he feels 'disconnected from reality'. Cassie suspects that he has not been taking his medications as prescribed. She suggests to Sam that they sit down and try to work out what to do about the problems he has described.

'Why don't we start by checking if it is the medications or something else that might be causing you to feel tired and disconnected? When do you think you started feeling this way?' Sam tells Cassie that he is not sure but thinks it has been a couple of weeks. Cassie says to Sam, 'You have been taking this same medication since you left hospital. Why do you think it is only affecting you now – could there be something else that is affecting the way you feel?' 'I don't know,' Sam responds. 'Maybe there is a delayed effect. Anyway, I am tired of taking medication all the time.'

Cassie asks Sam to list all the things he does not like about taking medication. 'Its not normal – other people don't have to take tablets all the time. I don't know what these things are doing to my head. It's hard to remember to take them the same time each day. I've seen people get fat just from taking these things.' Cassie says 'OK, they sound like pretty reasonable concerns – most people would probably be worried about these kinds of things. Can you think of any benefits you get from taking medication?' 'Well I guess I feel less stressed and less out of control – I don't get voices. I know my parents like me to take medication, and things are better at home.' 'So it sounds like medication is a mixed blessing,' says Cassie. 'There are some things that really bother you about it but there are also some benefits. Have you thought about discussing feeling tired and disconnected with your doctor?' Sam replies, 'She'll just tell me I have to keep taking it.' Cassie thinks for a moment and suggests, 'How about talking about your tired and disconnected feelings and asking if they could be caused by the medication, rather than just saying you want to stop taking it? Your doctor will know whether these are usual side effects and whether you might be better off with a different dose or a different type of medication.'

Working effectively with primary care clinicians/pharmacists

Mental health policies in Australia (Australian Health Ministers, 2003) and in the UK (Department of Health, 1990) stress the need to develop links between mental health services and other health and social services. An increasing number of people with mental health problems, including those with severe mental illness, seek help from primary care providers such as general practitioners and pharmacists (Andrews et al., 2001). GPs can provide a less stigmatising clinical environment and a more holistic approach to health care than specialist mental health services. During 2000 in Australia, 84.2% of scripts for oral antipsychotics and 81.2% of scripts for depot medications were written by GPs (Mond et al., 2003).

In areas that have few or no psychiatrists, the primary care physician is often the person who prescribes and monitors psychotropic medications. Harris (2000) noted that GPs (in Australia) were willing to engage in the care of people with mental illness, including those with severe illness, but required the support of specialist mental health services. This can be quite challenging for the rehabilitation practitioner, because GPs are usually much more comfortable relating professionally to medical specialists and may be unclear about the role of the rehabilitation practitioner. Similarly, rehabilitation practitioners often have limited understanding of the needs and priorities of GPs, who operate within very tight time constraints and require clear and concise communication of information.

Pharmacists can be a key source of information on medications and other health related issues. Pratt (2001) suggests that multidisciplinary teams should have access to a 'specialist' pharmacist who could provide information on issues surrounding the use of medications. They could also review previous medication regimes and 'identify gaps in treatment that may have produced partial response' (p. 258). Schmidt and colleagues (1998) demonstrated that it was possible to decrease the prescribing of antipsychotics and other medications through multidisciplinary teamwork, which included input from a pharmacist. The NHS in the UK promotes the review of treatment plans by a pharmacist before approving treatment with the more costly atypical antipsychotics (Pratt, 2001). In any event, most people have access to their community based pharmacist. Although they may not have specialist training in psychiatric medications, they can provide valuable information on the safe use of medications and other physical health conditions. Community pharmacists are well respected and the majority provide information at no cost to the consumer.

Conclusion

Core components of the treatment of mental illness are the amelioration of symptoms, the prevention of a relapse, and the restoration of social and vocational roles through rehabilitation. It is clear that the appropriate use of medications plays a major role in achieving these goals. While some individuals will demonstrate significant response to medications, a small subgroup of others will continue to struggle with their illness. The use of medication in itself is rarely adequate to reverse the effects of conditions such as schizophrenia. Among the majority who derive substantial benefit from psychotropic medications, many will be affected by side effects or by problems adhering to the standard regime. Medications are most effective when used in combination with counselling and psychosocial treatments. Practitioners can promote a recovery focused approach to use of medications by supporting active client engagement in decisions about choice of medications and strategies to manage side effects. Practitioners can also develop and foster collegial relationships with doctors and pharmacists so as to maximise the likelihood that clients will maintain clear channels of communication with those professionals best able to provide information and advice about medication.

References

Allison, D., Mentore, J., Heo, M., Chandler, L., Cappelleri, J., Infante, M., & Weiden, P. (1999). Anti-psychotic induced weight gain: A comprehensive research synthesis. *American Journal of Psychiatry, 156,* 1686–1696.

Andrews, G., Henderson, S., & Hall, W. (2001). Prevalence, comorbidity, disability and service utilisation: Overview of the Australian National Mental Health Survey. *British Journal of Psychiatry, 178,* 145–153.

Anthony, A. (2000). A recovery-oriented service system: Setting some system level standards. *Psychiatric Rehabilitation Journal, 24,* 159–168.

Australian Health Ministers. (2003). *National mental health plan 2003–2008.* Canberra: Australian Government.

Awad, G. (2004). Antipsychotic medications: compliance and attitudes towards treatment. *Current Opinion in Psychiatry, 17,* 75–80.

Awad, G., & Voruganti, L. (2004). New antipsychotics, compliance, quality of life, and subjective tolerability – are patients better off? *Canadian Journal of Psychiatry, 49,* 297–301.

Ayuso-Gutierrez, J., & del Rio Vega, J. (1997). Factors influencing relapse in the long-term course of schizophrenia. *Schizophrenia Research, 28,* 199–206.

Baldessarini, R., & Frankenburg, F. (1991). Clozapine: A novel antipsychotic agent. *New England Journal of Medicine, 324,* 746–754.

Baldwin, D.S., Anderson, I.M., Nutt, D.J., Bandelow, B., Bond, A., Davidson, J.R., den Boer, J.A., Fineberg, N.A., Knapp, M., Scott, J., & Wittchen, H.U. British Association for Psychopharmacology (2005). Evidence-based guidelines for the pharmacological treatment of anxiety disorders: Recommendations from the British Association for Psychopharmacology. *Journal of Psychopharmacology, 19,* 567–596.

Beck, C., Patten, S., Williams, J., Wang, J., Currie, S., Maxwell, C., & El-Guebaly, N. (2005). Antidepressant utilisation in Canada. *Social Psychiatry and Psychiatric Epidemiology, 40,* 799–807.

Blatt, S., Zuroff, D., Bondi, C., & Sanislow, C. (2000). Short- and long-term effects of medication and psychotherapy in the brief treatment of depression: Further analysis of data from the NIMH TDCRP. *Psychotherapy Research, 10,* 215–234.

Briffa, D., & Meehan, T. (1998). Weight changes during clozapine treatment. *Australian and New Zealand Journal of Psychiatry, 32,* 718–721.

Carpenter, W. Jr., & Buchanan, R. (1994). Medical progress: Schizophrenia. *The New England Journal of Medicine, 330,* 681–690.

Castle, D., Morgan, V., & Jablensky, A. (2002). Antipsychotic use in Australia: The patient's perspective. *Australian and New Zealand Journal of Psychiatry, 36,* 633–641.

Conley, R., & Johnson, D. (1991). British versus United States usage of depot neuroleptics. *Relapse, 1,* 1–2.

Day, J., Wood, G., Dewey, M., & Bentall, R. (1995). A self-rating scale for measuring neuroleptic side-effects. Validation in a group of schizophrenic patients. *British Journal of Psychiatry, 166,* 650–653

Department of Health. (1990). *Community care in the next decade and beyond.* London: HMSO.

Frangou, S., & Lewis, M. (2000). Atypical antipsychotics in ordinary clinical practice: A pharmo-epidemiologic survey in a south London service. *European Psychiatry, 15,* 220–226.

Gaebel, W. (1994). Intermittent medication – an alternative? *Acta Psychiatrica Scandinavica,* (Suppl. 382), 33–38.

Gray, R., & Howard, A. (1997). The Maudsley medication review clinic. *Journal of Psychiatric and Mental Health Nursing, 4,* 225–226.

Greil, W., Ludwig-Mayerhofer, W., & Erazo, N. (1997). Lithium versus carbamazepine in the maintenance treatment of bipolar disorders: A randomised study. *Journal of Affective Disorders, 43,* 151–161.

Hagan, J., & Jones, D. (2005). Predicting drug efficacy in schizophrenia. *Schizophrenia Bulletin*, *31*, 830–853.

Harris, M. (2000). General practice recruitment for schizophrenia prevention studies. *Australian and New Zealand Journal of Psychiatry*, *34* (Suppl. S137), 9.

Harris, M., Chandram, S., & Chakraborty, N. (2003). Mood-stabilisers: The archaeology of the concept. *Bipolar Disorders*, *5*, 446–452.

Haynes, R., Yao, X., Degani, A., Kripalani, S., Garg, A., & McDonald, H. (2005). Interventions to enhance medication adherence. *The Cochrane Database of Systematic Reviews*, *(Issue 4)*.

Healy, D. (2005). *Psychiatric drugs explained* (4th ed.). London: Elsevier.

Henderson, D., Cagliero, E., Grey, C. Nasrallah, R., Hayden, D., Schoenfield, D., & Goff, D. (2000). Clozapine, diabetes mellitus, weight gain, and lipid abnormalities: A five-year naturalistic study. *American Journal of Psychiatry*, *157*, 975–981.

Hogarty, G., & Ulrich, R. (1998). The limitations of antipsychotic medication on schizophrenia relapse and adjustment and the contributions of psychosocial treatment. *Journal of Psychiatric Research*, *32*, 243–250.

Hogarty, G., Schooler, N., Ulrich, R., Mussare, F., Ferro, P., & Herron, E. (1994). Fluphenazine and social therapy in the aftercare of schizophrenia patients. *Archives of General Psychiatry*, *36*, 1283–1294.

Hollon, S.D., & Fawcett, J. (1995). *Combined medication and psychotherapy in treatments of psychiatric disorders* (2nd ed.). Washington: American Psychiatric Press.

Kane, J., Safferman, A., Pollack, S., Johns, C., Szymanshi, S., Konig, M., & Liberman, J. (1994). Clozapine, negative symptoms and extrapyramidal side effects. *Journal of Clinical Psychiatry*, *55* (Suppl. B), 74–77.

Kaplan, H., & Sadock, B. (1993). *Pocket handbook of psychiatric drug treatment*. Baltimore: Williams & Wilkins.

Kessler, R., McGonagel, K., Zhao, S., Nelson, C., Hughes, M., Eshleman, S., Wittchen, H., & Kendler, K. (1994). Lifetime and 12 month prevalence of DSM-III-R psychiatric disorders in the United States. *Archives of General Psychiatry*, *51*, 8–19.

Kopelewicz, A., Zarate, R., Tripodis, K., Gonzalez, V., & Mintz, J. (2000). Differential efficacy of olanzapine for deficit and nondeficit negative symptoms in schizophrenia. *American Journal of Psychiatry*, *157*, 987–993.

Kupfer, D., & Sartorious, N. (2002). The usefulness and use of second-generation antipsychotic medications. *Current Opinion in Psychiatry*, *15* (Suppl. 1), 7–16.

Lehman, A., & Steinwachs, D. (1998). At issue: Translating research into practice. The schizophrenia patient outcomes research team (PORT) treatment recommendations. *Schizophrenia Bulletin*, *24*, 1–10.

Lewinsohm, P., Rohde, P., Seeley, J., & Fischer, S. (1993). Age-cohort changes in the lifetime occurrence of depression and other mental disorders. *Journal of Abnormal Psychology*, *102*, 110–120.

Marder, S. (2000). Integrating pharmacological and psychosocial treatments for schizophrenia. *Acta Psychiatrica Scandinavica*, *102* (Suppl. 407), 87–90.

Mattia, C., Paoletti, F., Coluzzi, F., & Boanelli, A. (2002). New antidepressants in the treatment of neuropathic pain. A review. *Minerva Anestesiologica*, *68*, 105–114.

McIntyre, R.S., Trakas, K., Lin, D., Balshaw, R., Hwang, P., Robinson, K., & Eggleston, A. (2003). Risk of weight gain associated with antipsychotic treatment: Results from the Canadian National Outcomes Measurement Study in Schizophrenia. *Canadian Journal of Psychiatry*, *48*, 689–694.

Meltzer, H. (1995). Treatment-resistant schizophrenia: The role of clozapine. *Current Medical Research and Opinion, 14*, 1–20.

Moller, H. (1995). The negative component of schizophrenia. *Acta Psychiatrica Scandinavica, 388* (Suppl. 91), 11–14.

Mond, J., Morice, R., Owen, C., & Korten, A. (2003). Use of antipsychotic medications in Australia between July 1995 and December 2001. *Australian and New Zealand Journal of Psychiatry, 37*, 55–61.

Morrison, P., Meehan, T., Gaskill, D., Lunney, P., & Collings, P. (2000). Enhancing case managers skills in the assessment and management of antipsychotic medication side-effects. *Australian and New Zealand Journal of Psychiatry, 34*, 814–821.

Murray, C., & Lopes, A. (1996). *The global burden of disease.* Geneva: World Health Organization.

Noordsy, D.L., Torrey, W.C., Mead, S., Brunette, M., Potenza, D., & Copeland, M.E. (2000). Recovery-oriented psychopharmacology: Redefining the goals of antipsychotic treatment. *Journal of Clinical Psychiatry, 61* (Suppl. 3), 22–29.

Pratt, P. (2001). The administration and monitoring of neuroleptic medication. In: C. Brooker & J. Repper (Eds.), *Serious mental health problems in the community: Policy, practice and research* (pp. 238–264). London: Bailliere Tindall.

Perlick, D., Rosenheck, R., Clarkin, J., Sirey, J., Salahi, J., Struening, E., & Link, B. (2001). Adverse effects of perceived stigma on social adaptation of persons diagnosed with bipolar disorder. *Psychiatric Services, 52*, 1627–1632.

Robinson, D., Woerner, M., McMeniman, M., Mendelowitz, A., & Bilder, R. (2004). Symptomatic and functional recovery from first episode of schizophrenia or schizoaffective disorder. *American Journal of Psychiatry, 161*, 473–479.

Rossler, W., & Hanker, H. (2003). Conceptualizing psychosocial interventions. *Current Opinion in Psychiatry, 16*, 709–712.

Schmidt, I., Claesson, B., Westerholm, B., Nilsson, L., & Svarstad, B. (1998). The impact of regular multidisciplinary team interventions on psychotropic prescribing in Swedish nursing homes. *Journal of the American Geriatrics Society, 46*, 77–82.

Smith, J., Hughes, I., & Budd, R. (1999). Non-compliance with anti-psychotic depot medications. Users' views on advantages and disadvantages. *Journal of Mental Health, 8*, 287–296.

Song, F., Freemantle, N., Sheldon, T., House, A., Watson, P., Long, A., & Mason, J. (1993). Selective serotonin reuptake inhibitors: Meta-analysis of efficacy and acceptability. *British Medical Journal, 306*, 683–687.

Svedberg, B., Backenroth-Ohsako, G., & Lutzen, K. (2003). On the path to recovery: Patients' experiences of treatment with long-acting injections of anti-psychotic medication. *International Journal of Mental Health Nursing, 12*, 110–118.

Thase, M., & Kupfer, D. (1996). Recent development in the pharmacotherapy of mood disorders. *Journal of Consulting and Clinical Psychology, 64*, 646–659.

Thase, M., Trivedi, M., & Rush, A. (1995). MAOIs in contemporary treatment of depression. *Neuropsychopharmacology, 12*, 185–219.

Walburn, J., Gray, R., Gourney, K., Quraishi, S., & David, A. (2001). Systematic review of patient and nurse attitudes to depot antipsychotic medication. *British Journal of Psychiatry, 179*, 300–307.

Chapter 8

FAMILY PSYCHOEDUCATION

Robert King and Chris Lloyd

Overview of chapter

This chapter begins with a brief history of relationships between mental health practitioners and families and carers of people with mental illness. It highlights progress from family blaming to collaboration with families and in particular the role of psychoeducation in this collaboration. Psychoeducation as a psychosocial intervention is explained and the role of family psychoeducation in deinstitutionalised mental health care is discussed. Confidentiality is a potential barrier to collaboration between families and mental health practitioners and strategies for overcoming this barrier are outlined. Different approaches to psychoeducation, including the use of problem solving, multiple family groups and brief interventions are identified and the evidence base concerning these approaches and what is known about the most effective components is discussed. The chapter ends by revisiting Sam and examining issues troubling his family and the response of his treatment team and, in particular, his psychosocial rehabilitation practitioner.

Early approaches

Up until the last 20 years there has been a tendency to see families as part of the problem rather than part of the solution in recovery from mental illness. Perspectives on the family ranged from theories about family interactions as causal agents in mental illness to theories about family interactions as contributing to relapse in mental illness.

The theory of the 'schizophrenogenic mother' (Hartwell, 1996; Neill, 1990) was popular during the 1950s and 1960s. It proposed that psychosis was the result of mothering that was intrusive, controlling and ultimately rejecting. This kind of mothering was thought to impede or prevent the development of individual identity and in extremity lead to psychosis. In Europe, Pankow (1961) also highlighted the mother–child relationship and proposed that schizophrenia was the expression in the child of unmanageable intrapsychic conflicts of one of the parents, usually the mother. Her approach to treatment therefore included the mother, focusing on her personal history and the place of her child in her unconscious life. Laing & Esterson (1964), who were highly influential during the 1960s and 1970s, also saw the family as responsible for the development of psychotic illness but emphasised interactional patterns within the whole family rather than the mother–child relationship. They suggested that families of people diagnosed with schizophrenia were characterised by intereactions described as 'double binds'. These were emotional conundrums imposed on the person with mental illness whereby any kind of rational response was unacceptable to the family – driving the person to responses that seemed irrational on the surface but made sense when you understood the double bind.

These theories were based on clinical observation rather than systematic research and did not distinguish between causality and behaviour which, while not causal might have the effect of exacerbating the condition. This important distinction formed the basis for later research and clinical application based on the theory of 'expressed emotion' (Wearden et al., 2000). This theory postulates that parents who are critical and overinvolved contribute to relapse in psychosis as a result of the emotional demands they place on a person vulnerable to stress. As Parker (1982) pointed out, 'expressed emotion' focused on similar hostile, rejecting and over-controlling characteristics as had been identified in the 'schizophrenogenic mother'. The important development was that these characteristics were not posited as causal agents in the illness but rather as factors that contributed to relapse.

While expressed emotion as a construct has been the subject of intensive research, and there is some evidence of cross-cultural validity (Kuipers, 1992; Marom et al., 2002; Yang et al., 2004), most of the evidence demonstrates an association rather than a causal relationship with relapse (Barrowclough & Hooley, 2003; Kavanagh, 1992). Those studies that have attempted to investigate causality have failed to find evidence that it is fundamentally linked with mental illness or with relapse (King, 2000; Subotnik et al., 2002). It is quite possible that high expressed emotion is a normal response to the symptoms and behaviour of the person affected by the mental illness (Kavanagh, 1992; van Os et al., 2001).

Although expressed emotion as a theory was less overtly blaming of families than some of the earlier theories, it nonetheless left families in the position of feeling responsible and even criticised (Hatfield et al., 1987). It made collaboration between professionals and family members difficult, and collaboration with families rather than changing families was increasingly being identified as the most productive approach to facilitating recovery (Hatfield, 1997). Failure to validate the theory of expressed emotion made it difficult to justify persevering with a framework that was of questionable scientific merit and risked alienating the very people it was designed to help.

Text box 8.1 Maintaining a recovery focus in family psychoeducation

- Families often provide the physical and emotional support that is essential to recovery
- Families desperately want their loved one to make the best possible recovery
- Families usually want to be included in the thinking and planning about how psycho-social rehabilitation will promote recovery
- The experience of hope is important for families as well as for people immediately affected by mental illness
- Families seek respect and understanding of their lived experience of mental illness

What is psychoeducation?

The term psychoeducation has been defined as *the education of a person with psychiatric disorder in subject areas that serve the goals of treatment and rehabilitation* (Pekkala & Merinder, 2002). The term has been used to describe a variety of clinical interventions designed to inform clients and family members about the characteristics of a mental health problem, as well as clinical strategies and strategies of general living that will contribute to recovery, promote stability and reduce the risk of relapse (Colom & Vieta, 2004). Psychoeducation aims to empower those who are directly affected by mental illness and those who are part of their daily life to become active agents of recovery through possession of accurate and useful information (Mericle, 1999).

Psychoeducation may be essentially didactic and informative (Hornung et al., 1996) or it may have a substantial therapeutic component. As Pekkala & Merinder (2002) point out, learning implies more than just changes in knowledge but rather changes that impact on cognitive, affective and even psychomotor processes. Cognitive behaviour therapy (CBT) is sometimes described as a psychoeducational therapy, but some studies have compared CBT as a psychotherapy with a non-psychotherapy form of psychoeducation. There is evidence that psychoeducation without a psychotherapy component is effective at enhancing recovery and reducing risk of relapse, but that a psychotherapy component probably increases the effectiveness of information alone (Bechdolf et al., 2004; Gonzalez-Pinto et al., 2004).

The focus of this chapter is on psychoeducation designed specifically for family members. This form of psychoeducation, as will be seen, often has both informational and therapeutic components (Anderson et al., 1986). These typically comprise provision of:

- Information about mental illness including scientific information concerning neurophysiological functioning, epidemiological information, information about the role of psychosocial stressors, and the use of medication
- A learning environment conducive to the development of a calm and rational problem solving approach within the family
- Interventions designed to modify interpersonal relations within the family that are characterised by hostility, intrusiveness or critical judgement

However, some family psychoeducation programmes (De Groot et al., 2003) are primarily didactic, with informal therapeutic components resulting from interaction between family members or different families in a structured environment.

Family psychoeducation represents a shift away from treatment of the individual who is suffering from the mental illness to the immediate milieu within which the individual lives and is supported. The underlying principle is that if the support network is stressed or uncertain, then this will have an adverse impact on the person with the illness. Psychoeducation seeks to address some of the environmental factors that contribute to mental illness.

Psychoeducation differs from earlier approaches to the families of people with mental illness in several important respects:

- It does not suppose a causal link between the structure or behavioural characteristics of the family and the development of mental illness
- While in some forms it proposes a link between family behaviour and exacerbation of symptoms or relapse into acute state, in other forms it avoids even this level of attribution
- It is not concerned with exploring in depth family dynamics or family relationships, but rather is concerned with focusing on very specific and often quite practical aspects of family life
- The focus is on providing the family with information and facilitating problem solving, rather than in making fundamental changes in the family as a structure or a system
- There is commitment to formal evaluation of the efficacy of the programmes with respect to impact on the functioning and mental stability of the person suffering from mental illness, and the impact on family burden of care

Text box 8.2 Maintaining a multidisciplinary focus in family psychoeducation

- Families often have a strong interest in medical interventions and want information about medications, their effects and side effects
- Families usually have little knowledge or understanding of the roles of different practitioners in psychosocial interventions and will appreciate a clear, plain language explanation of the roles of various people contributing to treatment and care
- If there is a case manager or some other designated person who is the point of first contact for family members, families need to be clear about the role of this person and how and when to contact
- Information sessions or 'survival skills workshops' provide an opportunity for families to have formal and informal exposure to a range of mental health practitioners and perspectives

Why has family psychoeducation become such a prominent approach to mental illness?

The emergence of psychoeducation as a major force, especially in public mental health services, probably derives from two factors:

- Evidence of efficacy, especially with reducing risk of early relapse but also with reducing family burden (Dixon et al., 2000; Lehman et al., 2003; Murray-Swank & Dixon, 2004)
- A changing relationship between mental health professionals and families, which has followed the movement away from hospital based care towards community based care (Riebschleger, 2002)

When institutional care was dominant, the institution took on a quasi-parental role and mental health workers were in a potentially rivalrous and conflictual position in relation to the real family. Families were often not encouraged to even maintain contact with family members in institutional care. In some instances, the institution may have aimed to provide a more successful 'family' milieu by contrast with the toxic milieu of the actual family. These kinds of approaches were particularly evident in the therapeutic community movement that was popular in inpatient settings during the 1960s and 1970s. By contrast, successful community based care of people with mental illness required an alliance with the family, which was often the primary care giver. Mental health professionals were therefore less inclined to adopt a position towards the family that was critical or likely to alienate them.

It became increasingly clear to clinicians that family members were looking to professionals as a source of useful information which could enable them to understand the often dramatic changes that had taken place within their son, daughter, sibling or sometimes parent. Family members were also often looking for ways in which they could make a contribution to recovery, but were also struggling to cope with a complex of emotional and practical burdens associated with caring for a mentally ill family member. These burdens included dealing with feelings of guilt and responsibility, dealing with feelings of anger and frustration and managing the demands of providing day-to-day care for an adult. In many cases, parents were aging and struggling with problems of impaired physical health. In some cases, one or other parent was also struggling with mental illness. Families were often dissatisfied with mental health professionals, who they experienced as either blaming or indifferent to their difficulties (Hatfield, 1997).

Confidentiality: a challenge in communication with families

Confidentiality is an ethical consideration with potential to inhibit communication between practitioners and families (Furlong & Leggatt, 1996; Petrila & Sadoff, 1992). Families often want information and advice, but practitioners may feel that communicating freely with families without the explicit permission of the client is ethically unacceptable. Practitioners may even avoid contact with families so as to minimise the risk of breaching confidentiality. There is evidence that practitioners tend to interpret legal provisions and ethical codes pertaining to confidentiality very conservatively, meaning that they make the minimal disclosures rather than the fullest possible disclosures (Marshall & Solomon, 2003). It is important that practitioners respect and adhere to the legal and ethical codes that apply to their profession and service delivery environment, but there are some useful strategies for maximising communication with families without violating confidentiality (Furlong & Leggatt, 1996; Zipple et al., 1990):

- Work with clients to secure permission for open communication with families.
- Permission should be formally granted and a signed copy, together with any specific exceptions (see below), kept in the client chart or file.

- Encourage clients to identify and specify issues or information they do not want discussed with families, and respect these.
- Whenever possible, maintain open communication with the client present. This minimises the risk of splitting and ensures that all parties know what the other has communicated.
- Become knowledgeable about the legal and ethical codes and their confidentiality provisions. Often, codes include a range of circumstances in which it is acceptable to breach confidentiality and these may apply in communication with families.
- When in doubt consult with peers, medical ethicists, professional associations and malpractice insurance advisors – but aim for maximally acceptable disclosure to families rather than minimally acceptable disclosure.
- When the client has not granted permission and a family wants information, don't just leave it with 'I can't tell you because it's confidential'. Instead, 'I would need to check with your son/daughter to make sure they are OK about me discussing this with you – how about I do that and then get back to you?' Or, 'How about we get together with your son/daughter and discuss this together? – I'm not sure how much they want me to pass on, so it would be best we discuss it together.'
- In meetings with the family and client together, address issues of privacy, consent and wish or need to know before dealing with the substance of the issue. It is important that all parties understand and respect both needs for privacy and needs for information. Most times, both can be respected and there is not a conflict between the two.

Family psychoeducation: from interventions designed to reduce expressed emotion to problem solving in multiple family groups

The early findings concerning the relevance of expressed emotion resulted in the design of family intervention and education programmes with the specific aim of reducing the level of expressed emotion (Leff et al., 1990). Family members were educated in the relationship between expressed emotion and relapse risk, as well as in other factors such as medication compliance thought to be important in stabilising schizophrenia. They were then taught approaches to managing and reducing expressed emotion, especially criticism of the family member. The family therapy sessions employed a rather eclectic set of techniques, drawing to some extent from the structural and systemic family therapy approaches as well as from behavioural, cognitive and problem solving approaches.

The outcome reports from these studies were that family interventions designed to lower expressed emotion were effective in reducing critical comments, hostility and overinvolvement, and relapse rates were reduced (Hogarty et al., 1991; Leff et al., 1990; Tarrier et al., 1994). However, meta-analyses of controlled studies of family interventions (Mari & Streiner, 1994; Pharoah et al., 2003) revealed at best modest benefits for family interventions with respect to reductions in expressed emotion, rate of relapse and social indicators.

The use of problem solving was an element of some early family psychoeducation approaches (Anderson et al., 1986). Problem solving involves identifying problems or stressors, brainstorming possible solutions and then selecting and implementing workable solutions. The benefit of problem solving is that it takes a lot of the emotional intensity out of difficulties and enables them to be formulated as problems with solutions, rather than sources of anger or blame. Problem solving in family groups became central to the approach developed by McFarlane et al. (1993). The benefits of multiple family psychoeducation are:

- Challenges involved in living with and supporting a person with severe mental illness have individual characteristics, but also much in common from family to family
- Families derive support and comfort from knowing that they are not alone with these challenges
- Families benefit from learning about solutions that others have found to common problems
- Linking up with other families develops social networks to the benefit of both the families and the person directly affected by mental illness

This approach to multiple family psychoeducation is broadly similar to that described by Anderson et al. (1986) for individual family work. Families are recruited through a 'survival skills workshop', which provides information about mental illness and about the benefits of multiple family psychoeducation. Families then meet on a regular basis in groups of 3–5 families. Each session is highly structured and includes informal socialisation at the beginning and end and systematic problem solving in the main part of the meeting. The person directly affected by mental illness is encouraged to attend, but this is not mandatory. From time to time, medical staff attend the groups to answer questions or discuss issues specifically related to medication or other medical aspects of treatment.

Text box 8.3 Family psychoeducation in action: Sam's parents attend a survival skills workshop

Sam's parents are getting exasperated with him. He is moody and uncooperative. He lazes about, sleeps during the day and they don't know what he is doing at night. He does not contribute to the household. They know that he has a diagnosis of schizophrenia, because that is what they were told by the doctors during his previous admissions. However, they don't know what this really means and the doctors seem very vague. Is he going to return to normal? Should they put more pressure on him or less pressure on him? Isn't it reasonable that if he is living at home he should help out?

Sam's mother calls his rehabilitation practitioner, who explains that because of confidentiality she cannot discuss Sam's situation without his permission. She says that she would be happy to meet with both parents and Sam together. She also suggests

Sam's parents attend an information evening that is coming up in a couple of weeks. 'Some of the doctors and other mental health professionals will be talking about mental illness and its treatment. You will also get a chance to meet with other parents in a similar situation.'

Sam's parents attend the information session. Some of the information is rather technical and they are not sure exactly what parts apply to Sam. 'It seems from what they are saying that anything could happen' says Sam's dad after the meeting. 'He could come good and just get on with his life or he could be on medication and a disability pension for the rest of his life. I wish I knew what we could do that would make a difference'. Sam's mum is really pleased that she got to meet some other parents during the coffee break. 'One thing I found out is that it is not just us,' she told her husband. 'I met a woman whose daughter took an overdose after she was asked to put her dirty clothes in the washing machine. She seemed like a perfectly normal woman so I guess it must be the illness that has this affect on some kids. It is reassuring to know there are other people in the same situation because sometimes I feel like what is happening with Sam is all my fault.'

Sam reluctantly agrees to his parents meeting with him and his rehabilitation practitioner. 'They are always on my back,' he says, 'You will see what they are like.' During the meeting, Sam's parents explain that they feel generally uncertain and worried about what is happening with Sam. The rehabilitation practitioner encourages them to identify concrete and immediate issues and problems. Sam's mother says that she cannot get him up out of bed and he does nothing around the house. Sam immediately responds 'All you ever do is yell at me – why should I do anything for you?' The rehabilitation practitioner asks Sam if he is bothered about his sleeping in or about not doing much around the house. Sam says he does more than they think – for example, they got a DVD recently and did not have a clue how to set it up so he did this for them. He also replaced the wiper blades on his father's car and got the lawn mower running by replacing the air filter. His parents agree that he did do these things, but he only does things when he feels like it, not when they ask him. By the end of the meeting, Sam has agreed that he is a bit concerned about his reversed sleep pattern because he does want to get a job when he is feeling better. Sam's parents agree that they have a tendency to nag Sam and to yell when they get frustrated.

Results obtained by McFarlane et al. (1995a; 1995b), in controlled trials comparing the efficacy of multiple family psychoeducation with single family psychoeducation, suggest a clear advantage for the multiple family approach with respect to relapse rate but not with respect to other outcome variables, such as number of hospitalisations, symptom reduction and medication compliance. A controlled study comparing multiple family groups with and without the information component showed no differences between the two on the outcome measures, but both multiple family groups had superior outcomes to single family groups (McFarlane et al., 1995a). This suggests that the critical factor in the success of the multiple family groups is the communication and interaction between families. The benefits of multiple family groups are most evident in the group of patients identified as having high risk of relapse (McFarlane et al., 1995b). Application of the multiple family approach to bipolar disorder has also been reported, but with limited outcome data and no evidence of enhanced rate of recovery relative to medication (Miller et al., 2004). However, there is at least one high quality study (Miklowitz et al., 2003) that shows single family psychoeducation applied to bipolar disorder is associated with lower rate of relapse when compared with case management and crisis intervention, so it is reasonable to expect that this would also be the case for multiple family psychoeducation.

Despite the encouraging findings reported by McFarlane's team, endorsement by family advocates and researchers and a programme of dissemination (McFarlane et al., 1993), subsequent research into this model and application in routine psychosocial rehabilitation services has been limited (Dixon, 1999). This may be because services have failed to accommodate the needs of families in their mode of service delivery (Dixon, 1999).

Brief family psychoeducation

Given the cost and burden of long term family therapy along the lines of the McFarlane model, it is not surprising that there have been several attempts to develop and evaluate focused brief family psychoeducation interventions. Glick et al. (1993) found that families who received eight weekly sessions of education and problem solving activities reported less family burden and more positive attitudes towards the family member with mental illness than families receiving standard care only. They also found some evidence that the clinical outcomes were better for people whose families participated in these groups, although these benefits tended to erode over time. Solomon et al. (1996) found that a 9-month programme of group psychoeducation had a positive impact on self efficacy among those families who had not been involved previously in family support or advocacy groups.

In a review of findings from six studies of brief family psychoeducation interventions, Pekkala & Merinder (2002) concluded that there was clear evidence of a positive impact on rate of readmission to hospital, and probable evidence of benefit with respect to medication compliance and psychosocial functioning on the part of the person immediately affected by mental illness. They found that there was probable evidence that families became more knowledgeable about mental illness and had more positive attitudes as a result of brief family psychoeducation.

Since then, De Groot et al. (2003), in a matched control study, found no impact for brief (6 month) family psychoeducation, with a mixture of didactic and problem solving components, on client functioning, admission rates or family burden, but a positive impact on family knowledge and understanding of mental health services. Chien & Chan (2004) found positive impact on client functioning and rehospitalisation for multiple family peer support (12 sessions over 6 months) but not for didactic psychoeducation. This lends weight to the proposition that peer support and problem solving, rather than information, are the active components of successful psychoeducation.

It is possible that benefits for brief interventions will be limited to knowledge unless there is sufficient scope for peer support and problem solving. It is also likely that current admission practices mean that there is generally less scope for any psychosocial intervention to impact on the frequency and duration of readmission than was the case during the 1980s and early 1990s (see also Chapter 9).

Text box 8.4 Evidence base for family psychoeducation

- Family psychoeducation contributes to knowledge of illness and knowledge of services
- Family psychoeducation has a positive impact on relapse and probably on other indicators of mental health
- Family psychoeducation is most powerful when it includes a significant component of peer interaction and support, and a significant component of problem solving or some other reality based therapeutic approach
- Longer term (i.e. more than 6 months) is probably more effective than short term family psychoeducation, but brief programmes are likely to have some beneficial effect
- Expressed emotion has weak validity as a mediating variable in family psychoeducation, and focus on expressed emotion does not promote collaboration

Conclusion

Families are central to the recovery of many people with mental illness. Families are a support system, as well as having an enormous personal stake in the best outcome for the person most immediately affected by mental illness. Historically, mental health service providers have often had negative attitudes to family members, seeing them as part of the problem rather than part of the solution. Today, family members are viewed as part of the recovery team. However, even today, barriers associated with confidentiality or unsympathetic service models mean that communication with families is often less than optimal.

Family psychoeducation provides a structured means of including families, providing them with information and, probably more importantly, opportunities to share experiences with peers and to problem solve. Family psychoeducation is regarded as an evidence-based psychosocial intervention with potential to reduce relapse and to bring benefits to the families and to the person most immediately affected by mental illness. It appears that family psychoeducation is less practised than indicated as desirable by contemporary practice standards and the evidence base. It is important for practitioners in psychosocial rehabilitation to include the family whenever possible, whether as part of a formal family psychoeducational programme, or in the course of planning and review of psychosocial interventions.

References

Anderson, C., Reiss, D., & Hogarty, G. (1986). *Schizophrenia and the family: A practitioner's guide to psychoeducation and management.* New York: The Guilford Press.

Barrowclough, C., & Hooley, J.M. (2003). Attributions and expressed emotion: A review. *Clinical Psychology Review, 23,* 849–880.

Bechdolf, A., Knost, B., Kuntermann, C., Schiller, S., Klosterkotter, J., Hambrecht, M., & Pukrop, R. (2004). A randomized comparison of group cognitive–behavioural therapy and group psychoeducation in patients with schizophrenia. *Acta Psychiatrica Scandinavica, 110,* 21–28.

Chien, W.T., & Chan, S.W. (2004). One-year follow-up of a multiple-family-group intervention for Chinese families of patients with schizophrenia. *Psychiatric Services*, 55, 1276–1284.

Colom, F., & Vieta, E. (2004). A perspective on the use of psychoeducation, cognitive–behavioral therapy and interpersonal therapy for bipolar patients. *Bipolar Disorders*, 6, 480–486.

De Groot, L., Lloyd, C., & King, R. (2003). Evaluation of a family psychoeducation program in community mental health. *Psychiatric Rehabilitation Journal*, 27, 18–23.

Dixon, L. (1999). Providing services to families of persons with schizophrenia: present and future. *Journal of Mental Health Policy and Economics*, 2, 3–8.

Dixon, L., Adams, C., & Lucksted, A. (2000). Update on family psychoeducation for schizophrenia. *Schizophrenia Bulletin*, 26, 5–20.

Furlong, M., & Leggatt, M. (1996). Reconciling the patient's right to confidentiality and the family's need to know. *Australian and New Zealand Journal of Psychiatry*, 30, 614–622.

Glick, I.D., Clarkin, J.F., Haas, G.L., & Spencer, J.H. (1993). Clinical significance of inpatient family intervention: Conclusions from a clinical trial. *Hospital and Community Psychiatry*, 44, 869–873.

Gonzalez-Pinto, A., Gonzalez, C., Enjuto, S., Fernandez de Corres, B., Lopez, P., Palomo, J., Gutierrez, M., Mosquera, F., & Perez de Heredia, J.L. (2004). Psychoeducation and cognitive–behavioral therapy in bipolar disorder: An update. *Acta Psychiatrica Scandinavica*, 109, 83–90.

Hartwell, C.E. (1996). The schizophrenogenic mother concept in American psychiatry. *Psychiatry*, 59, 274–297.

Hatfield, A.B. (1997). Working collaboratively with families. *Social Work in Health Care*, 25, 77–85.

Hatfield, A.B., Spaniol, L., & Zipple, A.M. (1987). Expressed emotion: A family perspective. *Schizophrenia Bulletin*, 13, 221–226.

Hogarty, G.E., Anderson, C.M., Reiss, D.J., Korblith, S.J., Greenwald, D.P., Ulrich, R.F., & Carter, M. (1991). Family psychoeducation, social skills training, and maintenance chemotherapy in the aftercare treatment of schizophrenia. II. Two-year effects of a controlled study on relapse and adjustment. Environmental–Personal Indicators in the Course of Schizophrenia (EPICS) Research Group. *Archives of General Psychiatry*, 48, 340–347.

Hornung, W.P., Kieserg, A., & Feldmann, R. (1996). Psychoeducational training for schizophrenic patients: Background, procedure and empirical findings. *Patient Education and Counseling*, 29, 257–268.

Kavanagh, D.J. (1992). Recent developments in expressed emotion and schizophrenia. *British Journal of Psychiatry*, 160, 601–620.

King, S. (2000). Is expressed emotion cause or effect in the mothers of schizophrenic young adults? *Schizophrenia Research*, 45, 65–78.

Kuipers, E. (1992). Expressed emotion research in Europe. Special Issue: European perspectives in clinical and health psychology. *British Journal of Clinical Psychology*, 31, 429–443.

Laing, R.D., & Esterson, A. (1964). *Sanity, madness and the family*. London: Tavistock.

Leff, J., Berkowitz, R., Shavit, N., Strachan, A., Glass, I., & Vaughn, C. (1990). A trial of family therapy versus a relatives' group for schizophrenia. Two-year follow-up. *British Journal of Psychiatry*, 157, 571–577.

Lehman, A.F., Buchanan, R.W., Dickerson, F.B., Dixon, L.B., Goldberg, R., Green-Paden, L., & Kreyenbuhl, J. (2003). Evidence-based treatment for schizophrenia. *Psychiatric Clinics of North America*, 26, 939–954.

McFarlane, W.R., Dunne, E., Lukens, E., Newmark, M., McLaughlin-Toran, J., Deakins, S., & Horen, B. (1993). From research to clinical practice: Dissemination of New York State's family psychoeducation project. *Hospital and Community Psychiatry*, 44, 265–270.

McFarlane, W.R., Link, B., Dushay, R., Marchal, J., & Crilly, J. (1995a). Psycho-educational multiple family groups: Four-year relapse outcome in schizophrenia. *Family Process*, 34, 127–144.

McFarlane, W.R., Lukens, E., Link, B., Dushay, R., Deakins, S.A., Newmark, M., Dunne, E.J., Horen, B., & Toran, J. (1995b). Multiple-family groups and psychoeducation in the treatment of schizophrenia. *Archives of General Psychiatry*, 52, 679–687.

Mari, J.J. & Streiner, D.L. (1994). An overview of family interventions and relapse on schizophrenia: Meta-analysis of research findings. *Psychological Medicine*, 24, 565–578.

Marom, S., Munitz, H., Jones, P.B., Weizman, A., & Hermesh, H. (2002). Familial expressed emotion: Outcome and course of Israeli patients with schizophrenia. *Schizophrenia Bulletin*, 28, 731–743.

Marshall, T., & Solomon, P. (2003). Professionals' responsibilities in releasing information to families of adults with mental illness. *Psychiatric Services*, 54, 1622–1628.

Mericle, B.P. (1999). Developing the therapeutic environment. In: N. Kelter, L.H. Swecke, & C.E. Bostrom (Eds.), *Psychiatric Nursing* (3rd ed.) (pp. 320–342). St. Louis: Mosby.

Miklowitz, D.J., George, E.L., Richards, J.A., Simoneau, T.L., & Suddath, R.L. (2003). A randomized study of family-focused psychoeducation and pharmacotherapy in the outpatient management of bipolar disorder. *Archives of General Psychiatry*, 60, 904–912.

Miller, I.W., Solomon, D.A., Ryan, C.E., & Keitner, G.I. (2004). Does adjunctive family therapy enhance recovery from bipolar I mood episodes? *Journal of Affective Disorders*, 82, 431–436.

Murray-Swank, A.B., & Dixon, L. (2004). Family psychoeducation as an evidence-based practice. *CNS Spectrums*, 9, 905–912.

Neill, J. (1990). Whatever became of the schizophrenogenic mother? *American Journal of Psychotherapy*, 44, 499–505.

Pankow, G. (1961). Dynamic structurization in schizophrenia. In: Burton A. (Ed.) *Psychotherapy of the Psychoses* (pp. 152–171). New York: Basic Books.

Parker, G. (1982) Re-searching the schizophrenogenic mother. *Journal of Nervous and Mental Disorders*, 170, 452–462.

Pekkala, E., & Merinder, L. (2002). Psychoeducation for schizophrenia. *The Cochrane Database of Systematic Reviews* 2002, Issue 2. Art. No. CD002831. DOI: 10.1002/14651858.CD002831.

Petrila, J.P., & Sadoff, R.L. (1992). Confidentiality and the family as caregiver. *Hospital and Community Psychiatry*, 43, 136–139.

Pharoah, F.M., Rathbone, J., Mari, J.J., & Streiner, D. (2003). Family intervention for schizophrenia. *The Cochrane Database of Systematic Reviews*, Issue 3. Art. No. CD000088.

Riebschleger, J. (2002). Community mental health professionals' theoretical assumptions about families: Responses to a practice simulation vignette. *Psychiatric Rehabilitation Journal*, 26, 91–96.

Solomon, P., Draine, J., Mannion, E., & Meisel, M. (1996). Impact of brief family psychoeducation on self-efficacy. *Schizophrenia Bulletin*, 22, 41–50.

Subotnik, K.L., Goldstein, M.J., Nuechterlein, K.H., Woo, S.M., & Mintz, J. (2002). Are communication deviance and expressed emotion related to family history of psychiatric disorders in schizophrenia? *Schizophrenia Bulletin, 28*, 719–729.

Tarrier, N., Barrowclough, C., Porceddu, K., & Fitzpatrick, E. (1994). The Salford Family Interventional Project: Relapse rates of schizophrenia at five and eight years. *British Journal of Psychiatry, 165*, 829–832.

van Os, J., Marcelis, M., Germeys, I., Graven, S., & Delespaul, P. (2001). High expressed emotion: Marker for a caring family? *Comprehensive Psychiatry, 42*, 504–507.

Wearden, A.J., Tarrier, N., Barrowclough, C., Zastowny, T.R., & Rahill, A.A. (2000). A review of expressed emotion research in health care. *Clinical Psychology Review, 20*, 633–666.

Yang, L.H., Phillips, M.R., Licht, D.M., & Hooley, J.M. (2004). Causal attributions about schizophrenia in families in China: Expressed emotion and patient relapse. *Journal of Abnormal Psychology, 113*, 592–602.

Zipple, A., Langle, S., & Spaniol, L. (1990). Client confidentiality and the family's need to know: Strategies for resolving the conflict. *Community Mental Health Journal, 26*, 533–545.

Chapter 9

INTENSIVE CASE MANAGEMENT IN PSYCHOSOCIAL REHABILITATION

Tom Meehan and Robert King

Overview of chapter

This chapter looks at case management as a framework for psychosocial rehabilitation. The evolution of case management in the context of de-institutionalisation of mental health services is considered, and different models of case management are examined. The primary focus is on intensive case management as a particularly well researched model with a strong emphasis on assertive rehabilitation. Intensive case management is described and illustrated and the evidence that indicates what it can and cannot achieve is examined.

Introduction

Since the 1950s there has been an almost worldwide trend towards the closure of asylums and institutions for the mentally ill. Coupled with these closures has been the development of a range of community alternatives for people with severe psychiatric disorders. Community based services, it was envisaged, would enable people with mental illness to move out of institutional care and live as independently as possible within their own homes or other 'homely settings' in the community (Durham, 1989). Demand for community based services grew in an attempt to meet the changing needs of people with mental illness.

It is now clear that the expanding array of community based services had both positive and negative consequences (Mueser et al., 1998). Tension developed between the stand-alone hospitals and the 'new' community services, which competed for limited resources. This resulted in a fragmented service system which was described in North America as 'a chaotic and incomplete patchwork of short-term inpatient units and inadequate outpatient care' (Bloch & Cournos, 1990, p. 389). Moreover, the growing complexity of service provision made it difficult for those with severe psychiatric conditions to seek out and access the necessary services (Mechanic, 1991). People with serious mental illness, particularly those with schizophrenia, showed little interest in keeping appointments and were frequently lost to the system (Melzer et al., 1991). Large numbers of mentally ill people received no treatment and among those that did, the treatment they received was frequently inappropriate or inadequate. The limitations of community based care for those with serious mental illness were becoming apparent from the sharply rising readmission rates (Franklin et al., 1987).

In response, case management was introduced as a means of coordinating the care for a small, but significant subgroup of people with serious mental illness. While the coordination of care has remained an integral part of the case manager's role, the responsibilities of the case manager have grown to include the provision of a variety of clinical, rehabilitative and social services (Mueser et al., 1998). At the same time, a number of variations of case management have emerged (e.g. broker, strengths, assertive, clinical) to meet the complex needs of individuals with mental illness.

Models of case management

A wide range of terms have been used to describe case management, e.g. standard, clinical, strengths-based, intensive, enhanced, assertive. However, they have similar goals: (i) to keep people in contact with services (Thornicroft, 1991); (ii) to reduce the frequency and duration of hospital admissions and hence costs (Kanter, 1989); and (iii) to improve outcome, especially social functioning and quality of life (Holloway, 1991). Although case management differs in focus and intensity, it relies on a combination of purposeful, goal-oriented care planning and the healing power of the therapeutic relationship between the case manager and client.

The primary focus of this chapter will be on intensive case management, which has a strong rehabilitation focus, but a brief overview of standard case management approaches will also be provided.

Standard case management models

Brief intervention case management

Brief intervention case management, as the name implies, was developed to provide a time limited service to clients with specific needs. Brief case management is usually provided by a triage team for a period of not greater than 6 weeks. It may be utilised for new clients during an assessment period in which a decision is made as to whether ongoing case management is required. It can also be utilised in association with a brief crisis intervention or during periods when a client, who usually manages well in the community with GP care or non-specialist support, requires short-term support when natural supports are not present due to holidays, etc. The advantage of using this type of case management is that the client can receive necessary treatment in their home environment without the long-term involvement of public mental health services.

Text box 9.1 Maintaining a recovery focus: tips for practitioners

- Remember that there is more to case management than just 'managing a case'; the therapeutic and rehabilitation focus is critical – your client is a person in the context of rehabilitation and is only a 'case' from a service system perspective
- Try not to be content with maintenance goals such as 'staying out of hospital', or maintenance strategies such as 'take medication'. Actively work with the client to set recovery oriented goals and identify strategies to achieve these goals
- Focus on client strengths and resources
- Allocate enough time to actively work with your client on recovery oriented goals and strategies. Avoid the trap of allocating time only when there is a crisis or problem

Broker case management

The brokerage model aims to achieve a separation of service needs assessment and service provision. Under this model a broker is responsible for assessing client needs and arranging for appropriate services (Curtis et al., 1992). The broker case manager is often the fund holder with the responsibility for managing a treatment budget, based on service needs, for each client. The major functions of the broker case manager include the assessment of patient needs, referral to appropriate agencies and the monitoring of care provided (Intagliata, 1982). Thus, the broker case manager does not personally provide the services required, but rather refers clients to specialist service providers.

The potential benefit of brokerage is that it minimises the overservicing potential inherent in a system where the clinician alone is responsible for deciding on the nature and quantity of services required. It also enables case managers to carry a larger caseload since much of the actual service provision is done by external agencies. The major weakness of this model in mental health service delivery is that there is little continuity in service provision, and client functioning must be at a level that enables them to cope with the inherent fragmentation. It is ineffectual when clients are ambivalent about services or resistant to service provision. The 'broker' must have an in-depth knowledge of all community services to ensure that the services brokered meet the needs of each individual.

Clinical case management

The clinical case management model was developed to address the shortcomings of the brokerage model. It assumes that the case manager will also carry a clinical role and provide clinical services in addition to linking clients to other service providers (Kanter, 1989; Lamb, 1980). The main activities of the clinical case manager include the assessment and planning of care, linking clients to required services (consultation with families, health professionals), providing patient interventions (skills training, psychotherapy, etc.), providing crisis intervention and monitoring. The clinical case manager will attempt to provide most of the required clinical services, and there is an expectation that case managers are clinicians with expertise in such areas as skill development and psychotherapy (Lamb, 1980). Clinical case management works best in multidisciplinary team settings where the case manager can access the specialist skills of team members. Clinical case management forms the cornerstone of publicly funded community mental health services throughout much of the developed world including the UK, USA and Australia.

The main advantages of clinical case management are clear clinical accountability, readily identifiable points of contact for clients and families or carers, continuity of care, and simplicity. The disadvantages are lack of objectivity of the clinical case manager with respect to decisions about continuing need for services, and a tendency for the clinical case manager to attempt interventions that might be better provided by a specialist.

Intensive case management

Background

As case management models developed during the initial wave of deinstitutionalisation, it was recognised that there was a subgroup of clients who were difficult to engage in treatment using standard case management practices (Test & Stein, 1976). This group of clients consumed large amounts of staff time and used the most expensive treatment options available, including inpatient care and emergency room visits (Surles & McGurrin, 1987). Such clients were often described as 'revolving door patients', because discharge from acute inpatient care would be quickly followed by readmission (Kent et al., 1995a). Characteristics of such clients included poor treatment compliance, itinerancy, lack of natural supports and multiple problems, usually involving some combination of mental illness with intellectual disability, personality disorder, physical illness, substance use or forensic problems (Kent et al., 1995b).

Standard case management was relatively ineffectual with this group because of limited capacity to follow up clients who missed appointments, since standard case management operates within normal working hours. Moreover, most standard case managers do not have the time or the capacity to develop an individualised intensive rehabilitation programme that would enable such people to survive successfully in the community.

Assertive community treatment

Assertive community treatment (ACT) is a form of intensive case management designed to overcome the limitations of standard case management. It had its origins in innovative and well publicised pilot programmes developed in Madison, Wisconsin by Stein & Test (1980), and in Sydney by Hoult and colleagues (1983).

In standard case management, the client is assumed to be a voluntary recipient of services and to have autonomy with respect to their decision as to whether or not to seek or accept services. If a client misses an appointment, the case manager will usually make a phone call or send a note, but will not take it further unless there is good reason to believe there is a psychiatric emergency. By contrast, ACT starts from the premise that clients are unable, as a result of their mental illness, to assume full responsibility for their continuing treatment and the service must accept this responsibility.

Whereas standard case management emphasises the individual therapeutic relationships between case managers and clients, ACT emphasises team working. Team members work with different clients as and when required, and several members commonly work together with the same client. The team approach is necessary because ACT operates seven days a week and into the evenings, with several client contacts each week and readiness to respond to client needs as they arise. A team approach enables continuity through team contact that would be impossible if a single individual was responsible for all the contact with a given client. The team approach also acknowledges the complexity and difficulty of the rehabilitation process with such clients and the need for a wide range of skills to be brought to bear in the implementation of a rehabilitation programme.

Finally, whereas standard case management is often based in a community mental health centre, with clients typically attending appointments, ACT teams are highly mobile and often provide interventions in clients' own homes or places of work (see Olfson, 1990; Scott & Dixon, 1995; Solomon, 1992 for discussion of characteristics of ACT teams). ACT teams always work with low staff to client ratios (usually 10–15 clients per staff member) and invariably practice 'assertive outreach', meaning that they continue to contact and offer services to reluctant or uncooperative clients. ACT teams also place particular emphasis on medication compliance and 24-hour emergency cover (McGrew & Bond, 1995).

Thus the main tenets of ACT include (i) low patient:staff ratios; (ii) services provided in the community (rather than the clinic); (iii) caseloads shared across case managers; (iv) 24-hour coverage; (v) most services provided by ACT team – not brokered out; (vi) time-unlimited service provision. The main advantages of assertive case management are that the client does not have to assume responsibility for their treatment, the treatment is less restrictive than inpatient care and there is scope for intensive rehabilitation focus that has the potential to develop truly independent living capacity. However, due to its intensity, it is costly to provide – although probably less expensive than extended inpatient rehabilitation.

The ACT model has been widely embraced in the UK, North America and Australia. In some states of Australia these teams are called Mobile Intensive Treatment Teams (MITT), while in others they practice under the title Mobile Support Teams (MSTs). The term Enhanced Case Management (ECM) has been used in the UK.

Intensive case management and assertive community treatment are similar in many ways: both serve clients at the severe end of the scale, and both focus on practical issues such as medication use (McGrew & Bond, 1995), accommodation and finances (Schaedle et al., 2002). However, while ACT has clear programme elements, intensive case management does not represent a single programme model. It includes a number of 'case management practice orientations' that are more intense than standard case management (Schaedle et al., 2002). Thus, while ACT is more clearly articulated than intensive case management, treatment goals and approaches are very similar in practice.

Psychosocial rehabilitation in the context of case management

While the primary purpose of case management is sometimes seen as maintenance within the community as distinct from long-term hospital care or frequent readmission for acute treatment, the underlying purpose is the development of capacity for independent living. This means capacity to manage daily living skills, utilise community resources and optimally become an active and productive member of the community through work or study (Mowbray et al., 1997). Achieving rehabilitation outcomes is probably more difficult than achieving maintenance outcomes. The interventions for maintenance are close monitoring of mental state, medication compliance and effective intervention in, or prevention of, crises. These interventions are congruent with the professional training of mental health nurses, who typically comprise the largest professional group within case management teams, and nurses in particular may need little additional training to achieve affective service delivery for maintenance outcomes within case management.

There is some risk that case management, whether standard or intensive, will focus excessively on maintenance of the person in the community at the expense of rehabilitation. Relatively low goals may be set by the case manager (e.g. avoiding hospital admission), and strategies may be confined to ensuring medication compliance and managing crises. Effective case management will focus on building capacity for successful independent living, not just on staying out of hospital.

Rehabilitation within the framework of case management requires motivation of the client and development of a systematic programme that supports achievement of client goals. This means that the rehabilitation oriented case management takes place within the rehabilitation framework described by Anthony et al. (1988) and Cnaan et al. (1988) and the strengths approach described by Rapp (1993), Bjorkman et al., 2002 and Barry et al., 2003. Much everyday case management is eclectic, being practised at varying levels of intensity and combining elements of the brokerage, clinical case management and strengths models (Thornicroft, 1991). High intensity case management with high fidelity to the ACT model is usually reserved for the most disabled clients who are at high risk of requiring extended periods of inpatient care. Rapp & Goscha (2004) identified ten components of effective case management (Table 9.1). The authors concluded that use of the ACT or strengths model provides the best base for meeting the 10 components. They claimed that 'the broker model of case management should be abandoned and resources reallocated' (Rapp & Goscha, 2004, p. 327).

Table 9.1 Components of effective case management

1. Case managers should take responsibility for delivering as many of the services as possible, rather than making referrals to multiple formal services
2. Natural community resources are the primary partners, i.e. building a life that is independent of the mental health system
3. Activities should be carried out with clients in normal community settings rather than in mental health centres
4. Individual and team case management are effective. Team delivered services tend to be no more successful in producing positive outcomes than individually provided services
5. Case managers have primary responsibility for the person's services – when case managers have increased control over important decisions (e.g. as in the ACT model), outcomes tend to be better
6. Case managers can be paraprofessionals, but they require quality, supervision experienced and fully credentialed professionals
7. Caseload size should be small enough to allow for a relatively high frequency of contact. It is suggested that the number of contacts rather than the duration of contact is important in preventing hospitalisation
8. Case management services should be time unlimited. In the absence of long-term contact, gains can evaporate, while others do not have sufficient time to be established
9. People need access to familiar persons 24 hours a day, 7 days a week. The effectiveness of crisis management is enhanced when provided by staff who have a relationship with the individual
10. Case managers should foster choice. Choice and self-determination are associated with improved outcomes

Adapted from Rapp & Goscha, 2004.

How effective is case management?

A considerable number of reviews and meta-analyses have now been published on the efficacy and effectiveness of case management services (for example, Bjorkman et al., 2002; Gorey et al., 1998; Holloway, 1991; Marshall et al., 1998; Mueser et al., 1998; Wykes et al., 1998; Ziguras & Stuart, 2000). Of these, the Cochrane review by Marshall et al. (1998) was the most controversial and widely debated. The authors concluded that case management maintained more people in contact with psychiatric services (one extra person remains in contact for every 15 people who receive case management), but it also increased hospital admission rates and duration of stay. People receiving case management had approximately twice as many admissions as those receiving standard community care. Whilst it improved compliance, it did not produce clinically significant improvement in mental state, social functioning or quality of life. There was no evidence that case management improved outcome on any other clinical or social variable. The review concluded that:

'Case management is an intervention of questionable value, to the extent that it is doubtful whether it should be offered by community psychiatric services. It is hard to see how policy makers who subscribe to an evidence-based approach

can justify retaining case management as the cornerstone of community health care' (Marshall et al., 1998, p. 1).

This scathing conclusion attracted the attention of policy makers and clinicians who promote the case management model of community care. Parker (1997) argued that the conclusion of ineffectiveness relied too heavily on data related to 'admissions', in that admission to hospital was considered a negative consequence of case management. The impact of case management on total length of hospitalisation was not reported – although people were more likely to be admitted, they may have had shorter periods in hospital. Parker also argued that there was too little information about the operation of the models in practice, and it was difficult to determine how well the reviewed models maintained fidelity.

A subsequent meta-analysis by Ziguras & Stuart (2000) provides a somewhat different conclusion to that of Marshall et al. (1998). Ziguras & Stuart agreed that case management does not impact on clinical symptoms and is associated with increased admission rates. However they found that the total of bed days was less for clients in case management (because admissions were briefer), and case management was generally effective in improving outcomes from mental health services as measured by social functioning, symptoms, client satisfaction and family burden of care. This was more consistent with the finding of Gorey et al. (1998) that overall, three quarters or more of people receiving case management did better than the average person not receiving case management in the areas of functional status, re-hospitalisation and quality of life.

On balance, the evidence suggests that standard case management does produce greater continuity of care by keeping people in contact with services. It is also likely to produce a small to moderate improvement in social functioning and symptoms. However, it may lead to an increase in admissions and, unless these admissions are brief, resultant increased treatment costs.

ACT versus standard case management or hospital based rehabilitation

The rationale for intensive case management is based on evidence suggesting that a reduced caseload will result in more comprehensive treatment (Harris & Begman, 1987; Thornicroft, 1991). Although intensive case management is more costly than standard care due to its intensity, the additional costs can be justified if there is reduction in use of other expensive services or if there are substantially improved outcomes for clients.

The Cochrane Review by Marshall et al. (1998) compared ACT to standard case management and found that those clients receiving ACT were more likely to remain in contact with services, less likely to be admitted to hospital, and spent less time in hospital than those receiving standard community care. In terms of clinical and social outcome, ACT clients demonstrated significantly better outcomes on (i) accommodation status; (ii) employment; and (iii) patient satisfaction. There were no differences between ACT and control treatments on mental state or social functioning. ACT reduced the cost of hospital care, but did not have a clear cut advantage over standard care when other costs were taken into account (Marshall et al., 1998). Latimer (1999) concluded that whether or not ACT is a cost effective treatment depends on the amount of inpatient care a client in ACT usually receives. He found that, based on inpatient costs in Quebec, a client would need prior hospital use of 50 days per annum or more for ACT to be cost effective.

When ACT was compared to hospital-based rehabilitation programmes, clients receiving ACT were more likely to remain in contact with services than those receiving hospital-based rehabilitation and were significantly less likely to be admitted to hospital (i.e. acute care) than those receiving hospital-based rehabilitation (Marshall et al., 1998). However, the favourable finding for intensive case management, while consistent with the bulk of the literature (Gorey et al., 1998; Mueser et al., 1998; Ziguras & Stuart, 2000) has not been reproduced in a number of more recent well designed studies (Burns et al., 2000; Clarke et al., 2000; Dekker et al., 2002; Harrison-Read et al., 2002; Issakidis et al., 1999).

Quality of implementation may be an issue in effectiveness of intensive case management (Essock & Kontos, 1995; McHugo et al., 1999; Resnick et al., 2003), but it is also possible that changes in both the practice of standard case management and inpatient treatment practices mean that there is less scope for intensive case management to outperform standard services than was the case when it was first developed. A number of publications have examined criteria for determining whether or not a specific implementation of intensive case management meets acceptable standards (McGrew & Bond, 1995; Salyers et al., 2003; Teague et al., 1998). There is some evidence that higher fidelity to standards, especially ACT standards, is associated with better outcomes, suggesting that programme implementation should closely replicate the original model features (Resnick et al., 2003). However, fidelity alone does not guarantee outcomes (Fiander et al., 2003). There is also evidence that even when programmes are implemented with high fidelity they tend to 'drift' over time to lower fidelity. This raises an important question as to how robust this model of care is, and King (2006) concluded that results from more recent trials bring into question a long standing view that intensive case management has clear benefits that outweigh its costs when compared with usual care of people with severe mental illness.

Text box 9.2 Case management: what the evidence shows

- Case management promotes continuity of care
- Case management may be (but is not always) associated with fewer and briefer hospital admissions
- Case management is associated with client and family satisfaction with services
- Case management can be associated with improved quality of life
- More intensive and assertive case management is indicated for clients with high disability, high rate of relapse or low service engagement
- Focus on client strengths enhances outcomes

In summary, there is some controversy surrounding the impact of case management on client outcomes. The weight of evidence suggests that it makes a positive contribution to continuity of care and can support client recovery. More intensive client contact and strengths focus are associated with better client outcomes. For a small subgroup of clients with severe problems, intensive case management with several contacts each week is likely to reduce the need for hospital admission and lead to more stable accommodation and increased satisfaction. Stand-alone programmes of intensive case management such as ACT have a strong track record of success with this client group, but recent evidence suggests the benefits of such programmes may be modest when compared with contemporary standard case management.

Notwithstanding its intensity, intensive case management is unlikely to produce significant improvement in clinical functioning, and the impact on psychosocial functioning and disability is uncertain. As noted by Solomon (1992), case management is really a system of care rather than a clinical intervention. Thus, case management is more likely to have an impact on the system (i.e. lower admission rates) rather than on the client (i.e. improved functioning, etc.). What the rehabilitation practitioner and client work on together within the framework of case management may be more decisive with respect to outcomes than the form of case management.

Text box 9.3 Intensive case management in action: Sam is referred to the ACT team

You will remember Sam from previous chapters. Sam was a young man with a diagnosis of schizophrenia and two admissions. His main aims were to get rid of the voices that persecuted him and to acquire some friends. He was rather suspicious of services and used medication rather erratically.

Sam's rehabilitation was initially provided through standard or clinical case management. Sam's case manager scheduled meetings at the community mental health centre every 2–3 weeks and also arranged occasional meetings with Sam's parents. Sam had a medical review with his psychiatrist once every 3 months. However, things did not go smoothly. Although Sam and his case manager both reported that they were getting on well, Sam often missed appointments. Sam's parents reported that he was awake all night and asleep during the day and they sometimes heard him talking angrily to himself late at night. They have checked his blister pack and noticed that he has often not taken his daily medication. When they confronted him he just got angry.

Things came to a crisis when Sam's mother found that the light fitting in Sam's bedroom has been dislodged. Sam refused to explain how it happened and his mother thinks that he might have tried to hang himself. Sam was admitted for a third time and the treating team decided to refer him to the ACT team for intensive case management. The following factors influenced this decision:

(1) Sam has remained symptomatic despite a standard course of rehabilitation – and this is probably due, in part at least, to non-compliance with medication
(2) Sam has not really engaged with the service – he is not sufficiently motivated to take responsibility for engaging
(3) There is reason to believe that Sam may be at significant risk if the current approach to rehabilitation is maintained
(4) There may also be risks to members of Sam's family
(5) The alternative to intensive case management would be extended inpatient treatment. This would be less satisfactory because it would be more restrictive, more stigmatising and more isolating as well as more expensive

Intensive case management (see Text box 9.3) brings important changes to the service environment for Sam. Until now, there has been quite a lot of responsibility left with Sam to maintain services. Standard case management with Sam relied on his own motivation and the development of a therapeutic alliance to engage Sam in treatment. By contrast, intensive case management accepts that, as a result of his mental illness, Sam may not be able to maintain an engagement with services. In the absence of regular monitoring, appropriate clinical treatment and recovery oriented psychosocial interventions, Sam is at risk of further deterioration and even of suicide. Intensive case management ensures that Sam's mental state is closely monitored and that he has the opportunity to benefit from both biological and psychosocial interventions. Because of the level of concern about Sam, he has been referred to a specialist team. His intensive case management is provided by a small team and not just a single case manager. The team can support Sam and his family over extended hours, 7 days a week, whereas, his previous case manager was only available during standard office hours 5 days a week.

In many jurisdictions, intensive case management can be given legal force by a community treatment order, which means that if Sam refuses to engage with his case manager he can be admitted to hospital as an involuntary patient. For the first few weeks after discharge, Sam's new case manager, or another member of the intensive case management team, will visit Sam daily. The visits will have two main goals: to develop an alliance with Sam, and to monitor his treatment compliance. Sam has been told that unless he is compliant with medication he will be readmitted under the Mental Health Act as part of his community treatment order. Sam's case manager will re-negotiate the rehabilitation plan, focusing as before on Sam's objectives and strengths, but this time with greater emphasis on team priorities, even when they are not the same as Sam's priorities. Sam's intensive case manager will have much more flexibility than his previous case manager, because of a much smaller caseload, and he can visit Sam at home or take him out for coffee or to a specialist rehabilitation activity. Sam's intensive case manager can provide active support to Sam's parents and can closely monitor his medication compliance.

Conclusion

Evaluations of deinstitutionalisation suggest that the 'mere discharge of mentally ill people into the community is far from being sufficient to bring about improvement in their condition' (Aviram, 1990, p. 70). In the aftermath of deinstitutionalisation, the mental health system is still struggling to meet the needs of people with mental illness living in the community. People with psychiatric disability frequently require input from a number of agencies to facilitate their access to accommodation, income security and to participate in community life. As suggested by Shepherd (1990), case management has become 'the cornerstone of community care' (p. 61).

However, it should be noted that case management is not a treatment, but a service structure through which treatments are delivered (Holloway, 1991). This means that it is important that the case manager be an active agent of rehabilitation, actively promoting recovery rather than just maintaining the client out of hospital. There is evidence that higher contact intensity and focus on client strengths contribute to recovery, and clients with high levels of disability and weak engagement with services may benefit from programmes of high intensity case management such as ACT.

References

Anthony, W., Cohen, M., & Farkas, M. (1988). The chronically mentally ill and case management – more than a response to a dysfunctional system. *Community Mental Health Journal*, 24, 21–28.

Aviram, U. (1990). Community care of the seriously mentally ill: Continuing problems and current issues. *Community Mental Health Journal*, 26, 69–88.

Barry, K.L., Zeber, J.E., Blow, F.C., & Valenstein, M. (2003). Effect of strengths model versus assertive community treatment model on participant outcomes and utilization: Two-year follow-up. *Psychiatric Rehabilitation Journal*, 26, 268–277.

Bjorkman, T., Hansson, L., & Sandlund, M. (2002). Outcome of case management based on strengths model compared to standard care. A randomised controlled trial. *Social Psychiatry and Psychiatric Epidemiology*, 37, 147–152.

Bloch, M., & Cournos, F. (1990). Mental health policy for the 1990's: Tinkering in the interstices. *Journal of Health Politics, Policy and Law*, 15, 387–411.

Burns, T., Fiander, M., Kent, A., Ukoumunne, O., Byford, S., Fahy, T., & Kumar, K. (2000). Effects of case-load size on the process of care of patients with severe psychotic illness (UK 700 Trial). *British Journal of Psychiatry*, 177, 427–433.

Clarke, G.N., Herinckx, H.A., Kinney, R.F., Paulson, R.I., Cutler, D.L., Lewis, K., & Oxman, E. (2000). Psychiatric hospitalizations, arrests, emergency room visits, and homelessness of clients with serious and persistent mental illness: Findings from a randomized trial of two ACT programs vs. usual care. *Mental Health Services Research*, 2, 155–164.

Cnaan, R., Blankertz, L., Messinger, K., & Gardner, J. (1988). Psychosocial rehabilitation: Toward a definition. *Journal of Psychosocial Rehabilitation*, 11, 61–77.

Curtis, D., Millman, E., Struening, E., & D'Ercole, A. (1992). Effect of case management on rehospitalisation and utilisation of ambulatory care services. *Hospital and Community Psychiatry*, 43, 895–899.

Dekker, J., Wijdenes, W., Koning, Y.A., Gardien, R., Hermande-Willenborg, L., & Nusselder, H. (2002). Assertive community treatment in Amsterdam. *Community Mental Health Journal*, 38, 425–434.

Durham, M. (1989). The impact of deinstitutionalization on the current treatment of the mentally ill. *International Journal of Law and Psychiatry*, 12, 117–131.

Essock, S., & Kontos, N. (1995). Implementing assertive community treatment teams. *Psychiatric Services*, 47, 679–683.

Fiander, M., Burns, T., McHugo, G., & Drake, R. (2003). Assertive community treatment across the Atlantic: Comparison of model fidelity in the UK and USA. *British Journal of Psychiatry*, 182, 248–254.

Franklin, J., Solovitz, B., Mason, M., Clemons, J., & Miller, L. (1987). An evaluation of case management. *American Journal of Public Health*, 77, 674–678.

Gorey, K., Leslie, D., Morris, T., Carruthers, W., John, L., & Chacko, J. (1998). Effectiveness of case management with severely and persistently mentally ill people. *Community Mental Health Journal*, 34, 241–250.

Harris, M., & Begman, H. (1987). Case management with the chronically mentally ill: A clinical perspective. *American Journal of Orthopsychiatry*, 57, 296–302.

Harrison-Read, P., Lucas, B., Tyrer, P., Ray, J., Shipley, K., Simmonds S., Knapp, M., Lowin, A., Patel, A., & Hickman, M. (2002). Heavy users of acute psychiatric beds: Randomized controlled trial of enhanced community management in an outer London borough. *Psychological Medicine*, 32, 403–416.

Holloway, F. (1991). Case management for the mentally ill: Looking at the evidence. *International Journal of Social Psychiatry*, 37, 2–13.

Hoult, J., Reynolds, I., Charbonneau-Powis, M., Weekes, P., & Briggs, J. (1983). Psychiatric hospital versus community treatment: A controlled study. *Australian and New Zealand Journal of Psychiatry*, 17, 160–167.

Intagliata, J. (1982). Improving the quality of community care for the chronically mentally disabled: The role of case management. *Schizophrenia Bulletin*, 8, 655–674.

Issakidis, C., Sanderson, K., Teesson, M., Johnston, S., & Buhrich, N. (1999). Intensive case management in Australia: a randomized controlled trial. *Acta Psychiatrica Scandinavica*, 9, 360–367.

Kanter, J. (1989). Clinical case management: definition, principles, components. *Hospital and Community Psychiatry*, 40, 361–368.

Kent, S., Fogarty, M., & Yellowlees, P. (1995a). A review of studies of heavy users of psychiatric services. *Psychiatric Services*, 46, 1247–1253.

Kent, S., Fogarty, M., & Yellowlees, P. (1995b). Heavy utilization of inpatient and out-patient services in a public mental health service. *Psychiatric Services*, 46, 1254–1257.

King, R. (2006). Intensive case management: A critical re-appraisal of the scientific evidence for effectiveness. *Administration and Policy in Mental Health and Mental Health Services Research* (in press).

Lamb, H. (1980). Therapist–case managers: More than brokers of services. *Hospital and Community Psychiatry*, 31, 762–764.

Latimer, E.A. (1999). Economic impacts of assertive community treatment: a review of the literature. *Canadian Journal of Psychiatry*, 44, 443–454.

McGrew, J., & Bond, G. (1995). Critical ingredients of assertive community treatment: Judgments of the experts. *Journal of Mental Health Administration*, 22, 113–125.

McHugo, G., Drake, R., Teague, G., & Xie, H. (1999). Fidelity to assertive community treatment and client outcomes in the New Hampshire dual disorders study. *Psychiatric Services*, 50, 818–824.

Marshall, M., Grey, A., & Lockwood, A. (1998). *Assertive community treatment for people with severe mental disorders* (Cochrane Review). In: The Cochrane Library, Issue 2, Update Software, Oxford.

Mechanic, D. (1991). Strategies for integrating public mental health services. *Hospital and Community Psychiatry*, 42, 797–801.

Melzer, D., Hale, A., Malik, S., Hogman, G., & Wood, S. (1991). Community care for people with schizophrenia one year after hospital discharge. *British Medical Journal*, 303, 1334–1335.

Mowbray, C., Collins, M., Plum, T., Masterton, T., Mulder, R., & Harbinger, I. (1997). The development and evaluation of the first PACT replication. *Administrative Policy Mental Health*, 25, 105–123.

Mueser, K., Bond G., Drake, R., & Resnick, S. (1998). Models of community care for severe mental illness: A review of the research on case management. *Schizophrenia Bulletin*, 24, 37–74.

Olfson, M. (1990). Assertive community treatment: An evaluation of the experimental evidence. *Hospital and Community Psychiatry, 41*, 634–641.

Parker, G. (1997). Case management: An evidence based review fails to make its case. *Current Opinion in Psychiatry, 10*, 261–263.

Rapp, C. (1993). Theory, principles, and methods of the strengths model of case management. In: Harris, M., & Bergman, H. (Eds.), *Case management for mentally ill patients: Theory and practice* (pp. 143–164). Langhorne: Harwood Publishers.

Rapp, C., & Goscha, R. (2004). The principles of effective case management of mental health services. *Psychiatric Rehabilitation Journal, 27*, 319–333.

Resnick, S., Neale, M., & Rosenheck, R. (2003). Impact of public support payments, intensive psychiatric community care, and program fidelity on employment outcomes for people with severe mental illness. *Journal of Nervous and Mental Disease, 191*, 139–144.

Salyers, M., Bond, G., Teague, G., Cox, J., Smith, M., Hicks, M., & Koop, J. (2003). Is it ACT yet? Real-world examples of evaluating the degree of implementation for assertive community treatment. *Journal of Behavioural Health Services and Research, 30*, 304–321.

Schaedle, R., McGrew, J., Bond, G., & Epstein, I. (2002). A comparison of experts' perspectives on assertive community treatment and intensive case management. *Psychiatric Services, 53*, 207–210.

Scott, J., & Dixon, L. (1995). Assertive community treatment and case management for schizophrenia. *Schizophrenia Bulletin, 21*, 657–668.

Shepherd, G. (1990). Case management. *Health Trends, 22*, 59–61.

Solomon, P. (1992). The efficacy of case management services for severely mentally disabled clients. *Community Mental Health Journal, 28*, 163–180.

Stein, L., & Test, M. (1980). Alternative to mental hospital treatment: Conceptual model, treatment program, and clinical evaluation. *Archives of General Psychiatry, 37*, 392–397.

Surles, R., & McGurrin, M. (1987). Increased use of psychiatric emergency services by young chronic mentally ill patients. *Hospital and Community Psychiatry, 38*, 401–405.

Teague, G., Bond, G., & Drake, R. (1998). Program fidelity in assertive community treatment: development and use of a measure. *American Journal of Orthopsychiatry, 68*, 216–232.

Test, M., & Stein, L. (1976). Practice guidelines for the community treatment of markedly impaired patients. *Community Mental Health Journal, 12*, 72–82.

Thornicroft, G. (1991). The concept of case management for long-term mental illness. *International Review of Psychiatry, 3*, 125–132.

Wykes, T., Leese, M., Taylor, R., & Phelan, M. (1998). Effects of community services on disability and symptoms. *British Journal of Psychiatry, 173*, 385–390.

Ziguras, S., & Stuart, W. (2000). A meta-analysis of the effectiveness of mental health case management over 20 years. *Psychiatric Services, 51*, 1410–1419.

Chapter 10

COMMUNITY PARTICIPATION

Chris Lloyd and Frank P. Deane

Overview of chapter

This chapter looks at how people with a mental illness are marginalised and often denied opportunities to participate fully in the community of their choice. The importance of adopting a recovery focus is discussed. This is followed by exploring the implications for service delivery and the role of rehabilitation practitioners in providing a recovery oriented service, which targets access to a range of community activities. Practical strategies for developing a community participation focus are outlined.

Deinstitutionalisation

Deinstitutionalisation has shifted the focus of care from institutional settings to the community. The expectation was that people would receive psychiatric care in their own communities and reduce the segregation of people with mental illness. For many people with mental illness, the implementation of community based care has not adequately met their needs or reduced segregation and isolation. Living in the community they face economic and social barriers, which impact upon life quality. They find themselves excluded from many aspects of life that are basic rights of citizens, including employment, family and social support, health care, and community life. Exclusion has a substantial impact upon individuals, families, and society. Focusing on recovery has the potential to assist individuals in developing new meaning and purpose in their lives and to promote social inclusion, thereby lessening the devastating impact of mental illness on all concerned.

Social exclusion

Johnstone (2001) stated that people with a mental illness are among the most stigmatised, discriminated against, marginalised, disadvantaged and vulnerable members of society. People with mental illness are over-represented in all socially excluded groups, including those who are poor, unemployed, homeless and isolated (Bonner et al., 2002). Huxley & Thornicroft (2003) stated, 'It has been argued that people with a significant mental illness are among the most excluded in society'

(p. 289). They go on to define the various meanings of social exclusion, and identify exclusion from citizen status of a given nation state that might deny equality in terms of social, political and legal rights. This often involves discrimination that prevents access to help such as 'social security, employment, housing, health, education, and community services' (p. 289). It may also relate to access to the democratic process (e.g. voting) or legislation. Huxley & Thornicroft (2003) also identify exclusion at the level of community that includes 'membership, influence, integration and fulfilment of needs, and a shared emotional connection.' (p. 289). Exclusion at this community level reduces access to the degree of individual identification and participation in the wider social community (Huxley & Thornicroft, 2003).

People with mental illness should be entitled to the things in life that people without disability take for granted, for example access to roles, relationships with others, happiness and peace of mind and access to services (Johnstone, 2001; Meddings & Perkins, 2002). Many of the basic human needs of people with a mental illness are not met and their recovery is constantly compromised by social disadvantage (Ellis, 2003). A report released by the UK based Social Exclusion Unit (Office of the Deputy Prime Minister [ODPM], 2004) identified five main reasons why mental health problems lead to and reinforce social exclusion. These include: (i) stigma and discrimination against people with mental health problems; (ii) low expectations by professionals of what people with mental health problems can achieve; (iii) lack of clear responsibility for promoting vocational and social outcomes; (iv) lack of ongoing support to enable people with mental health problems to work; and (v) barriers to engaging in the community and with accessing the basic services they need.

Twenge et al. (2003) found that people who are socially excluded experience an altered sense of time, loss of meaning, lethargy and avoidance of self-awareness. Social exclusion thwarts a basic human drive and challenges one's self-worth and confidence to participate in the life of the community. Perceived stigma is thought to be a major contributor to the social exclusion process. Perlick et al. (2001) evaluated the relationship between social withdrawal by people with mental illness in response to concerns about stigma and anticipated discrimination or rejection by others. They found that clients with strong concerns about stigma showed greater impairment in their social and leisure functioning over a 7-month period. Specifically, there was greater psychological isolation and behavioural avoidance in those with greater stigma concerns (Perlick et al., 2001). Such findings are consistent with a cycle of exclusion whereby the person withdraws from society and is vulnerable to unemployment, homelessness, debt and social isolation. This in turn can lead to worsening mental health and can trigger a long-term cycle of exclusion (ODPM, 2004).

Service delivery utilising a recovery focus

A recovery orientation emphasises the importance of positive, trusting relationships in bringing people back to living fully in society. Principles include peer support, empowerment and holistic health, which acknowledge the importance of relationships, beliefs, self and identify, community participation or social inclusion, and skills for meaningful participation in the community. Recovery requires the presence of a positive sense of self and social identity. In order to regain a valued role, people with a mental illness need to feel that they are worthwhile and capable of entering a community of their choice. People with a mental illness can acquire many of the skills needed to manage their own lives and possible emotional distress after they come to believe in themselves and in their capacity to recover (Ahern & Fisher, 2001). Hope contains the seeds of recovery as it enables people with a mental illness to imagine a better life. Loss of hope by themselves, carers and mental health professionals can halt recovery (Mental Health Commission, 2002). ← Ref.

Reorienting services based on recovery and empowerment necessitates the old entrenched cultures, which many practitioners may find difficult go. The challenge is for practitioners to think about people with a mental illness as individuals and to explore alternate means of delivering services that are more directly in tune with what clients want and need to assist them in their recovery. This involves practitioners thinking about recovery, the importance of hope and collaborative relationships, and providing interventions or strategies that emphasise social inclusion (specific strategies are outlined later in this chapter).

However, attitudes of service providers have been described as impeding mental health service reforms and perpetuating stigma for people with mental illness. Many clinical service providers still believe that a diagnosis of schizophrenia is a 'life sentence' that inevitably has negative consequences over the course of the person's life (Rickwood, 2004). Attitude change among service providers is seen as 'fundamental to working within a recovery orientation' (Rickwood, 2004, p. 3).

Casper et al. (2002) developed an instrument to measure practitioners' beliefs, goals and practices in psychosocial rehabilitation. This measure may be utilised to (i) enable service directors to evaluate their staff's current beliefs, goals and practices to provide baseline information about what areas of practice need changing, and (ii) for staff members to self-assess how up to date they are. Information is provided in the following:

- Practices that emphasise consumer preferences, choice and individualised assessments, which include community integration in normalised settings
- Beliefs about the limiting effects of the illness
- Housing, employment and educational goals, support skills development, and a strengths focus
- Individualised plans and services that incorporate the strengths and aspirations of each client
- Humanistic goals and beliefs that reflect current recovery oriented psychosocial rehabilitation

Support for reintegration into the community should be an integral part of the work of an effective mental health service (ODPM, 2004). This goes beyond the provision of supported housing and supported employment. Inclusion involves a feeling of belonging, of having a niche or a meaningful role to play in the life of the community. Davidson et al. (2001) suggested that there are three dimensions intrinsic to this broader sense of inclusion that are not typically addressed in existing clinical rehabilitative or recovery paradigms. According to Davidson et al. (2001) these dimensions involve experiences of: (i) social inclusion through friendship, (ii) feeling like a worthwhile human being through meaningful activity, and (iii) hopefulness through an affirmative stance. They suggest that these dimensions provide a cornerstone for improvement, and are fundamental to the inclusion of people with mental illness.

Role of rehabilitation practitioners

It has been found that the stigma associated with mental illness harms the self-esteem of many people with mental illness (Link et al., 2001) and that social rejection is a persistent source of stress (Wright et al., 2000). These experiences increase feelings of self-depreciation, which in turn weakens their sense of mastery and alters their identity (Markowitz, 1998). Wright et al. (2000) highlighted the need for practitioners to identify ways to help clients cope with these experiences to counter negative self-related changes. Opportunities for clients should be facilitated to involve them in activities that increase their sense of self-mastery, improve self-esteem and participate in socially inclusive activities. The following section will include some examples of the types of activities that practitioners may consider when working with clients to promote their community participation.

Voting

Nash (2002) raised the issue that people with mental illness are often disenfranchised from many functions of society, and suggest that voting is one area where disenfranchisement and exclusion are unnecessarily experienced. He suggested that is important that practitioners act as advocates for their client's rights. This includes making information about voting available, for example registering to vote, voting rights and mental illness, postal voting, proxy voting and voting when in hospital. Social inclusion may be realised by facilitating social integration and voting. It is important for practitioners to be aware that having the right to vote is one thing, and being able to exercise it is another (Nash, 2002).

Community gardening

Community garden projects are a useful strategy to develop partnerships with staff members, peers and the broader community (Myers, 1998). In her description of a 6-month gardening project involving 10 gardens and 18 people with a mental illness, Myers describes the process of initiating such projects, which also highlights the opportunities for community participation. Preparation involved attending a garden fair with clients, gardening lectures, book store sales to find gardening books on sale and chatting over lunch with other gardeners. The project had an initial US$400 as 'seed money', but when visiting garden clubs some plants were donated and staff members provided seedlings from their own gardens. One of the local nurseries donated shrubs and plants with minor flaws. They attended the local flower show and practised some gardening skills at the group home. On one of the projects, as they were installing a rock garden one of the neighbours introduced themselves and plant exchange resulted. The staff worked side by side with clients and role modelled conversations with people who passed by the gardens. The highlight of the project was inclusion of one of the gardens on a local annual garden tour. The project enhanced the clients' living environment and prompted friendships with a landlord and over five neighbours as they stopped by to admire the gardens and talk (Myers, 1998).

We are aware of other gardening projects that produce potted plants and vegetables, which are sold at market days, providing another opportunity for consumers to interact with the public. The proceeds from these sales are then returned to support the gardening activities. Many local governments in Australia also provide free courses on recycling and composting (e.g. http://www.wollongong.nsw.gov.au/EnvironmentDevelopment/WasteAndRecycling/Index_Glengarry.html).

A qualitative study by Fieldhouse (2003) found that participants in an allotment group valued the natural, outdoors, green environment, which provided them with a sense of peace. They described that they noted improved concentration, a fascination with growing plants and increased self-mastery. Participants were afforded the opportunity to form social networks and generate goals. Fieldhouse (2003) stressed the importance of providing groups within ordinary settings to promote social inclusion and recovery.

Community arts

The arts have had a long connection with mental health. Both the creative and performing arts programmes provide opportunities and structure for self-exploration during the recovery process. Useful approaches include such events as art exhibitions and poetry recitals, where people with a mental illness are able to display their work in the mainstream community (Lloyd & Chandler, 1999). People with a mental illness have commented that being able to use one's gifts and talents, to be needed, and to be productive are all part of recovery (Schiff, 2004). A study by Wong et al. (2004) found that both the creation of art and involvement in a community arts programme helped to facilitate internal changes, as outlined in the conceptual model of recovery. The perceived value of their contribution to society increased as artists experienced increased ability to influence their surroundings. Participants in this study felt that through their art, they had an impact on those who bought their pieces, and found it satisfying to be a creator of something that was useful, meaningful and brought enjoyment to others in society. As one participant said, 'And they were just impressed with the three pieces I had, which were only the beginning, which I regret now that I've sold. But they sold! The response to my type of art for therapy must have attached itself to somebody who wanted to buy it and keep it'.

Holistic health

It is useful for rehabilitation practitioners to focus on wellness and work closely with people with a mental illness to explore strategies for keeping well. They need assistance to develop mastery over symptoms, so that they may assume self-management for their illness and take increased responsibility for their own wellness. A useful strategy to use is the Wellness Recovery Action Plan (WRAP), which was developed by Mary Ellen Copeland (2001). The WRAP builds on the principles of hope, personal responsibility, education, self-advocacy and support. It is a tool that provides a self-help framework for people who experience psychiatric symptoms. The WRAP provides a structured way in which people are empowered to take control of their life and move beyond the consequences of their mental illness and the effects of discrimination. For further information on the steps involved in developing a WRAP refer to www.mentalhealthrecovery.com

It is important for practitioners to work with clients to improve their health and physical wellbeing. People with psychiatric disabilities are at risk from various diseases that are linked to poor nutrition and physical inactivity (Catapano & Castle, 2004). Freeley et al. (2004) suggested that wellness would seem an appropriate course of treatment for people with psychiatric disabilities, in order for them to achieve their highest potential for wellbeing. Wellness programmes may include such components as individual nutritional counselling, group weight loss programmes, aerobics, yoga, tai chi, and various sports such as volleyball, basketball and softball. In addition, other areas may be addressed, such as communication skills, stress reduction, advocacy and empowerment (Freeley et al., 2004).

Supported education

Higher education is becoming more of a necessity for the employability of people. Access to post-secondary education is important for people with mental illness, since many of these people have had their career goals and educational aspirations interrupted by onset of their illness (Mowbray et al., 2001). Following a similar model to supported employment and supported accommodation, psychosocial rehabilitation practitioners have developed supported education programmes. These programmes provide assistance, preparation, and/or support to people with mental illness wishing to pursue post-secondary education or training (Mowbray et al., 2001). Supported education programmes may be found associated with clubhouses, community colleges and universities, and private providers (Mowbray et al., 2003). Unger (1993) described three prototypes of supported education: (i) the self-contained classroom, where students attend a separate class with a specialised curriculum; (ii) on-site support where students attend regular classes and receive support on site; and (iii) mobile support, where students attend regular classes with support from mental health staff. Mowbray et al. (2001) suggested that supported education programmes need to address the availability of support groups (e.g. self-help groups), choosing a course of study, study skills, vocational choice and scheduling of classes.

Unger and colleagues described the outcomes of a 5-year research and demonstration project related to supported continuing education at the Boston University campus (Unger, 1993; Unger et al., 1991). Those participating in the programme had increased participation in postsecondary education, increased employment, decreased hospitalisation and increased self-esteem (Unger et al., 1991). It was also observed that when clients became identified as students, 'The change in label often led to corresponding changes in attitude and behavior on the part of the human service provider as well as the clients themselves' (Unger, 1993, p. 18). Thus, there appeared to be a destigmatising effect. In developing their programmes, Unger and colleagues focused on using existing community resources such as local community grants or service club monies, as well as mental health and education staff. A range of campus services were used to support these programmes, which included financial aid, academic counselling, the career centre, tutoring, and disability related counselling.

One of the main problems identified in servicing students with mental illness was stigma (Unger, 1993). However, somewhat surprisingly, they described some instructors as too tolerant of disruptive behaviours (e.g. excessive classroom comments) and mental health staff as tending to unilaterally make decisions about who is not capable of returning to school rather than encouraging clients to try (Unger, 1993). Whilst stress was alluded to as a potential problem it was not emphasised, but it is likely to be a consideration that requires planning and preparation.

In a large study of 70 students with schizophrenia in a supported education programme, the students with schizophrenia (SWS) reported higher emotional distress than a comparison group of 55 adult students without schizophrenia who were also in a supported education programme (Ponizovsky et al., 2004). In this study there was recognition that SWS may have impaired capacity to enter into and maintain interpersonal relationships, particularly those related to the learning process (e.g. group classroom projects). This may contribute to the development of stress. It was argued that social support from family, friends and significant others would provide a buffer or adaptive coping strategy to manage stress. This hypothesis was confirmed by finding that the psychological distress experienced by SWS was associated with higher use of ineffective emotion oriented coping and insufficient social support from friends and family (Ponizovsky et al., 2004). It was notable that the overall levels of emotional stress found among SWS were 'modest in magnitude' (p. 405). The study suggested the need to strengthen social support systems as much as possible prior to enrolling in supported education programmes. In addition, it was suggested that more adaptive task oriented coping, combined with problem solving, social skills and communication training might all help prevent emotional distress.

Peer support and supported socialisation

Peer support is defined as 'a system of giving and receiving help founded on key principles of respect, shared responsibility, and mutual agreement of what is helpful' (Mead et al., 2001, p. 135). The importance of peer support lies in the fact that it can offer a culture of health and ability, and challenge the assumptions about mental illness, while at the same time validating the individual for who they really are and where they have come from. Supportive relationships help contribute to positive adjustment, offer a sense of belonging, and feedback of a person's own self worth (Solomon, 2004). It allows people to experience and make meaning of their lives. Practitioners need to consider the ways in which peer support might be provided to clients participating in psychosocial rehabilitation programmes. This may include providing the room and space for peer support programmes to be conducted, and introducing clients to peer support programmes. Peer support should also be available on an individual basis. This could be fostered by such means as consumer consultants, or developing relationships with services that provide peer support, to build up mechanisms to enable clients to have access to peer support.

Many people with a mental illness experience diminished social networks and social isolation, and fewer opportunities for social support. For example, it has been found 31% live alone, 59% have an impaired ability to socialise, 39% have no best friend to share thoughts and feelings with, 64% are single and 59% had no sexual relationships in the past year (Jablensky et al., 1999). A study that compared the social networks of 27 severely mentally ill clients (SMI) with 19 clients who had less severe disorders found that the social networks of clients with SMI were smaller, less reciprocal and contained fewer family members. In addition, SMI clients' networks were more likely to involve social service providers (Meeks & Murrell, 1994). This highlights both the relative disadvantage, and also the important role that rehabilitation practitioners have in filling the social support gap.

Obstacles to developing social relationships include stigma, rejection, loss, poverty, unemployment, and a lack of opportunities for establishing meaningful, reciprocal relationships with peers outside the mental health system (Davidson et al., 2001). Stigma is one of the major barriers to development of social relationships. For example, in a large study of 5025 German adults, it was found that beliefs that people with mental illness were unpredictable and dangerous were related to a desire for greater social distance (Angermeyer et al., 2003).

Davidson et al. (2001) developed a supported socialisation approach to addressing the community needs of individuals with psychiatric disabilities. In this programme, individuals who were socially isolated and withdrawn were paired with volunteer partners with whom they were able to participate in social and recreational activities for a few hours per week. Fostering opportunities such as this enables participation in a range of naturally occurring activities within the community.

Perhaps one of the most common examples of such volunteer friendship models is the Compeer model (Skirboll, 1994), which can now be found in a number of countries. Unfortunately, there is little empirical data regarding the effectiveness of such programmes. The available research suggests that there are high levels of satisfaction amongst both volunteers and clients, and descriptive data suggests improved self-esteem and decreased loneliness (e.g. Pickard & Deane, 2000; Skirboll, 1994). No randomised controlled trials of volunteer friendship interventions could be found, but a trial that compared individual cognitive–behavioural therapy (CBT) with non-specific befriending for people with persistent symptoms of schizophrenia suggested promising short term effects for befriending. Both the CBT and befriending interventions led to significant improvement in psychiatric symptoms at the end of 9 months of individual treatment. There were no significant differences between the two interventions at the end of treatment, but 9 months after treatment only the CBT group had sustained the improvements (Sensky et al., 2000).

Leisure participation

Social disadvantage and particularly low incomes amongst people with mental illness likely limits access to a range of leisure activities (Huxley & Thornicroft, 2003). For example, a study comparing the leisure activities of individuals with schizophrenia to a control group without a mental illness found that fewer people with schizophrenia owned a cassette, record or CD player to listen to music (McCreadie et al., 2001). A study of time use in 229 adults diagnosed with schizophrenia residing in London found that 'Few of the participants were engaged in work, active leisure, education or volunteer occupations, their predominant occupations being sleeping, personal care and passive leisure.' (Shimitras et al., 2003, p. 46).

Neumayer & Wilding (2005) highlighted the importance of leisure to health and that practitioners should incorporate concepts of leisure as part of their everyday practice. Indeed, they go so far as to say that leisure should be a cornerstone consideration of all health professional practice. Leisure is defined as 'those activities which people do because they want to for their own sake, for fun, entertainment, self improvement, for goals of their own choosing, but not for material gain' (Argyle, 1996, p. 3). It is important for practitioners to assist people to live in ways that are health sustaining and community building (Neumayer & Wilding, 2005). Leisure includes a diverse range of cultural/social practices and activities. For example, arts, sports, outdoor pursuits, shopping, bushwalking, travel, hobbies, social interaction, and solitary activities such as reading, listening to music and watching television. Encouraging participation in leisure pursuits is important, since leisure provides a forum where relationships develop between people and a sense of community is produced (Neumayer & Wilding, 2005).

There are numerous approaches to improving engagement to leisure activities but most will involve cognitive processing, practical implementation and problem solving (e.g. Roder et al., 1998). Roder et al. described goals in the cognitive processing stage as including the generation of ideas about organising one's free time and comparing various leisure activities. Practical implementation includes goals such as learning about and checking out leisure time activities (e.g. finding where it is located) and then planning and engaging in an activity. In their group format, problem solving was used to address issues such as perseverance (Roder et al., 1998).

Participation in religious and spiritual activities

Overall, a positive relationship between religiosity and mental health has been found following meta-analysis (r = 0.10; Hackney & Sanders, 2003). However, this summary finding disguises the variation in results, which suggests support for positive, negative and no relationship between religiosity and mental health. The mixed findings are likely a function of the variation in definitions of religiosity (e.g. institutional religion to personal devotion) and mental health (e.g. psychological distress, life satisfaction or self actualisation) (Hackney & Sanders, 2003). From a practical perspective it is recommended that practitioners 'guide clients toward an increased participation in those aspects of their spiritual lives that are most psychologically beneficial, while cautioning them about those aspects found to be less beneficial (or detrimental)' (Hackney & Sanders, 2003, p. 52). For example, there are many examples of religious content in delusions, and hyperreligiosity in psychotic disorders, that may suggest caution in excessive focus on religious activities (e.g. Brewerton, 1994). However, religious or spiritual activities are commonly reported coping strategies amongst people with serious mental illness and have been reported as beneficial for promoting recovery (e.g. Russinova et al., 2002).

In a sample of 406 individuals with mental illness (predominantly psychotic disorders), more than 80% used religious beliefs or activities to cope with day-to-day difficulties (Tepper et al., 2001). Prayer was the most frequent religious coping strategy (59%) followed by attending religious services and worshipping God (both 35%). The authors concluded by calling for 'more intentional out-reach to persons who desire greater contact with religious communities and organisations' (p. 664), particularly churches, clergy and pastoral counsellors (Tepper et al., 2001). Rehabilitation practitioners have a major role in facilitating connections between individuals with mental illness and the various formal and informal opportunities for religious or spiritual activity.

Volunteer work

Interviews with 43 clients with schizophrenia in Hamilton, Canada revealed 30 had been volunteers in the past and considered this work as 'meaningful' (Woodside & Luis, 1997). However, a number of clients also felt they needed support in order to be successful volunteers. In their example of developing a supported volunteering project Woodside & Luis described assessment, planning and implementation stages.

In the assessment stage, information is gathered from the client regarding preferred types of volunteering work, and what is hoped to be achieved by volunteering. In addition, an assessment of the effects of illness on performance is needed, along with the client's views about disclosing his or her mental health status. Details regarding the preferred tasks, times, place and locations, along with needed supports, is developed (Woodside & Luis, 1997).

The planning stage involves locating possible volunteer jobs. Resources such as the Volunteering Australia website and associated search engines are good places to start (http://www.volunteeringaustralia.org/). During the planning stage, it is recommended sufficient time is spent finding a good match and then checking on the openness of the volunteer site to working with someone who has a mental illness (Woodside & Luis, 1997). The rehabilitation practitioner should meet with the manager of the volunteer site to clarify confidentiality and any necessary support for the volunteer.

When appropriate supports are in place, the implementation stage can commence, which involves the volunteer starting their job (possibly on a trial basis to begin). A plan for regular monitoring and meetings with the manager and other key people should be arranged to review progress (Woodside & Luis, 1997). Following consent from the volunteer, it is recommended that the site manager also have appropriate contact names and numbers of rehabilitation practitioners.

In their one-year pilot project Woodside & Luis (1997) found that three of the four client volunteers were still volunteering at the end of the one-year period. All four clients reported improvements in their self-esteem and confidence as a result of their volunteer work. The support persons for the volunteers felt that the fit between the job and volunteer was critical to success and that their main role 'was to help the new volunteer feel secure on the job' (Woodside & Luis, 1997, p. 71). The commitment of the host organisations to supporting volunteers with special needs was also important for success. Whilst case studies suggest supported volunteering can be a very positive experience for clients, there is little other empirical evidence and this is clearly an area in need of further research.

Text box 10.1   Sam and the Skyliners

Sam's mother maintains regular contact with his rehabilitation practitioner, Cassie from the ACT team. She mentions that she has been feeling a bit concerned because Sam seems to be spending a lot of time on the Internet lately. She does not feel comfortable asking what he is doing because she is concerned about being intrusive.

Cassie chats informally with Sam about the Internet and they swap information about useful sites. Sam tells her he has found a Nissan Skyline chat group. Members swap information about how to solve restoration problems and where to get parts. Sam said he is finding it really useful and has made quite a bit of progress with his car. He has also learned there is a local group of Skyline enthusiasts who call themselves the 'Skyliners'. One of the members of the Skyliners sent Sam a message with details of a BBQ next weekend. A couple of members have recently finished restorations and they plan to bring the cars along. Sam tells Cassie he would really like to see the cars but he is not sure he could cope with the people. 'It's much easier on the Internet. No-one knows who you are or what you are like. They all think I am just another "car nut". If I go along to the BBQ they will probably discover I am actually a "nut case".'

'Why don't you say you can only call by for 30 minutes or so because you have something else on? That will give you a chance to look at the cars and you can get a feel for what the group is like without having to spend too much time with them. If you feel comfortable there you can stay a little longer – otherwise, there will be other opportunities,' suggests Cassie. Sam thinks he might give it a go.

Conclusion

People with a mental illness are amongst the most marginalised and socially excluded groups in society. This chapter offers some suggestions as to how services can be modelled to better meet what clients see as being vital in their recovery journey. Recovery is possible, but this is often dependent upon practitioners being open to changing how they view serious mental illness, being prepared to empower clients, and how receptive they are to changing customary models of service delivery. Directions for service delivery need to focus on health and wellbeing, collaboration, recovery and facilitating opportunities for community participation. Through the provision of such rehabilitation programmes, clients are able to develop social networks, participate in meaningful activities of their choice and develop a sense of hope through the achievement of valued goals. It is through assisting clients to participate in socially inclusive community activities that they are enabled to become fully participatory members of the community, and decrease their marginalisation and social exclusion.

References

Ahern, L., & Fisher, D. (2001). Recovery at your own PACE (personal assistance in community existence). *Journal of Psychosocial Nursing and Mental Health Services, 39*, 22–32.

Angermeyer, M.C., Beck, M., & Matschinger, H. (2003). Determinants of the public's preference for social distance from people with schizophrenia. *Canadian Journal of Psychiatry, 48*, 663–668.

Argyle, M. (1996). *The social psychology of leisure*. London: Penguin Books.

Bonner, L., Barr, W., & Hoskins, A. (2002). Using primary care-based mental health registers to reduce social exclusion in patients with severe mental illness. *Journal of Psychiatric and Mental Health Nursing, 9*, 585–593.

Brewerton, T.D. (1994). Hyperreligiosity in psychotic disorders. *Journal of Nervous and Mental Disease, 182*, 302–304.

Casper, E., Oursler, J., Schmidt, L., & Gill, K. (2002). Measuring practitioners' beliefs, goals, and practices in psychiatric rehabilitation. *Psychiatric Rehabilitation Journal, 25*, 223–234.

Catapano, L., & Castle, D. (2004). Obesity in schizophrenia: What can be done about it? *Australasian Psychiatry, 12*, 23–25.

Copeland, M.E. (2001). Wellness recovery action plan: A system for monitoring and eliminating uncomfortable or dangerous physical symptoms and emotional feelings. In: C. Brown (Ed.), *Recovery and wellness: Models of hope and empowerment for people with mental illness* (pp. 127–150). New York: The Haworth Press.

Davidson, L., Stayner, D., Nickou, C., Styron, T., Rowe, M., & Chinman, M. (2001). 'Simply to be let in': Inclusion as a basis for recovery. *Psychiatric Rehabilitation Journal, 24*, 375–388.

Ellis, G. (2003). Prevention, promotion or just survival? A consumer's perspective. *Australasian Psychiatry, 11*, 65–69.

Fieldhouse, J. (2003). The impact of an allotment group on mental health clients' health, wellbeing and social networking. *British Journal of Occupational Therapy, 66*, 286–296.

Freeley, T., Servoss, T., & Fox, C. (2004). The effects of an outpatient wellness program on subjective quality of life in people with psychiatric disabilities. *Psychiatric Rehabilitation Journal, 27*, 275–278.

Hackney, C.H., & Sanders, G.S. (2003). Religiosity and mental health: A meta-analysis of recent studies. *Journal for the Scientific Study of Religion*, 42, 43–55.

Huxley, P., & Thornicroft, G. (2003). Social inclusion, social quality and mental illness. *British Journal of Psychiatry*, 182, 289–290.

Jablensky, A., McGrath, J., Herrman, H., Castle, D., Gureje, O., Morgan, V., & Korten, A. (1999). *People living with psychotic illness: An Australian study 1997–98 – an overview*. Canberra: Commonwealth of Australia.

Johnstone, M. (2001). Stigma, social justice and the rights of the mentally ill: Challenging the status quo. *Australian and New Zealand Journal of Mental Health Nursing*, 10, 200–209.

Link, B., Struening, E., Neese-Todd, S., Asmussen, S., & Phelan, J. (2001). The consequences of stigma for the self-esteem of people with mental illness. *Psychiatric Services*, 52, 1621–1626.

Lloyd, C., & Chandler, L. (1999). Girrebala: An Australian rehabilitation program. *Psychiatric Rehabilitation Skills*, 3, 173–192.

McCreadie, R., Farrington, S., Halliday, J., Macdonald, S., MacEwan, T., & Sharkey, V. (2001). Leisure activities of people with schizophrenia: Listening to music and playing the National Lottery. *Psychiatric Bulletin*, 25, 277–278.

Markowitz, F. (1998). The effects of stigma on the psychological well-being and life satisfaction of persons with mental illness. *Journal of Health and Social Behaviour*, 39, 335–347.

Mead, S., Hilton, D., & Curtis, L. (2001). Peer support: A theoretical perspective. *Psychiatric Rehabilitation Journal*, 25, 134–141.

Meddings, S., & Perkins, R. (2002). What 'getting better' means to staff and users of a rehabilitation service: An exploratory study. *Journal of Mental Health*, 11, 319–325.

Meeks, S., & Murrell, S. (1994). Service providers in the social networks of clients with severe mental illness. *Schizophrenia Bulletin*, 20, 399–406.

Mental Health Commission (2002). *Recovery competencies for New Zealand mental health workers*. Wellington: Mental Health Commission.

Mowbray, C., Bybee, D., & Collins, M. (2001). Follow-up client satisfaction in a supported education program. *Psychiatric Rehabilitation Journal*, 24, 237–247.

Mowbray, C., Megivern, D., & Holter, M. (2003). Supported education programming for adults with psychiatric disabilities: Results from a national survey. *Psychiatric Rehabilitation Journal*, 27, 159–167.

Myers, M.S. (1998). Empowerment and community building through a gardening project. *Psychiatric Rehabilitation Journal*, 22, 181–183.

Nash, M. (2002). Voting as a means of social inclusion for people with a mental illness. *Journal of Psychiatric and Mental Health Nursing*, 9, 697–703.

Neumayer, B., & Wilding, C. (2005). Leisure as commodity. In: G. Whiteford & V. Wright-St Clair (Eds.), *Occupation and practice in context* (pp. 317–331). London: Elsevier.

Office of the Deputy Prime Minister (2004). *Mental health and social exclusion*. Wetherby, UK: ODPM Publications.

Perlick, D.A., Rosenheck, R.A., Clarkin, J.F., Sirey, J., Salahi, J., Struening, E.L., & Link, B.G. (2001). Adverse effects of perceived stigma on social adaptation of persons diagnosed with bipolar affective disorder. *Psychiatric Services*, 52, 1627–1632.

Pickard, J.A., & Deane, F.P. (2000). Evaluation of the 'Helping Hands' volunteer program for people with mental illness. *Australian Journal of Rehabilitation Counselling*, 6, 45–56.

Ponizovsky, A., Grinshpoon, A., Sasson, R., & Levav, I. (2004). Stress in adult students with schizophrenia in a supported education program. *Comprehensive Psychiatry, 45,* 401–407.

Rickwood, D. (2004). Recovery in Australia: Slowly but surely. *Australian e-Journal for the Advancement of Mental Health, 3,* 1–3. Retrieved November 24, 2004, from http://www.auseinet.com/journal/vol3iss1/rickwoodeditorial.pdf

Roder, V., Jenull, B., & Brenner, H.D. (1998). Teaching schizophrenic patients recreational, residential and vocational skills. *International Review of Psychiatry, 10,* 35–41.

Russinova, Z., Wewiorski, N.J., & Cash, D. (2002). Use of alternative health care practices by persons with serious mental illness: Perceived benefits. *American Journal of Public Health, 92,* 1600–1603.

Schiff, A. (2004). Recovery and mental illness: Analysis and personal reflections. *Psychiatric Rehabilitation Journal, 27,* 212–218.

Sensky, T., Turkington, D., Kingdon, D., Scott, J.L., Scott, J., Siddle, R., O'Carroll, M., & Barnes, T.R.E. (2000). A randomized controlled trial of cognitive–behavioral therapy for persistent symptoms in schizophrenia resistant to medication. *Archives of General Psychiatry, 57,* 165–172.

Shimitras, L., Fossey, E., & Harvey, C. (2003). Time use of people living with schizophrenia in a North London catchment Area. *British Journal of Occupational Therapy, 66,* 46–54.

Skirboll, B. (1994). The Compeer model: Client rehabilitation and economic benefits. *Psychosocial Rehabilitation Journal, 18,* 89–94.

Solomon, P. (2004). Peer support/peer provided services underlying processes, benefits, and critical ingredients. *Psychiatric Rehabilitation Journal, 27,* 392–401.

Tepper, L., Rogers, S.A., Coleman, E.M., & Malony, H.N. (2001). The prevalence of religious coping among persons with persistent mental illness. *Psychiatric Services, 52,* 660–665.

Twenge, J., Catanese, K., & Baumeister, R. (2003). Social exclusion and the deconstructed state: Time perception, meaninglessness, lethargy, lack of emotion, and self-awareness. *Journal of Personality and Social Psychology, 85,* 409–423.

Unger, K.V. (1993). Creating supported education programs utilizing existing community resources. *Psychosocial Rehabilitation Journal, 17,* 11–23.

Unger, K., Anthony, W., Sciarappa, K., & Rogers, E.S. (1991). Development and evaluation of a supported education program for young adults with long-term mental illness. *Hospital and Community Psychiatry, 42,* 838–842.

Wong, S., Lloyd, C., & Petchkovsky, L. (2004). *Art and recovery: A qualitative investigation.* Unpublished honours report, Division of Occupational Therapy, University of Queensland.

Woodside, H., & Luis, F. (1997). Supported volunteering. *Psychiatric Rehabilitation Journal, 70,* 70–74.

Wright, E., Gronfein, W., & Owens, T. (2000). Deinstitutionalization, social rejection, and the self-esteem of former mental patients. *Journal of Health and Social Behaviour, 41,* 68–90.

Chapter 11

VOCATIONAL REHABILITATION

Robert King and Chris Lloyd

Overview of chapter

Entering or re-entering the workforce is a key component of recovery of social functioning. Vocational rehabilitation is a complex role that involves assisting the client to overcome both internal and external barriers to employment. It requires both advanced counselling skills as well as capacity to either link the client to specialist vocational rehabilitation service or to work in a highly practical fashion with the client. There is a substantial body of research to support the efficacy of supported employment as an approach to vocational rehabilitation and there is also evidence that transitional employment can be a bridge to supported and independent employment. In this chapter, two programmes that deliver evidence-based vocational rehabilitation for people recovering from mental illness are examined and guidelines are provided for the practitioner working with a client to achieve employment outcomes. We revisit Sam as he takes tentative steps to enter the workforce.

Why is vocational rehabilitation important?

Work is central to both the identity and community participation of adults in our community. It is also fundamental to economic wellbeing. Lack of work, loss of work or insufficient work have adverse psychological, social and economic consequences, regardless of whether or not an individual has a mental illness. For people who have a mental illness, especially when that illness is at the more severe end of the spectrum, access to work is extremely difficult. For example, a national survey in Australia (Waghorn et al., 2004) found that only 21% of householders with a probable psychosis were engaged in the workforce. Similar findings have been reported for the UK by the Social Exclusion Unit (2004) (see Figure 11.1).

The reasons for low participation are partly to do with impairments associated with the mental illness that impact on concentration, communication, reliability, or other attributes important to participation in the workforce. Poor self-rated functioning, negative psychiatric symptoms and recent hospitalisation have all been found associated with poorer employment outcomes (Razzano et al., 2005). However, low participation is also a function of social and community attitudes and structures that have limited access despite policy and legislative intentions (Stefan, 2002).

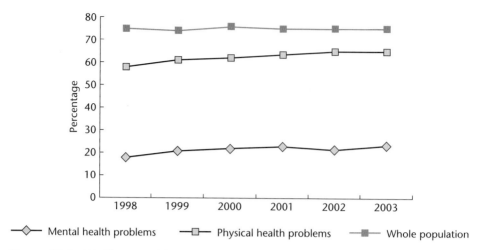

Figure 11.1 Workforce participation in England for people with mental health problems, physical health problems and the whole population. Source: Social Exclusion Unit (2004); reproduced with permission. © Crown copyright.

Source: Labour Force Survey, figures for England only.

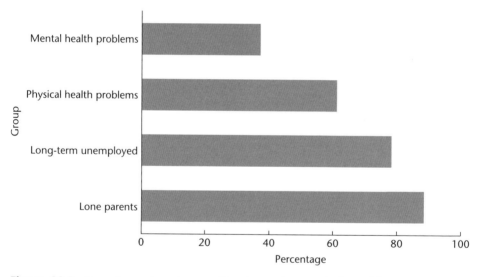

Figure 11.2 Percentage of employers willing to employ people from different backgrounds or problem areas. Source: Social Exclusion Unit (2004); reproduced with permission. © Crown copyright.

Data source: ONE Evaluation: Department for Work and Pensions, 2001.

The Social Exclusion Unit (2004) reported that only 40% of employers indicated that they would employ a person with a mental illness, and this was a much lower number than would employ from other groups at risk of disadvantage resulting from stigma, such as people with physical illness, the long-term unemployed and single mothers (see Figure 11.2). Only 25% of employers would be prepared to employ a person with schizophrenia. It is not surprising that the Social Exclusion Unit (2004) also reported that two-thirds of a sample of people with mental illness indicated that they had been put off from applying for jobs because of fear of unfair treatment.

As noted in Chapter 2, recovery of social functioning among people affected by mental illness in western societies appears poorer than recovery of social functioning among people in less developed societies. While the reasons for this are a matter for speculation, one possibility is that less developed societies are better able to provide meaningful productive social roles for people with mental illness, for example harvesting rice and in the production of village goods (Harnois & Gabriel, 2000). One of the characteristics of our technologically advanced, highly competitive societies is that people whose productivity is adversely affected for any reason can easily be isolated or marginalised. It may require significant accommodation on the part of society and the various organisations and individuals who are central to the organisation of work, to enable people with mental illness to actively participate in productive employment (Kirsh, 2000).

Text box 11.1 Employment for people with severe mental illness: what the evidence shows

- Some form of paid employment is a key goal for many people with severe mental illness
- A range of illness-related barriers and social barriers result in poor employment outcomes for most people with severe mental illness
- Intensive assistance, using a supported employment approach, increases access to employment
- A high level of integration between specialist employment services and clinical services is a key factor in achieving employment outcomes
- A flexible and assertive approach to providing employment services probably contributes to successful outcomes

Not only is lack of work detrimental to the wellbeing of people with mental illness, there is evidence that obtaining work, especially competitive work, is associated with improvement in wellbeing and mental health status (Bond et al., 2001; Van Dongen, 1996). It is likely that work impacts favourably on mental health because it provides a stable structure, a social network, and has positive impact on self esteem and identity (Bond et al., 2001). However, it cannot be assumed that work in itself is sufficient to improve mental health, because it is also likely that people whose mental health is improving are better able to work. Whether or not employment can directly contribute to recovery, it is clear that mental health and work are interlinked, which makes it important to ensure that people affected by mental illness have access to work and support during the process of adapting to a work environment (Grove, 1999).

A number of qualitative studies have explored, with people affected by severe mental illness, their hopes, fears and experiences regarding work. These studies provide the rehabilitation practitioner with valuable information about some of the issues that clients might be struggling with when considering entering the workforce. Bassett et al. (2001) conducted a focus group investigation of young people wishing to rejoin the workforce. A number of issues were identified that had an impact on their employment opportunities beyond labour market opportunities, or lack of them. The participants focused primarily on issues related to personal losses, low self-esteem and self-confidence, the impact of stigma, symptom management and the experience of being unwell, and a lack of direction as to how they could achieve their vocational goals.

Honey (2004) found that participants in focus groups identified six categories of benefit associated with employment:

- Money – greater independence and increased resources
- Purposeful and meaningful activity – doing something constructive during the day
- Growth and development – enhancing capacities, fulfilling potential
- Social participation and belonging – being accepted as part of a normal social group
- Self image and self-esteem – being perceived to be a productive member of the community
- Mental health – work can provide stability and purpose

However, participants also identified a number of negatives, including the tedium of the work itself, feeling different from work colleagues, experiencing a sense of failure because of inability to hold jobs, and feeling as if the stress of work contributed to deteriorating mental health. This means that, while people with mental illness can be strongly motivated towards work, they also have to deal with concerns and barriers that are often quite reality based.

Henry & Lucca (2002) interviewed both clients and service providers in psychosocial rehabilitation services providing vocational rehabilitation. They found that while a range of individual and illness factors were impediments to employment, there were also major systemic factors, including the social security system, the service system and stigma that affected employment outcomes. They concluded that it was equally important for practitioners to address social impediments as it was to work at the level of the individual. In a study conducted by Mallick et al. (1998), participants indicated that financial resources, employment resources and vocational skills presented the greatest barriers to community integration. Vocational adjustment skills included such aspects as interpersonal skills required to function in the workplace, the ability to follow directions, make judgements, complete tasks, maintain orientation to a task and comply with rules and regulations.

Secker & Membrey (2003) interviewed people with mental illness who had experienced supported employment to find out what factors were critical in enabling them to retain their jobs. The main themes identified were issues that might be expected by any person starting a new job: orientation to workplace culture, training, developing relationships with colleagues and support from management.

They referred to these as 'natural supports' in the workplace and highlighted the importance of ensuring that these were in place when a person with mental illness enters employment. They also identified accommodations on the job – especially with respect to work schedule and hours of work – and the role of their vocational support workers as being important.

Facilitating access to employment for people affected by mental illness

The importance of employment has long been recognised, and even during the period when institutional care dominated treatment of mental illness, there was usually some form of structured activity such as farm work or craft included in the daily routine (McGurrin, 1994). Early approaches to community based vocational rehabilitation centred on 'sheltered workshops' and other kinds of pre-vocational training programmes integrally linked with the clinical service environment. Other vocational approaches include social firms and social collectives. Social firms are small to medium-sized firms which have been developed with the primary purpose of providing employment for people with disability in a context that replicates ordinary firms but provides the required support for workers who need it. People with disability work alongside people without disability and are paid regular wages and work on the basis of a regular work contract (Harnois & Gabriel, 2000). Social cooperatives function independently from mental health services but maintain a close working relationship with them. They aim to provide social and health assistance and promote job opportunities for people with disabilities (Harnois & Gabriel, 2000).

The contemporary vocational rehabilitation environment is dominated by just two models: supported employment (Bond, 2004) and transitional employment (Beard et al., 1963; Henry et al., 2001). While these models both have pre-vocational components, they both prioritise rapid entry or re-entry into the workforce and support in retaining work. There are a number of well developed service programmes designed to deliver supported and/or transitional employment. In this chapter, we will pay particular attention to two such programmes: Individual Placement and Support (IPS), which delivers supported employment as a component of a clinical programme, and Clubhouse, which delivers both supported and transitional employment as components of a non-clinical rehabilitation programme. Each programme has specific strengths and weaknesses as a vehicle for vocational rehabilitation. If employment outcome alone is the measure of success, then supported employment (Bond et al., 1999) and in particular supported employment using the IPS approach (Mueser et al., 2004) have higher impact than transitional employment or supported employment in the Clubhouse model. On the other hand, Clubhouses provide affiliation, peer support and a structured environment in a non-clinical setting as well as access to employment. While employment outcomes may not be as strong as those of IPS, the other benefits may more than compensate (Warner et al., 1999).

Individual placement and support programme

The IPS programme of vocational rehabilitation (Becker & Drake, 1993) has been more systematically researched than any other. The key features are that vocational rehabilitation (VR) specialists work as part of the clinical treatment team, typically within an assertive case management (assertive community treatment or ACT) framework (see Chapter 9). The VR specialists work individually with clients, usually in their own home or environment to assist them locate and obtain a job. Once a job has been found, the VR specialist stays actively involved, providing continuing support, liaising with employers when necessary and assisting the client to deal with difficulties or problems as they arise. It is similar to other forms of supported employment in that the focus is not on pre-vocational training but on obtaining and maintaining a job. It is different from other forms of supported employment in that the VR specialist works within the clinical team and uses an assertive outreach rather than office based framework for service delivery. The IPS model has been successfully adapted to other social and cultural environments (Wong et al., 2001).

Two substantial and well-designed studies (Lehman et al., 2002; Mueser et al., 2004) have demonstrated that the IPS model is superior to less focused approaches to vocational rehabilitation in achieving employment for people with mental illness. The evidence suggests that people taking part in an IPS programme may be twice as likely to obtain employment as people engaged in other approaches to vocational rehabilitation.

It should be noted, however, that while IPS is very effective in assisting people obtain jobs, its advantage over other approaches in helping people sustain jobs is less pronounced. In the Lehman et al. (2002) study, many more people in the IPS programme obtained jobs but, among those who obtained jobs, hours worked and job retention was no different for IPS and standard psychosocial rehabilitation clients. In both groups, job retention was typically low (approximately 15 weeks). In the study conducted by Mueser et al. (2004), IPS clients not only obtained more jobs than clients of standard supported employment or of psychosocial rehabilitation programmes, but they also had better job retention. Nonetheless, among those who obtained employment, the average job retention was modest (20 weeks) and the majority worked less than 20 hours per week. There is no evidence that any other approach is superior to IPS in assisting clients retain jobs, but these data are a reminder that job retention is just as important and difficult as access into the workforce.

There is evidence that augmenting IPS supported employment with focused rehabilitation such as social skills training (Tsang, 2001) or cognitive training (McGurk et al., 2005) can enhance employment outcomes.

Clubhouse

Clubhouse is the most internationally extensive programme of vocational rehabilitation (Macias et al., 1999). It developed in the 1950s in New York, and there are today more than 300 Clubhouses in 25 countries in all parts of the world. While not as single-mindedly focused on vocational rehabilitation, as IPS, vocational rehabilitation is the major focus of Clubhouse. Clubhouse operates as a member operated organisation, with a collection of work units that follow what is termed the 'work-ordered day'. When a person becomes a Clubhouse member, they join a group that has an ethos of work within the Clubhouse and work outside the Clubhouse. All members are expected to participate in the work-ordered day and for many members this leads to participation in transitional employment, a Clubhouse sponsored education or supported employment programme, or independent employment (McKay et al., 2005; Henry et al., 2001; Masso et al., 2001).

Transitional employment is most distinctive to the Clubhouse approach. Clubhouse negotiates jobs with employers. The jobs are held by Clubhouse, which in turn fills them, 6 months at a time, with members who are supported by staff. Staff members work alongside members until such time as they are ready to take full responsibility for the job. If a member is unable to meet job requirements, the job is completed by a staff member. The member is paid at award wages while doing the job. There is evidence that transitional employment is valuable in providing members with real work experience and is a bridge to either supported employment or independent employment (Henry et al., 2001).

The main differences between transitional employment and supported employment are that in supported employment the job belongs to the person, not the Clubhouse, and the employer may not know that the person has a mental illness. Typically, the degree of hands-on support at the workplace is higher with transitional employment than is the case with supported employment. Transitional employment may be suitable for people with a higher level of disability. In practice, the differences between transitional employment and supported employment may be less fundamental than the principles suggest. For example, the research shows that supported employment positions in practice do not last longer than transitional employment positions and that hours and wages of supported employment positions are not higher. Anecdotal evidence suggests that from the perspective of clients, a job is a job and whether it is transitional employment or supported employment is more an issue for the rehabilitation service than the client.

Vocational rehabilitation in practice

The starting point for the rehabilitation practitioner is thinking vocationally. There is now a substantial amount of evidence that rehabilitation practitioners do not focus clearly on working with clients to achieve vocational outcomes (Blankertz & Robinson, 1996). This may be because of lack of expertise, lack of practitioner confidence in the capacity of the client to manage a work environment or client ambivalence about work. The first barrier to cross is the mindset of the practitioner who must believe that the client:

- Has the capacity to work
- Has the right to work, and
- Will benefit from work

Equipped with these core beliefs, the practitioner has some important tasks. These can be summarised as working with the client to identify:

- Benefits of obtaining work
- Work related goals
- Work related strengths or interests
- Fears or concerns about work
- Barriers to return to work
- Barriers to job retention
- Relapse management strategies

When clients lack motivation for work or have high levels of ambivalence concerning work, the use of motivational interviewing (see Chapter 12) is likely to be helpful. The aim is not to 'browbeat' the client into accepting vocational rehabilitation, but rather to assist the client to identify benefits and deal realistically with problems or issues associated with seeking and maintaining work. Mannock et al. (2002) suggested the Transtheoretical Model (TTM) as offering an empirically based approach to conceptualising and assessing readiness to return to work. They developed the University of Rhode Island Change Assessment–Vocational Counseling (URICA–VC) measure, which was designed specifically to assess clients' readiness to engage in job seeking behaviours. The URICA-VC is composed of three four-item scales that measure constructs representing precontemplation, contemplation, and action. Mannock et al. (2002) suggested that this enables practitioners to measure client progress along a stage-based continuum towards return to work.

Text box 11.2 Maintaining a recovery focus in vocational rehabilitation: tips for practitioners

- Remain alert to employment aspirations
- Assist your client to identify employment relevant strengths
- Assist your client to identify jobs that would be both enjoyable and make use of strengths and capacities
- Work with your client on strategies for overcoming work related fears and concerns
- Assist your client to make decisions regarding disclosure after weighing up the benefits and risks
- Remember that education, voluntary work and other structured social activities can be important stepping stones to employment

When the client has established motivation for work, indicated some goals and made a realistic but positive assessment of capacities and barriers, the practitioner is faced with a choice. This choice involves either handing over the major part of the VR to a specialist individual or agency, or to undertake the VR personally. We recommend that, whenever practical, the VR should be handled by a specialist. Not only does the research suggest that specialists achieve better outcomes, but there are obvious practical advantages that a specialist has. These include:

- Knowledge of the various forms of assistance available both to clients and employers
- Knowledge of the job market and the most efficient ways of accessing the market
- Contacts with employers, and
- Knowledge of current standards for resumes, presentation at interview, interview style

The specialist also preserves a clear work focus and is less likely to be distracted by clinical issues. They understand that return to work is stressful for everyone, regardless of mental illness and are less likely to pathologise normal anxiety. However, referral to a specialist does not mean that the psychosocial rehabilitation practitioner ceases to be part of the VR process.

One of the major findings from the evaluation of a range of demonstration projects implementing vocational rehabilitation for people with severe mental illness is that close liaison between the VR specialist and the rehabilitation practitioner is a key to success (Cook et al., 2005). The rehabilitation practitioner has a key role in supporting the client through the transition to employment focus. It is important that the client does not feel abandoned. There is a lot of merit in the rehabilitation practitioner accompanying the client to initial VR meetings while the client is developing a relationship with the VR specialist and closely monitoring continuing participation. The rehabilitation practitioner must be prepared to assist the client to work through concerns or ambivalence about participating in the VR process. It is also important that the VR specialist feels comfortable consulting with the rehabilitation practitioner if she or he has concerns about the mental state of the client. This needs to be clearly negotiated with the client at the beginning of the VR process and should be subject to written agreement.

A second important lesson from the success of IPS is that VR is most successful when it is done in the context of the assertive community treatment model. In the IPS programme, this means the VR practitioner home visiting and ensuring that the pace of VR is not dependent on client motivation or initiative. Many supported and transitional employment services are unable to provide this kind of service, and it may be up to the rehabilitation practitioner to assume responsibility for making sure the client gets to appointments and follows through with tasks. According to Boardman et al. (2003), vocational support cannot be simply handed over to specialists, and once people are in work any continuing support should remain the responsibility of the key worker.

A key consideration in the roles and responsibilities of the rehabilitation practitioner is the level of experience that the VR specialist has working with people who have severe mental illness. The less experience the VR specialist has in working with this population, the more important it will be for the rehabilitation practitioner to be available and to be an educator. The practitioner is able to suggest strategies for managing the illness and to provide the necessary mental health support for the client (Bassett & Lloyd, 2000).

VR will be most successful when the client, the mental health practitioner and the VR specialist are all clear about expectations and roles. Setting these out through the establishment of a service agreement is the best way of ensuring there is no misunderstanding. Documentation needs to be supported with regular communication. One such strategy is to develop a network meeting between VR specialists and psychosocial rehabilitation practitioners. An 'arm's length' brokerage approach to VR is much less likely to be effective than a 'hands on' teamwork approach.

In many instances there will be a lack of specialist VR services (Boardman et al., 2003). When psychosocial rehabilitation practitioners do not have access to specialised services, they will need to take on the primary responsibility for VR. The process that could be followed includes: (i) determining need for employment; (ii) assessing level of social and work related impairment; (iii) determining work related goals; (iv) assessing vocational status and degree of confidence in seeking work; (v) strengthening relapse prevention strategies and building coping skills; (vi) enhancing social networks; (vii) providing practical support; and (viii) resource development.

Text box 11.3   Maintaining a multidisciplinary focus in vocational rehabilitation

- Whatever your skills as a rehabilitation practitioner, it is likely that an employment specialist will add value and increase the likelihood of your client obtaining work
- Remember that frequency and quality of communication between clinical practitioners and employment specialists is one of the strongest predictors of successful employment outcomes
- Think about what other members of the rehabilitation team can contribute to your client's capacity and readiness for work. Can a psychologist assist your client to manage fears? Can an occupational therapist assist with personal presentation and interpersonal skills? Can a nurse or doctor advise on how to explain the illness to an employer?

Caspar (2003) suggested using the Need For Change (NFC) self-rating scale to determine satisfaction and the felt need to make a change now in employment status. This five-item measure provides clients with a simple, brief, and practical means of expressing their feelings about their current employment status. This type of tool helps practitioners make decisions about referrals to supported employment programmes and assists in addressing issues of under-utilisation, attrition and job termination. It is important to be able to determine clients' interests in work and the supporting beliefs that are needed to make a change now in employment status. If the client does wish to pursue work, the practitioner needs to consider conducting a prevocational interview to gain an understanding of the person's past experiences of work and what impact the illness has had on his or her work experiences. Topic areas would cover: pension status; finances; social and family support; transport; accommodation; education and work history; how the illness has impacted on ability to both seek and maintain work; issue of disclosure; type of work interests; what the person perceives as their strengths; and what assistance they require from the practitioner. It is important to find out the manner in which they wish to be assisted, for example, in group work, one-to-one, or referral on to another agency or service.

The Work and Social Adjustment Scale (WSAS) is a simple, reliable and valid measure of self-reported functional impairment attributable to an identified problem (Mundt et al., 2002). Items address work, home management, leisure activities and social relationships. This tool can be used to assess clients' level of functioning, for individual treatment planning to maximise functioning, and for the evaluation of treatment or intervention. It is important to prevent the development of further activity limitations and participation restrictions in order to assist clients obtain work related goals. At this stage the practitioner might refer the client to a psychosocial rehabilitation group to improve the client's level of functioning prior to focusing on work.

It is necessary to determine clients' work related goals from the clients' perspective. For example, the client might identify assistance with the use of public transport as important to him or her in being able to seek work. The practitioner would then work with the client to improve their confidence in using public transport. There may be a wide range of goals that clients have in connection with rejoining the work force, which may include such aspects as assistance with social security benefits, gaining awareness of agencies or support services which are available for people with disability, or finding out about appropriate courses and attending college.

Text box 11.4 Vocational rehabilitation in action: Sam attends a Clubhouse

You will recollect from Chapter 9 that Sam is now receiving intensive case management. He is generally more settled and the suicidal behaviour is less prominent, mainly taking the form of occasional thoughts of killing himself. Sam has not previously worked, but he has demonstrated some clear work relevant skills and interests (restoring cars). His parents have been on his back about work, but less so since becoming involved with family psychoeducation. Sam is now receiving social security (disability) benefits, but he is complaining about being bored. He has made a connection with the Skyliners, a local car club, but he does not feel confident he will be accepted by other members of the Skyliners.

Sam's rehabilitation practitioner raises the possibility of employment with Sam. His immediate response is, 'Who'd want to employ a psycho?' Further discussion with Sam reveals:

● He is very fearful of being humiliated by work colleagues – it has not occurred to him that people at work need not know about his background
● Sam does not know much about what an ordinary work environment is like and he is afraid of failing
● Sam has not given much thought to the kind of work he would like to do. He was bored at school and he thinks he would probably be bored at work
● There are aspects of work – especially getting paid and getting his parents off his back and 'showing people' – that appeal to him

Sam agrees that he is sufficiently bored hanging around at home to attend his local Clubhouse. His rehabilitation practitioner accompanies him as he gets a tour. At the end of it, he is feeling uncertain. Joining the Clubhouse would give him something to do, but he is not sure about getting to know a lot of other people. There are also a lot of older people there and in some ways it reminds him of being in hospital.

His rehabilitation practitioner encourages him to attend a few times at least, and offers to take him in and pick him up whenever Sam gives a call. Sam joins the kitchen work unit and finds time passes reasonably quickly preparing vegetables. He is impressed that the place runs pretty smoothly and that members, and not just staff, have a fair bit of responsibility. He also likes the fact that staff seem like ordinary people, not nurses or social workers.

After a few weeks, Sam notices an old lawnmower that appears to be disused. A staff member tells him that they took it in for repair but the shop said it was not worth fixing. Sam says he thinks he might be able to do something with it. The staff member tells Sam the Clubhouse has a transitional employment position as a storeman at a motor wrecking yard. The member currently in the job finishes in 6 weeks. He asks Sam if he would be interested in learning a bit more about the job and what he would need to do to have a chance of getting it.

Waghorn et al. (2005a) developed an instrument designed to capture participation in vocationally relevant activities, other than paid employment, which may later contribute to a vocational recovery pathway. Five major role categories are addressed, which include home duties and self-care; participation in psychosocial rehabilitation, voluntary work, vocational rehabilitation or personal development programmes; caring for others; education; and employment. This type of tool is useful in maintaining the focus on clients' vocational recovery goals and providing a basis for discussing vocational assistance options with local rehabilitation and disability employment support providers.

Clients may often experience varying degrees of confidence in their ability to carry out a range of employment activities, for example, identifying personal work values, arranging stress in the workplace, dressing appropriately or participating appropriately in an interview. The Self-confidence for Employment Activities consists of 38 questions on activities required in most forms of employment and how confident the person feels in their ability to do the task or activity (Waghorn et al., 2005b). This will assist practitioners with specific work activities that the client has identified as not feeling confident with, in order to increase their level of confidence.

Relapse prevention is a specific component of the recovery process and involves maximising for clients by reducing the likelihood and impact of relapse. Steps include identifying the relapse signature and developing a relapse prevention plan. This is particularly important when clients are looking for work and commencing a job, as these are both stressful work related activities. The rehabilitation practitioner may work with clients to educate them about relaxation and stress reduction. Clients may be assisted with strategies for staying well, for example doing yoga, tai chi, and exercise, developing interests, hobbies and enjoyable activities, and having a peer support network.

Corrigan & Phelan (2004) found that both objective and subjective measures of social support were significantly associated with a process perspective of recovery. People who report more friends and practitioners also report better recovery. These findings suggest the importance of interventions that facilitate social networks.

Hardiman & Segal (2003) suggested that peer knowledge and expertise is often an untapped source of support for people with psychiatric disabilities. They highlighted the importance of self-help participation in leading to increased peer support and strengthening social networks. It has been suggested that a broader approach needs to be taken in vocational rehabilitation, which is complemented by interventions that strengthen and support the clients' social networks (Shankar & Collyer, 2003). This may involve practitioners linking clients into peer support groups, and with the development of such groups as a worker support group for clients who have recently found work.

The following practical support strategies may be utilised to increase the likelihood of successful outcomes:

- Working alongside the client to locate suitable job opportunities
- Assisting the client to prepare letters of application, resumes, make phone calls, etc.
- Assisting the client present for interview (dress, grooming, hygiene, etc.)
- Helping the client make decisions regarding disclosure of mental health status (working through benefits and disadvantages of disclosure)
- Practicing simulated phone calls, interviews, etc., until both you and the client feel that competence has been achieved (overpractice is desirable because the real thing will be more stressful)
- Assisting the client with first day challenges – waking up, getting ready, getting to work
- High availability for phone consultation and after-hours support during first days of work

Resource development involves the practitioner becoming aware of exactly what types of services and supports are available in the local community. They may need to spend a substantial amount of time talking with other service providers in an attempt to increase their willingness to assist clients with finding and keeping work. It may also be likely that practitioners may need to provide education and information about mental illness and vocational rehabilitation for people with psychiatric disability. Practitioners may find it useful to develop an employment support network, where service providers may meet regularly and discuss issues and options related to employment for clients who want to join the workforce. It is important to bear in mind that the best evidence is that individualised, practical job-focused rehabilitation is the most effective. Extended prevocational preparation in group settings with a broad focus on communication skills or other generic capacity is less effective. Such processes may be helpful when the primary goals are peer acceptance or peer support or affiliation, but if the client wants to work it is much more effective to develop a clear work focus.

Because, as we have seen above, the average tenure of jobs is less than 6 months, the practitioner must be prepared not only to provide support when the client is working but also to support clients through the loss of jobs, and work on reengaging clients in the workforce at various times.

Conclusion

Assisting people with severe mental illness to obtain work is one of the greatest challenges in psychosocial rehabilitation. Mental illness often has a direct impact on work capacity and it has profound indirect effects through its impact on personal confidence, stigma and continuity of work history. Successful vocational rehabilitation requires a capacity to address barriers at all these levels and to work with the individual to develop motivation and self-belief. There is a well-developed evidence base for specific programmes that have been developed to assist people to return to work. Where such programmes are available, the primary role of the practitioner is to facilitate access to a specialist programme and to provide continuing support, working closely with the specialist vocational rehabilitation practitioner. However, even the best programmes have limited success in sustaining people affected by severe mental illness in work for extended periods. This means that vocational rehabilitation is often a continuing process rather than a one-off entrance point to employment.

References

Bassett, J., & Lloyd, C. (2000). Employment and young people with a mental illness: A review. *British Journal of Therapy and Rehabilitation, 7,* 480–485.

Bassett, J., Lloyd, C., & Bassett, H. (2001). Work issues for young people with psychosis: Barriers to employment. *British Journal of Occupational Therapy, 64,* 66–72.

Beard, J.H., Schmidt, J.R., & Smith, M.M. (1963). The use of transitional employment in the rehabilitation of the psychiatric patient. *Journal of Nervous and Mental Disorders, 136,* 507–514.

Becker, D.R., & Drake, R.E. (1993). *A working life: The individual placement and support (IPS) program.* Concord, NH: New Hampshire–Dartmouth Psychiatric Research Center.

Blankertz, L., & Robinson, S. (1996). Adding a vocational focus to mental health rehabilitation. *Psychiatric Services, 47,* 1216–1222.

Boardman, J., Grove, B., Perkins, R., & Shepherd, G. (2003). Work and employment for people with psychiatric disabilities. *British Journal of Psychiatry, 182,* 467–468.

Bond, G.R. (2004). Supported employment: evidence for an evidence-based practice. *Psychiatric Rehabilitation Journal, 27,* 345–359.

Bond, G.R., Drake, R.E., Becker, D.R., & Mueser, K.T. (1999). Effectiveness of psychiatric rehabilitation approaches for employment of people with severe mental illness. *Journal of Disability Policy Studies. Special Rehabilitation for People with Psychiatric Impairments, 10,* 18–52.

Bond, G.R., Resnick, S.G., Drake, R.E., Xie, H., McHugo, G.J., & Bebout, R.R. (2001). Does competitive employment improve nonvocational outcomes for people with severe mental illness? *Journal of Consulting and Clinical Psychology, 69,* 489–501.

Caspar, E. (2003). A self-rating scale for supported employment participants and practitioners. *Psychiatric Rehabilitation Journal, 27,* 151–158.

Cook, J.A., Lehman, A.F., Drake, R., McFarlane, W.R., Gold, P.B., Leff, H.S., Blyler, C., Toprac, M.G., Razzano, L.A., Burke-Miller, J.K., Blankertz, L., Shafer, M., Pickett-Schenk, S.A., & Grey, D.D. (2005). Integration of psychiatric and vocational services:

A multisite randomized, controlled trial of supported employment. *American Journal of Psychiatry*, *162*, 1948–1956.

Corrigan, P., & Phelan, S. (2004). Social support and recovery in people with serious mental illnesses. *Community Mental Health Journal*, *40*, 513–523.

Grove, B. (1999). Mental health and employment: Shaping a new agenda. *Journal of Mental Health*, *8*, 131–140.

Hardiman, E., & Segal, S. (2003). Community membership and social networks in mental health self-help agencies. *Psychiatric Rehabilitation Journal*, *27*, 25–33.

Harnois, G., & Gabriel, P. (2000). *Mental health and work: Impact, issues and good practices*. Geneva: World Health Organization and the International Labour Organization.

Henry, A.D., Barreira, P., Banks, S., Brown, J.M., & McKay, C. (2001). A retrospective study of Clubhouse-based transitional employment. *Psychiatric Rehabilitation Journal*, *24*, 344–354.

Henry, A.D., & Lucca, A.M. (2002). Contextual factors and participation in employment for people with serious mental illness. *Occupational Therapy Journal of Research*, *22* (Suppl. 1), 83S–84S.

Honey, A. (2004). Benefits and drawbacks of employment: Perspectives of people with mental illness. *Qualitative Health Research*, *14*, 381–395.

Kirsh, B. (2000). Factors associated with employment for mental health consumers *Psychiatric Rehabilitation Journal*, *24*, 13–21.

Lehman, A.F., Goldberg, R., Dixon, L.B., McNary, S., Postrado, L., Hackman, A., & McDonnell, K. (2002). Improving employment outcomes for persons with severe mental illnesses. *Archives of General Psychiatry*, *59*, 165–172.

McGurk, S.R., Mueser, K.T., & Pascaris, A. (2005). Cognitive training and supported employment for persons with severe mental illness: one-year results from a randomized controlled trial. *Schizophrenia Bulletin*, *31*, 898–909.

McGurrin, M.C. (1994). An overview of the effectiveness of traditional vocational rehabilitation services in the treatment of long term mental illness. *Psychosocial Rehabilitation Journal*, *17*, 37–53.

Macias, C., Jackson, R., Schroeder, C., & Wang, Q. (1999). What is a Clubhouse? Report on the ICCD 1996 Survey of USA Clubhouses. *Community Mental Health Journal*, *35*, 181–190.

McKay, C., Johnsen, M., & Stein, R. (2005). Employment outcomes in Massachusetts Clubhouses. *Psychiatric Rehabilitation Journal*, *29*, 25–33.

Mallick, K., Reeves, R., & Dellario, D. (1998). Barriers to community integration for people with severe and persistent psychiatric disabilities. *Psychiatric Rehabilitation Journal*, *22*, 175–180.

Mannock, T.J., Levesque, D., & Prochaska, J. (2002). Assessing readiness of clients with disabilities to engage in job seeking behaviours. (Readiness of clients). *Journal of Rehabilitation*, *68*, 16–24.

Masso, J.D., Avi-Itzhak, T., & Obler, D.R. (2001). The Clubhouse model: An outcome study on attendance, work attainment and status, and hospitalization recidivism. *Work*, *17*, 23–30.

Mueser, K.T., Clark, R.E., Haines, M., Drake, R.E., McHugo, G.J., Bond, G.R., Essock, S.M., Becker, D.R., Wolfe, R., & Swain, K. (2004). The Hartford study of supported employment for persons with severe mental illness. *Journal of Consulting and Clinical Psychology*, *72*, 479–490.

Mundt, J., Marks, I., Shear, K., & Greist, J. (2002). The Work and Social Adjustment Scale: A simple measure of impairment in functioning. *British Journal of Psychiatry*, *180*, 461–464.

Razzano, L.A., Cook, J.A., Burke-Miller, J.K., Mueser, K.T., Pickett-Schenk, S.A., Grey, D.D., Goldberg, R.W., Blyler, C.R., Gold, P.B., Leff, H.S., Lehman, A.F., Shafer, M.S., Blankertz, L.E., McFarlane, W.R., Toprac, M.G., & Ann Carey, M. (2005). Clinical factors associated with employment among people with severe mental illness: findings from the employment intervention demonstration program. *Journal of Nervous and Mental Disorders, 193*, 705–713.

Secker, J., & Membrey, H. (2003). Promoting mental health through employment and developing healthy workplaces: The potential of natural supports at work. *Health Education Research, 18*, 207–215.

Shankar, J., & Collyer, F. (2003). Vocational rehabilitation of people with mental illness: The need for a broader approach. *Australian e-journal for the Advancement of Mental Health 2* (2), www.auseinet.com/journal/vol2iss2/shankar.pdf

Social Exclusion Unit (2004). *Mental health and social exclusion.* London: Office of the Deputy Prime Minister.

Stefan, S. (2002). *Hollow promises: Employment discrimination against people with mental disabilities. The law and public policy.* Washington, DC, US: American Psychological Association.

Tsang, H.W. (2001). Applying social skills training in the context of vocational rehabilitation for people with schizophrenia. *Journal of Nervous and Mental Disorders, 189*, 90–98.

Van Dongen, C.J. (1996). Quality of life and self-esteem in working and nonworking persons with mental illness. *Community Mental Health Journal, 32*, 535–548.

Waghorn, G., Chant, D., White, P., & Whiteford, H. (2004). Delineating disability, labour force participation and employment restrictions among persons with psychosis. *Acta Psychiatrica Scandinavica, 109*, 279–288.

Waghorn, G., Chant, D., & King, R. (2005a). Classifying socially-valued role functioning among community residents with schizophrenia or schizoaffective disorder. *Australian and New Zealand Journal of Psychiatry, 39*, 288–299.

Waghorn, G., Chant, D., & King, R. (2005b). Work-related self-efficacy among community residents with psychiatric disabilities. *Psychiatric Rehabilitation Journal, 29*, 105–113.

Warner, R., Huxley, P., & Berg, T. (1999). An evaluation of the impact of Clubhouse membership on quality of life and treatment utilization. *International Journal of Social Psychiatry, 45*, 310–320.

Wong, K.K., Chiu, S.N., Chiu, L.P., & Tang, S.W. (2001). A supported competitive employment programme for individuals with chronic mental illness. *Hong Kong Journal of Psychiatry, 11*, 13–18.

Chapter 12

MENTAL ILLNESS AND SUBSTANCE MISUSE

Chris Lloyd

Overview of chapter

This chapter aims to acquaint practitioners with the literature covering mental illness and comorbid substance misuse, epidemiological studies, and the prevalence of dual diagnosis. Models of care in service provision are described. The steps in identifying clients' substance misuse, encouraging change and in motivational interviewing are discussed. Finally, dual diagnosis assessment and treatment approaches are outlined.

Impact of substance misuse

Individuals with psychotic disorders are more likely than the general population to smoke, and to have a lifetime history of alcohol or other substance misuse or dependence. The abuse of alcohol and other substances has a negative impact on the course and severity of their psychotic illness, while smoking, alcohol and substance misuse are known risk factors for physical ill health (World Health Organization, 2001). The burden to society of mental disorders and substance use disorders is considerable. The WHO burden of disease report estimates that mental illness and substance misuse contribute 20% to the burden of disease in society (World Health Organization, 2001). The epidemiological data suggest that prevention of comorbidity would reduce a substantial proportion of all lifetime psychiatric disorders and an even greater proportion of ongoing disorders. Comorbidity presents substantial treatment problems. These include lack of systematic screening, individuals with comorbid disorders being excluded from treatment, lack of specialist resources, sequential or parallel treatment, lack of knowledge of what elements of treatment are producing results and a narrow research base (Kavanagh, 2001). It is important that psychosocial rehabilitation practitioners have a thorough understanding of comorbidity and its treatment, since many of the clients seen in rehabilitation programmes will have a comorbid condition. Substance misuse is a risk factor that adversely influences the pathway to recovery.

Dual diagnosis

What does the term mean?

The term dual diagnosis or comorbidity refers to the co-occurrence of two or more disorders affecting an individual at the same time. It indicates a vulnerability to illness and points to disability and a higher need to use health services (Andrews et al., 2001). It is common for two or more mental disorders to occur together in an individual. Mental disorders also tend to occur much more frequently with physical disorders (World Health Organization, 2001). Anxiety and depressive disorders commonly occur together, with such morbidity being found among about half of all those individuals with these disorders. Another common situation is the presence of mental disorders associated with substance use and dependence (World Health Organization, 2001).

Harmful use and dependence

ICD-10 harmful use criteria require a pattern of substance use that causes damage to health (World Health Organization, 1993). The damage may be either physical or mental. ICD-10 dependence requires that three or more of the following are present: a strong desire to take the substance; impaired control over the use; a withdrawal syndrome on ceasing or reducing use; tolerance; a disproportionate amount of the user's time spent in obtaining, using and recovering from use; and continued use despite associated problems. These problems should have been experienced during the previous year for at least a month (World Health Organization, 1993).

What is the prevalence?

Comorbidity of mental disorders and substance use disorders is widespread. It is often associated with poor treatment outcome, severe illness course and high service use as compared with those with mental disorders alone. People with dual diagnosis are more likely to experience a range of negative outcomes including increased levels of medication non-compliance, psychosocial problems, depression, suicidal behaviour, re-hospitalisation, homelessness, poorer mental health, and higher family burden (Hall et al., 2001).

Why does comorbidity matter?

There are a number of reasons why comorbidity matters. These include the following:

- Comorbidity is the rule rather than the exception with mental disorders
- Comorbidity may result in inadequate treatment of one or both disorders – substance use may mask mental illness or vice versa and attitudes of practitioners may be more negative towards people with comorbid disorders

- Understanding why different disorders co-occur provides opportunities for prevention
- Persons with comorbid mental disorders often have a poorer treatment response and a worse course of illness over time; they are more impaired, suffer greater social disability and generate large social costs
- Comorbidity has important implications for treatment
- Having one disorder may worsen the symptoms and course of the other and may impair compliance with treatment

The presence of substantial comorbidity has serious implications for the identification, treatment and psychosocial rehabilitation of those individuals. The disability of individuals and the burden on families also increase correspondingly (World Health Organization, 2001).

The workforce

Services have typically been poor at detecting substance misuse in mental disorders. There are several possible reasons for this problem, including training of practitioners, ambiguity in the cause of some symptoms, and the lack of routine screening (Kavanagh, 2001; Treatment Protocol Project, 1997). Williams (1999) conducted a study examining the attitudes of mental health practitioners to comorbidity between mental health problems and substance misuse. This study highlighted the diversity of beliefs and views of roles that exist between the different professional groups. A significant percentage of the respondents expressed a need for specialist training. He recommended that training strategies be designed and implemented to enable mental health teams to develop a range of skills, attitudes and expertise, which would include the abilities to deal with the problems of comorbid substance misuse.

Difficulties in the management of comorbid substance misuse and mental disorders have also been identified. A survey conducted by Kavanagh et al. (2000) found that one or more issues presented a substantial clinical management problem for 98% of respondents. Problems identified included lack of accommodation or respite care, work and rehabilitation programmes, resource information for families, coordination of care, and difficulties with intersectoral liaison. There are a number of practical solutions to improve the assessment and treatment of comorbid substance misuse and mental disorders. These include:

- Staff training in identification and management of dual disorders
- Routine screening for dual diagnosis at intake
- Collaboration between service sectors in managing dual diagnosis clients
- Use of brief interventions adapted from motivational interviewing
- Provision of psychosocial rehabilitation
- Involvement of family and friends to support the therapeutic plan

Service provision

Why provide two services at once?

Comorbidity presents a substantial challenge associated with the most appropriate identification, prevention and management strategies. No single method of treatment for people with comorbid disorders is universally accepted. However, the literature indicates that models of care can be linked to poor outcomes (Drake et al., 1998; Mercer-McFadden et al., 1997). These include sequential and parallel models in which mental health and alcohol and drug abuse are treated separately, either one after the other, or at the same time but with no integration (Kavanagh, 2001; Welch & Mooney, 2001).

Text box 12.1 Multidisciplinary focus

- Avoid judging a person for using drugs
- Provide integrated treatment by assuming responsibility for treating substance misuse and other areas of mental health need
- Undertake a detailed functional analysis of substance use
- Provide support, encouragement and open communication
- Learn about the forces that maintain substance abuse, including biological, social and psychological factors
- Make use of the expertise of colleagues – there is no single solution and people with substance use problems often have a range of other medical, social and psychological problems

The present trend in treatment for people with comorbid disorders is towards integration of services (Treatment Protocol Project, 1997). In an integrated treatment model, practitioners treat both the mental disorder and substance misuse. Practitioners are encouraged to take responsibility for treating the substance abuse problem as well as the individual's other areas of need (Treatment Protocol Project, 1997). An approach such as this is more holistic in that substance misuse is not seen as the only problem, but one of a number of problems that have impacted on the life of the person. Additionally, this form of treatment aims to reduce conflicts between service providers, and to eliminate the client's burden of attending two programmes and hearing potentially conflicting messages (Drake et al., 1998; Ziedonis et al., 2001). Integrated treatment usually includes specialised assessment, assertive outreach to clients in treatment, intensive management, case management, family interventions, and substance misuse treatment groups (Mercer-McFadden et al., 1997; Welch & Mooney, 2001). Jerrell & Ridgely (1999) reported that it leads to high rates of engagement, reduced problematic substance use and psychiatric symptomatology and reduced need for hospitalisation.

Identifying substance use and encouraging change in clients

How to tell if someone is using substances

The presentation of substance misuse is often non-specific, for example anxiety, sleeplessness, dysphoria or restlessness, or it may appear as a psychotic symptom, for example paranoia or hallucinations. Given the high prevalence rates of substance use in people with psychotic disorders, systematic enquiry should be made as to whether your client is using substances.

There are a number of indicators that your client may be using substances. It is important to observe a combination of these indicators over a period of time before a substance use problem may be identified. Additionally, individuals with dual diagnosis may exhibit some of the following indicators in response to changes or exacerbations in their mental status.

- A marked personality change
- Extreme mood swings
- Change in physical appearance or wellbeing
- Change in mental status
- Medication non-compliance
- Change in job or school performance
- Change in friends or peer groups
- Unexplained accidents
- An excessive need for money
- Interpersonal relationship difficulties
- Contact with the law

How to define someone's substance use

Patterns of substance use can be explained on a spectrum that ranges from no use of substances to the dependent use of one or more substances. A person can move along the spectrum in either direction and stop at any point. While it can sometimes be the case that a person progresses, for example from one substance to another and increases their level of use, there is no evidence to confirm that this happens in every situation. There appear to be six different categories of substance use. They can be explained as:

- Life-time abstainer: a person has never used any substances.
- Ex-user: a person has not had any substances during a specified time period but did so previously.
- Experimental use: this type of use happens when a person tries out different drugs or alcohol for the first time to find out what they are like. Experimenting with drugs is common in adolescence. They may only try a drug once off, or may continue to use for a short period of time. They may decide to stop using some drugs, but continue to try using others.

- Recreational use: this type of use occurs when a person makes a deliberate decision to use a drug and/or alcohol in order to enhance particular leisure activities. In this type of use, the person makes a conscious choice as to where, when and how much they will use. They are unlikely to suffer psychologically or physically if they have to go without the drug and/or alcohol, although they may experience consequences associated with overdose or intoxication.
- Regular use: this occurs when a person starts to use the substances more often outside of recreational activities. They have made the decision to use the substances in order to help cope with other situations in their life, for example emotional distress, relationship problems, school or work pressures. Using the substance provides the person with some relief or the opportunity to avoid or escape from issues they don't want to deal with. However, they may be able to continue with other activities in their life, for example work or study. A person would experience psychological distress if they were to stop using the substance, but not necessarily strong physical withdrawal symptoms, although they may experience consequences associated with overdose or intoxication.
- Dependent use: this type of use is evident when a person has little or no control over their substance use. In this situation they feel compelled to use substances in order to feel normal or to cope. Substance dependent people can experience financial, legal, housing, health, school, work, social, emotional, relationship and psychological problems. The person is likely to experience substantial physical withdrawal symptoms if they stop using the substance, although this will depend on the type of substance they have been using. Psychological dependence can be longer lasting and more difficult to overcome than physical dependence.

People with psychotic disorders often use substances to deal with negative symptoms, sleeping problems, dysphoria and other adverse effects of antipsychotic medication. Recreational and social reasons for substance use are also important. Substance use is a social event and non-psychotic users may be more accepting of odd behaviours and limited conversation than non-users. Also, people with psychotic disorders often lack skills in social problem solving and drug refusal, thereby making them more vulnerable to this social influence (Kavanagh et al., 2002).

Harm minimisation strategies

Most drug and alcohol programmes have abstinence as their treatment goal. However, for some people who have a psychotic disorder as well as a substance use problem, abstinence may be too difficult a goal to work towards. They may perceive few positive aspects to their lives and may have little motivation to become abstinent (Treatment Project Protocol, 1997). Harm minimisation is a simple statement of policy that emphasises the reduction of drug related harm as the ultimate objective of interventions, rather than the traditional goals of eliminating or reducing use. Harm minimisation does not dictate a particular legal, preventative or treatment approach. The policy of harm minimisation does not require practitioners to accept or condone unsanctioned use of drugs. Rather, this approach recognises that within our society, there are people who choose to use alcohol and drugs, and that there is a continuum of levels of drug use and related harms. It recognises that people continue to use drugs no matter what the risks are. Harm minimisation recognises that different harm reduction approaches are appropriate for different drugs, people and situations (Ministry of Health, 2003).

Abstinence and consumption reduction approaches are important strategies to reduce harm. These approaches are only part of a comprehensive range of strategies, including health promotion, early intervention, access to health services, support for others affected by drug use, rehabilitation, law enforcement initiatives, community development activities, legislative reform and public policy, drug courts and customs imports/exports (Department of Health, 2001; Ministry of Health, 2001). People respond more positively to strategies that recognise and respect their ability to make their own decisions regarding their drug use. Harm minimisation avoids judging a person for using drugs. It provides practical information and strategies to help individuals and communities reduce health and social problems related to drug use (Ministry of Health, 2001).

Harm minimisation strategies are simple and should be used when working with people who use drugs. The practitioner should consider the following harm minimisation strategies:

- Encourage moderation (not necessarily expecting abstinence)
- Recreational rather than constant drug use
- Provide information about not sharing needles, syringe disposal and needle exchange programmes
- Ensure adequate nutrition, housing and clothing
- Encourage regular health checks, such as blood testing, diet, etc.

How to tell if someone wants to change

People who present with alcohol and drug issues range from those who identify no problems with their drug use at all and as such do not want to change, through to those able to link substance use with serious negative effects, who are highly motivated to change. When working with clients who misuse substances, it is important to assess how they view their drug use as well as their motivation to change. Readiness to change may be measured by a questionnaire developed by Rollnick et al. (1992).

Process of change

A model that was developed by Prochaska & DiClemente (1982) is useful in describing a person's motivation to change and in identifying a client's readiness for change. This model describes a series of stages through which people move when making behavioural change. During each stage of the process, a person thinks and feels differently about the behaviour in question and will benefit from different interventions according to the stage they are in. The Prochaska & DiClemente 'process of change' model can be applied to any behaviour, any age group and is relevant to all patterns of drug use. The stages include the following:

Stage 1. Precontemplation. This is the stage at which there is no intention to change behaviour in the foreseeable future (Prochaska et al., 1992). Many individuals in this stage are unaware of their problems. Often, the people around the individual can see the harm the person is doing to him or herself. However, the individual ignores or does not acknowledge these harms. At this stage, it is important that practitioners build rapport and offer to be available, and to provide information.

Stage 2. Contemplation. This is the stage in which people are aware that a problem exists and are seriously thinking about overcoming it, but have not yet made a commitment to action (Prochaska et al., 1992). It is during this stage that the person begins to realise or experience some of the costs or negative consequences of their ongoing drug use. The consequences are usually reflected in the areas of personal, social, health, worsening psychiatric symptoms, relationship difficulties and contact with the criminal justice system (Department of Health, 2001). The consequences are recognised by the user as problematic; however they are not severe enough for the contemplator to begin to change, or they lack the motivation to initiate change. Contemplators appear to struggle with their positive evaluations of the addictive behaviour and the amount of effort, energy and loss it will cost to overcome the problem (Prochaska et al., 1992). Again, it is important for practitioners to build rapport, offer to be available and give information. In addition, they need to engage in discussions using motivational interviewing, enlist other support networks and plan for high risk situations.

Stage 3. Preparation. During the preparation stage, the person acknowledges that the consequences outweigh the benefits of his or her continued drug use, and wants to do something about the drug use. They are planning to take action soon and often tell others of the intention to change (Prochaska et al., 1992). The person in the preparation stage begins to consider how they will achieve change, the degree of change they want, for example abstinence or reduction, and when they will commence with implementing these changes. During this stage, as with the previous stage, the practitioner engages in discussion using motivational interviewing, enlists other support networks and plans for high risk situations.

Stage 4. Action. In action, a person is beginning to modify their behaviour, experiences, or environments in order to overcome their problems (Prochaska et al., 1992). A person in the action stage is making visible changes and investing a lot of effort in doing so. What is important at this stage is that the person has made the decision to change and is acting on this. The person is consciously trying to avoid using drugs and is utilising strategies for preventing or minimising drug use, for example avoiding certain people, places or situations, leaving drug buddies behind, and focusing on saying NO to offers of drugs. This can be a difficult stage for a person as they may be experiencing withdrawal symptoms, feel strong cravings and experiencing varying degrees of psychological distress. Often during the action stage, a person will seek help from professionals or self-help groups. During this stage, it is important that the practitioner offers support, encouragement and open communication. It is necessary they provide help with trouble shooting for challenging situations.

Stage 5. Maintenance. During the maintenance stage, the changes in behaviour, which began during the action stage, are continued and consolidated (Prochaska et al., 1992). Changes become more of a settled pattern. A person in maintenance no longer feels a great desire to succumb to cravings, and generally feels strong in their ability to abstain from or control their use, and has made the lifestyle changes to support this. The practitioner assists the person to find a balanced lifestyle and affirm positive changes. The practitioner also monitors the potential for relapse and educates the person about relapse.

In addition to readiness to change, client self-efficacy is an important consideration. Clients may want to change, but feel unable to do anything about their pattern of dependence. Maintaining a strong and positive therapeutic alliance can assist low self-efficacy clients to make long-term gains with their substance use problems (Ilgen et al., 2006).

Relapse

Relapse and recycling through the stages occur quite frequently as individuals attempt to modify or cease addictive behaviours (Prochaska et al., 1992). According to the model, relapse can occur at any of the above-mentioned stages. Unfortunately, most people rarely make permanent change during their first attempt. Change takes time, and for a variety of reasons, many people go back to past levels of drug use. In line with this, a person can go back to any of the previous stages, i.e. precontemplation, contemplation, preparation or action after a relapse. Relapse is an important stage in the process of change and it is important that the person embarking on change not consider relapse as failure, but rather as a valuable learning experience, designed to teach the person to do things differently next time. At this stage, the practitioner discusses the benefits of change and brainstorms alternatives. It is necessary to reinforce that relapse is only a slip-up and not failure.

Motivational interviewing

Working from a background in motivational interviewing, Rollnick et al. (1999) proposed a method to use to help clients make decisions about health behaviour change. The initial tasks are to establish rapport and to set an agenda. Having agreed to discuss a particular change in behaviour, the goal is to understand exactly how the client feels about this by assessing importance (personal values and expectations of the importance of change) and confidence (self-efficacy). Other tasks that run throughout the intervention process include exchanging information and reducing resistance.

Text box 12.2   Recovery focus

- Comorbidity poses a considerable challenge to practitioners
- Comorbidity may result in a range of negative outcomes for clients
- People with comorbidity require a holistic approach to treatment
- Focus on life goals and aspirations is a key component of motivational enhancement
- Maintaining a strong therapeutic alliance is important, especially when clients lack self-efficacy
- Overcoming or controlling substance dependence is a major achievement and promotes general self-efficacy
- Peer and family supports may be as important as professional interventions

Motivational interviewing is a non-directive, client-centred counselling style to enhance behaviour change by helping people explore and resolve ambivalence about change (Rollnick & Miller, 1995). It is based on exploring the competing forces between a person's ongoing drug use and desire to change behaviour. The differences between what they are doing and what they want to do highlights a discrepancy in their belief and value system, resulting in discomfort that they are inherently seeking to resolve. The greater the discrepancy between the forces, the greater the motivation for change.

The aim of motivational interviewing is to get the person to tell the practitioner why they should change, rather than vice versa. It has been found that practitioners' consulting behaviour can affect the degree of resistance that emerges, and subsequent outcome. A client's motivation to change can be enhanced using a negotiation method in which the client, not the practitioner, articulates the benefits and costs involved (Rollnick et al., 1993). The motivational interviewing style is a collaborative method using distinct principles and techniques. The basic premises behind motivational interviewing are that:

- A client is someone who can acknowledge that drug use causes problems but who knows it provides some very real benefits
- The session focus is to elicit any concerns the client may have about drug use and any other problems
- The session aim is to have the client consider the pros and cons of changing current drug use
- The session style is practitioner directed yet client centred
- The practitioner's role is to facilitate a client generated inventory or problem list and help the client make decisions about future drug use.

The brief steps of motivational interviewing include the following:

1. Good things: 'What are the good things about drinking or drug use? What do you like about the effects? What would you miss if you weren't using?'

- Get specific examples
- Summarise when the client has finished

2. *Less good things*: 'What about the reverse side – what are some of the less good things? What are the things you wouldn't miss? How do you feel about these less good things? Do you have any concerns about your drug use?'

- Get specific examples
- Check if the person believes these negatives apply to them personally
- Use counselling skills to get the client in touch with their feelings about these consequences
- Summarise both the good and less good things

3. *How would you like things to be?* 'How would you like things to be in the future? If things work out for you, what would you be doing? If a miracle happened tonight, how would things be different?'

- Keep the client positive
- Be ready to prompt him or her and have some positive attributes ready

4. *How are things now?* 'How would you describe things at the moment? How does drug use fit in with how things are?'

- People often come up with the negatives faster than they come up with the positives

5. *Highlight the discrepancy*: 'How do these two images fit together? How does your drug use fit with how things are going now? How would things be in a year if you stayed the same?'

- Highlight the discrepancy between how things are versus how they like things to be

6. *Summary*: 'Let's see; so far you have said (summarise all). Where does that leave us now? What would you like to see happen with your drug use? What will be your next step?'

- Plan the next step
- Make arrangements for follow-up

In summary, while using client-centred techniques to build trust and reduce resistance, the practitioner focuses on increasing readiness for change. The principles of motivational interviewing include understanding the client's view accurately, avoiding or de-escalating resistance and increasing the client's self-efficacy and their perceived discrepancy between their actual and ideal behaviour. The techniques include listening reflectively and eliciting motivational statements from clients, examining both sides of clients' ambivalence and reducing resistance by monitoring clients' readiness and not forcing change prematurely (Rollnick & Miller, 1995).

Text box 12.3 Sam gets a dose of motivational interviewing

Sam has commenced transitional employment with a car wrecker (see Chapter 11). Sam has been mostly enjoying the work and finding the 12 hours per week manageable. However, his mother is concerned because she has noticed an unusual smell (which she thinks might be marijuana) around his room. Whenever she notices the smell, Sam seems to be more distant and uncommunicative than usual. She asks Cassie, his rehabilitation practitioner, if she can speak with Sam.

When Cassie next meets up with Sam, she detects a faint but distinctive smell and asks him if he has been smoking. 'What if I have been?' says Sam. 'I am earning my own money and it helps me relax. It gets pretty stressful being around people for hours.' 'OK,' Cassie responds, I can understand that it relaxes you and lots of people your age use marijuana. Maybe it is not a big issue, but I am wondering if you have noticed it causes any problems.'

'One time I had a smoke before work,' Sam replies, and I got really confused and disorganised and paranoid. They had to call the Clubhouse. That really freaked me – I don't want to lose this job'. 'That's not so unusual,' responds Cassie. 'Many people get disorganised when affected by marijuana and it is not a good idea to combine it with work or other demanding activities. People like you who have been affected by mental illness are especially vulnerable and it can even trigger a psychotic episode.'

'I really don't want to go back to hospital,' says Sam. 'I feel I am just getting over all that – I couldn't cope with being locked up and sedated and all that kind of thing.' 'Maybe we could look at other ways of coping with getting stressed out when you are with people at work,' suggests Cassie.

In a systematic review of 29 randomised trials of motivational interviewing interventions, there was substantial evidence that motivational interviewing is an effective substance abuse intervention method when used by practitioners who are non-specialists in substance abuse treatment, particularly when enhancing entry to and engagement in more intensive substance misuse treatment programmes (Dunn et al., 2001). In a randomised control trial, Barrowclough et al. (2001) demonstrated the effectiveness of a programme of routine care integrated with motivational interviewing, cognitive behaviour therapy and family interventions for people with comorbid schizophrenia and alcohol or drug use.

Assessment and treatment

Dual diagnosis assessment

A correct objective diagnosis is fundamental for the planning of individual care, and for the choice of appropriate treatment. A detailed functional analysis of substance use needs to be undertaken with the client. This includes gathering information about the substance used, how much is being used, at risk behaviour, and the situations, consequences and skill deficits that are currently maintaining the substance use. Information is also sought about attempts to abstain, control use or cut back, and past treatment. Attention must be paid to the role of alcohol and

Table 12.1 Substance use measures

Title	Description	Use
Alcohol Use Disorders Identification Test screening instrument (AUDIT)	Ten items measuring three domains: alcohol consumption, alcohol dependence, alcohol-related consequences Takes 2–5 min to complete	Screening instrument Suitable for use with a range of cultures Can be used with people with a minimum reading level
Drug Abuse Screening Test (DAST)	Twenty items addressing the use of drugs (excluding alcohol), physical and medical complications, and emotional and personal problems Takes less than 5 min to complete	Screening instrument to identify people with drug abuse problems in the past 12 months Predominantly used in North America; applicability to other cultural groups unknown
Short Alcohol Dependence Data questionnaire (SADD)	Fifteen items measuring severity of dependence on alcohol; reflects behavioural and subjective change associated with problem drinking Takes less than 5 min to complete	Instrument to measure severity of alcohol dependence Suitable for use with a range of ethnic groups and cultures Can be used in interview format with illiterate populations

drugs in the onset of mental illness and in subsequent relapses. The use and effects of all psychoactive substances, including nicotine and caffeine, is assessed.

Collateral information concerning psychotic symptoms and substance used should be obtained from relatives and health professionals involved in the client's management. Routine drug tests may be used to increase the validity of the self-report, especially when it appears that there are discrepancies between self-report and other evidence. Hulse (2001) suggested that to be effective in the general hospital psychiatric setting, alcohol screening needs to be incorporated into the routine ward assessment procedures. Measures that may be employed are outlined in Table 12.1.

Treatment approaches

Psychological approaches continue to represent the mainstay of treatment for most types of substance abuse problems (Ziedonis et al., 2001). A review of empirical studies found the most effective treatments included approaches based on behavioural and cognitive–behavioural theoretical models (Grabowski & Schmitz, 1998). However, major trials of treatment for alcohol dependence (Project Match) and cocaine abuse (NIDA Collaborative Cocaine Treatment Study) failed to detect major differences between a variety of interventions that included 12-step programmes and supportive expressive therapy as well as motivational enhancement and cognitive behaviour therapy (Siqueland & Crits-Cristoph, 1999). Capacity to provide flexible and responsive services with a range of options may be more important than discrete treatment packages.

Elements that have emerged in the literature as being important include avoidance of drug/alcohol stimuli in the environment, use of contingency management procedures, concurrent integrated treatment of other psychiatric conditions, providing therapeutic settings that are matched to the clients' normal daily functioning, and identifying optimal medication–behavioural strategies (Grabowski & Schmitz, 1998).

Successful treatment of substance use disorders may involve the use of multiple specific interventions, which may vary over time for any individual client. Specific psychotherapy approaches have been developed for treating substance misuse and have been demonstrated to improve treatment outcomes (Ziedonis et al., 2001). In 12-step facilitation, the practitioner assists the client understand addiction as a chronic disease and educates him or her about the basic philosophy and Twelve Steps, originally of Alcoholics Anonymous, including the important role of spirituality in recovery. In motivational enhancement therapy, the practitioner aims to help the client develop a commitment and motivation to change. In relapse prevention, the practitioner aims to help the client to better understand substance use triggers and to improve coping skills and self-efficacy (Ziedonis et al., 2001).

Motivation is an important prognostic and treatment matching factor in substance misuse treatment (Ziedonis & Trudeau, 1997). Awareness of a client's motivational level can help clinicians develop more realistic treatment goals and appropriate treatment techniques. The motivation based treatment model matches treatment to clients based on their motivational levels (Ziedonis & Trudeau, 1997).

Skills training interventions have been developed based on social learning theory models. These interventions focus on coping skills designed to cope with precipitants for relapse. In cue exposure treatment, clients are taught to identify urge triggers, are exposed to the identified stimuli, and practice coping with urges during exposure (Rohsenow et al., 2001). In communication skills training, topics covered include drink refusal skills, giving praise, giving effective criticism, receiving criticism, listening skills, conversation skills, developing supports and conflict resolution (Rohsenow et al., 2001).

Text box 12.4   Evidence base for substance misuse interventions

- Integrated treatment leads to high rates of engagement
- Motivational interviewing is an effective substance misuse intervention
- Motivation is an important prognostic and treatment matching factor in substance misuse treatment
- A wide range of treatments, including 12-step programmes, cognitive behavioural interventions, supportive expressive therapies and skills training interventions may usefully contribute to outcomes
- Substance misuse is difficult to treat and no intervention is reliably effective

A number of cognitive–behavioural interventions to treat substance misuse have been developed and tested. These interventions have differed in their length, modality, content and treatment setting (Morgenstern & Longabaugh, 2000). However, despite differences, cognitive–behavioural treatments share two core elements. These include adopting the principles of social–cognitive theory and employing some form of coping skills training to address cognitive and behavioural coping deficits (Morgenstern & Longabaugh, 2000). For example, Kavanagh et al. (1998) developed an intervention known as Substance Treatment Options in Psychosis (STOP), which integrates pharmacological and psychological treatments for psychotic symptoms with cognitive–behavioural approaches to substance misuse. STOP is tailored to clients' problems and abilities. Training in relevant skills is augmented by bibliotherapy, social support and environmental change (Kavanagh et al., 1998).

Finally a word of caution is warranted. Substance use treatment outcomes are typically modest and the amount of outcome attributable to treatment may be quite small. Cutler & Fishbain (2005) found that, in the Project Match study, a zero treatment drop-out group had outcomes nearly as good as those in any of the three treatment conditions. Practitioners can encourage and support client change, and the techniques and approaches discussed in this chapter will assist with this. However, it is likely that client factors will have be the major determinants of outcome.

The therapist should consider the following when designing an intervention programme:

- Identifying what is known about the person's situation
- What is needed to be known about the person and why the information is needed
- Based on the difficulties being experienced, the need to address the issues in the situation
- Determining the issues being identified as initially being of the highest priority
- Deciding on some strategies that could be implemented for each of the issues
- Linking strategies to service principles and evidence
- Deciding if the strategies were effective
- Deciding on the means of evaluation

Conclusion

Comorbidity of mental disorders with substance use is common. Individuals with comorbid conditions often have poor treatment outcomes, increased service utilisation and contribute to family and society burden. No single method of treating people with comorbid disorders is universally accepted. Current trends suggest that an integrated approach to comorbid conditions based on motivational interviewing and the stages of change indicate that there is the potential to engage clients and assist them reduce substance abuse and attain remission. Early recognition of problem drinking, early intervention, psychological interventions, treatment of the harmful effects of alcohol (including withdrawal and other medical consequences), teaching new coping skills in situations associated with a risk of drinking and relapse, family education and rehabilitation are the main strategies proven to be effective for the treatment of alcohol abuse problems. For people who abuse psychoactive substances, strategies include early diagnosis, identification and management of risk of infections as well as other medical and social problems, stabilisation and maintenance with pharmacotherapy (for opioid dependence), counselling, access to services and opportunities to achieve social integration.

References

Andrews, G., Issakidis, C., & Slade, T. (2001). The clinical significance of mental disorders. In: M. Teesson & L. Burns (Eds.), *National comorbidity project* (pp.19–30). Canberra: Mental Health and Special Programs Branch.

Barrowclough, C., Haddock, G., Tarrier, N., Lewis, S., Moring, J., O'Brien, R., Schofield, N., & McGovern, J. (2001). Randomized controlled trial of motivational interviewing, cognitive behaviour therapy, and family intervention for patients with comorbid schizophrenia and substance use disorders. *American Journal of Psychiatry, 158,* 1706–1713.

Cutler, R.B., & Fishbain, D.A. (2005). Are alcoholism treatments effective? The Project MATCH data. *BMC Public Health, 14* (5), 75.

Department of Health (2001). *Mental health policy implementation guide – dual diagnosis good practice guide.* London: Department of Health.

Drake, R., Mercer-McFadden, C., Mueser, K., McHugo, G., & Bond, G. (1998). Review of integrated mental health and substance abuse treatment for patients with dual disorders. *Schizophrenia Bulletin, 24,* 589–608.

Dunn, C., Deroo, L., & Rivara, F. (2001). The use of brief interventions adapted from motivational interviewing across behavioral domains: A systematic review. *Addiction, 96,* 1725–1742.

Grabowski, J., & Schmitz, J. (1998). Psychologic treatment of substance abuse. *Current Opinion in Psychiatry, 11,* 289–293.

Hall, W., Lynskey, M., & Teesson, M. (2001). What is comorbidity and why does it matter? In: M. Teesson & L. Burns (Eds.), *National comorbidity project* (pp. 11–18). Canberra: Mental Health and Special Programs Branch.

Hulse, G. (2001). Impediments to screening for hazardous alcohol use and dependence in general hospital psychiatric inpatients. *Australian and New Zealand Journal of Psychiatry, 35,* 606–612.

Ilgen, M., Tiet, Q., Finney, J., & Moos, R.H. (2006). Self-efficacy, therapeutic alliance, and alcohol-use disorder treatment outcomes. *Journal of Studies on Alcohol, 67,* 465–472.

Jerrell, J., & Ridgely, M. (1999). Impact of program implementation on outcomes of clients in dual diagnosis programs. *Psychiatric Services, 50,* 109–112.

Kavanagh, D. (2001). Treatment of comorbidity. In: M. Teesson & L. Burns (Eds.), *National comorbidity project* (pp. 60–70). Canberra: Mental Health and Special Programs Branch.

Kavanagh, D., Greenaway, L., Jenner, L., Saunders, J., White, A., Sorban, J., & Hamilton, G. (2000). Contrasting views and experiences of health professionals on the management of comorbid substance misuse and mental disorders. *Australian and New Zealand Journal of Psychiatry, 34,* 279–289.

Kavanagh, D., McGrath, J., Saunders, J., Dore, G., & Clark, D. (2002). Substance misuse in patients with schizophrenia. *Current Therapeutics, October,* 12–19.

Kavanagh, D., Young, R., Boyce, L., Clair, A., Sitharthan, T., Clark, D., & Thompson, K. (1998). Substance treatment options in psychosis (STOP): A new intervention for dual diagnosis. *Journal of Mental Health, 7,* 135–143.

Mercer-McFadden, C., Drake, R., Brown, N., & Fox, R. (1997). The community support program demonstrations of services for young adults with severe mental illness and substance use disorders, 1987–1991. *Psychiatric Rehabilitation Journal, 20,* 13–24.

Ministry of Health (2001). *National alcohol strategy.* Wellington: Ministry of Health.

Ministry of Health (2003). *Drug policy update,* 2 (2). Wellington: Ministry of Health.

Morgenstern, J., & Longabaugh, R. (2000). Cognitive–behavioral treatment for alcohol dependence: A review of evidence for its hypothesized mechanisms of action. *Addiction, 95,* 1475–1490.

Prochaska, J., & DiClemente, C. (1982). Stages and processes of self-change of smoking: Toward an integrative model of change. *Journal of Consulting and Clinical Psychology, 51,* 390–395.

Prochaska, J., DiClemente, C., & Norcross, J. (1992). In search of how people change – applications to addictive behaviours. *American Psychologist, 47,* 1102–1114.

Rohsenow, D., Monti, P., Rubonis, A., Gulliver, S., Colby, S., Binkoff, J., & Abrams, D.B. (2001). Cue exposure with coping skills training and communication skills training for alcohol dependence: 6- and 12-month outcomes. *Addiction, 96,* 1161–1174.

Rollnick, S., Heather, N., Gold, R., & Hall, W. (1992). Development of a short 'readiness to change' questionnaire for use in brief, opportunistic interventions among excessive drinkers. *British Journal of Addictions, 87,* 743–754.

Rollnick, S., Kinnersley, P., & Stott, N. (1993). Methods of helping patients with behaviour change. *British Medical Journal, 307,* 188–190.

Rollnick, S., Mason, P., & Butler, C. (1999). *Health behavior change. A guide for practitioners.* Edinburgh: Churchill Livingstone.

Rollnick, S., & Miller, W. (1995). What is motivational interviewing? *Behavioural and Cognitive Psychotherapy, 23,* 325–334.

Siqueland, L., & Crits-Christoph, P. (1999). Current developments in psychosocial treatments of alcohol and substance abuse. *Current Psychiatry Reports, 1,* 179–184.

Treatment Protocol Project (1997). *Management of mental disorders,* Part 1 & 2. Sydney: World Health Organization Collaborating Centre for Mental Health and Substance Abuse.

Welch, M., & Mooney, J. (2001). Managing services that manage people with coexisting mental health and substance use disorder. *Australasian Psychiatry, 9,* 345–349.

Williams, K. (1999). Attitudes of mental health professionals to co-morbidity between mental health problems and substance misuse. *Journal of Mental Health, 8,* 605–613.

World Health Organization (1993). *The ICD-10 classification of mental and behavioural disorders – diagnostic criteria for research.* Geneva: World Health Organization.

World Health Organization (2001). *The world health report 2001. Mental health: New understanding, new hope.* Geneva: World Health Organization.

Ziedonis, D., Krejci, J., & Atdjian, S. (2001). Integrated treatment of alcohol, tobacco, and other drug addictions. In: J. Kay (Ed.), *Integrated treatment of psychiatric disorders* (pp. 79–111). Washington: American Psychiatric Publishing.

Ziedonis, D., & Trudeau, K. (1997). Motivation to quit using substances among individuals with schizophrenia: Implications for a motivation-based treatment model. *Schizophrenia Bulletin, 23,* 229–238.

Useful resources

A copy of the Alcohol Use Disorders Identification Test (AUDIT) and manual is available free of charge from http://www.who.int/substance_abuse/docs/audit2.pdf

Dawe, S., Loxton, N., Hides, L., Kavanagh, D., & Mattick, P. (2000). *Review of diagnostic screening instruments for alcohol and other drug use and other psychiatric disorders* (2nd ed.). Canberra: Publications Production Unit, Commonwealth Department of Health and Ageing. (ISBN 0 642 821240).

Department of Health (2001). *Mental health policy implementation guide – Dual diagnosis good practice guide.* London: Department of Health Publications. Available on the Department's website at www.doh.gov.uk/mentalhealth

Key assessment instrument references

AUDIT

Saunders, J., Aasland, O., Babor, T, de le Fuente, J., & Grant, M. (1993). Development of the Alcohol Use Disorders Identification Test (AUDIT). WHO collaborative project on early detection of persons with harmful alcohol consumption – II. *Addiction, 88,* 791–804.

DAST

Gavin, D., Ross, H., & Skinner, H. (1989). Diagnostic validity of the Drug Abuse Screening Test in the assessment of DSM-III drug disorders. *British Journal of Addiction, 84,* 301–307.

RFTQ

Tate, J. & Schmidt, J. (1993). A proposed revision of the Fagerstrom Tolerance Questionnaire. *Addictive Behaviors, 18,* 135–143.

SADD

Raistrick, D., Dunbar, G., & Davidson, R. (1983). Development of a questionnaire to measure alcohol dependence. *British Journal of Addiction, 78,* 89–95.

Chapter 13

EARLY INTERVENTION, RELAPSE PREVENTION AND PROMOTION OF HEALTHY LIFESTYLES

Chris Lloyd and Robert King

Overview of chapter

This chapter provides an overview of early psychosis as a rationale for early intervention. A distinction is drawn between early intervention that aims to provide intensive services once a psychotic disorder is detected and early intervention that aims to identify 'at risk' individuals and provide interventions prior to the onset of a psychotic disorder, or during the 'prodrome'. A model of early psychosis and the stages of recovery are described. Risk and protective factors are examined. A number of key principles for early intervention are outlined and strategies for early intervention are provided, including family involvement, psychotherapy, psychoeducation and group work. The controversy regarding intervention in 'prodromal psychosis' is discussed. The evidence base for the effectiveness of early intervention in psychosis is reviewed.

Introduction

Internationally there has been growing interest in promotion, prevention and early intervention in mental health. For example, Australia's third National Mental Health Plans (Australian Health Ministers, 2003) have emphasised this approach and New Zealand's 'Like Minds, Like Us' campaign (http://www.likeminds.govt.nz/) was a successful major national initiative using mass media to destigmatise mental illness.

Mental disorders are a major cause of chronic disability. There is a public health burden associated with mental disorders. This includes the person directly involved, families and communities. Mental disorders affect the psychosocial functioning of individuals, thereby diminishing their capacity in their social role and productivity in society (Commonwealth Department of Health and Aged Care, 2000). For young adults, there is evidence of increasing psychological morbidity, illustrated by increasing rates of substance abuse, risk of developing depression and incidence of suicide (Davis et al., 2000).

Promotion, prevention and early intervention in mental health form a vast area. In this chapter, our focus is in on that aspect of most direct relevance to psychosocial rehabilitation, which is early intervention and relapse prevention in psychosis. We examine the principles that underpin early intervention and relapse prevention in psychosis and examine the limited empirical evaluation of early intervention services. We also consider some of the issues associated with early intervention as a preventative strategy, rather than a response to an episode of psychosis. You will note a number of references to Australian policy and practice. This reflects both national policy and the presence in Melbourne of a state-wide early psychosis service that has also served as a centre of excellence and disseminator of training and research. However, early psychosis demonstration projects have also been established in Canada (Malla et al., 2003) and the United Kingdom (Kuipers et al., 2004).

Early intervention and prevention in psychotic disorders is increasingly seen as having the potential to produce better outcomes for people who have developed these disorders. According to the National Early Psychosis Project Clinical Guidelines Working Party (1998), there are four principles that underpin the early intervention paradigm in psychosis. These include the following:

- Better outcomes have been associated with the reduction in duration of untreated psychosis
- During the early phase of illness, intensive and sophisticated interventions may assist in the recovery process and may also minimise iatrogenic damage
- Targeting early treatment resistance with recently developed and psychosocial interventions may result in lower rates of relapse, treatment resistance and disability
- Maintaining remission and preventing or limiting relapse contribute to improving outcomes

Rationale

Early intervention is defined as interventions targeting individuals displaying the early signs and symptoms of mental disorder (Commonwealth Department of Health and Aged Care, 2000). Early intervention can have a narrower or broader target group. The narrower target group is people who have experienced a clear episode of psychosis. The broader target group is people who show prodromal signs but have not clearly experienced an episode of psychosis. There is a reasonable consensus around the value of providing targeted services to the narrower group, but some controversy about the merits of attempting to intervene with the broader group (McGlashan et al., 2001). The focus of this chapter is on services targeting the narrower group. Later in the chapter we look at some of the issues associated with targeting the broader group.

Early intervention aims to reduce the dependency and disabilities associated with mental disorders and with co-existing mental health problems, substance use problems or secondary morbidity (Gardiner-Caldwell Communications Limited, 1997). Early and reliable recognition and the provision of effective treatments and rehabilitation can assist individuals in maintaining optimal functioning, and reducing the likelihood of family, social and work disruption. The aim is to provide the most effective treatment and interventions in order to achieve recovery (Commonwealth Department of Health and Aged Care, 2000).

Text box 13.1 Recovery focus in early psychosis

- Psychosis typically presents during adolescence and young adulthood, an important period for emotional and social development. Disruption of educational, vocational and social pursuits as a result of a psychotic episode can cause disability and social exclusion
- The early period following a psychotic episode presents the greatest opportunity to introduce measures that prevent the development of psychosocial disability
- After an episode of psychotic illness, a person needs a sense of purpose and structure, physical activity, opportunities to maintain social skills, opportunities to develop new skills, peer group contact, confidence building and a positive attitude about the future

It is necessary that risk factors are identified and strategies determined to support recovery and wellbeing. Recently, there has been growing awareness that it is not inevitable that a first episode will lead to further illness and disability, and that it is possible for people with a psychotic disorder to live full and meaningful lives. Relapse prevention is a critical issue for young people with psychotic disorders, their families, mental health services and the wider community. According to Melle et al. (2005), early intervention has the potential to prevent the deterioration in quality of life characteristic of chronic schizophrenia. Early intervention so as to reduce the likelihood and impact of future episodes of illness, and maximise clients' wellness and wellbeing is emerging as a 'best practice' component of contemporary mental health services (Bertolote & McGorry, 2005). However, for reasons that will become clearer later in the chapter, it is not entirely clear at present what kind of early intervention is warranted, and there are potential disadvantages as well as benefits.

Mental disorders typically present during adolescence and young adulthood, and are at their most common among young adults aged 18–25 years. This is an important period when the young person is developing emotionally and socially, and actively pursuing educational and vocational aspirations. It is a period of rapid change and can be highly stressful for young people as they go through periods of transition from one life stage to another (Raphael, 2000).

Many young people make significant improvements in mental state and functioning once appropriate antipsychotic medication has been initiated. The key point, however, is that they have been sidetracked from their developmental pathway. Disruptions to a person's health can affect educational attainment, vocational maturation, occupational capacity and integration into adult society. In addition, they have to struggle with the fact that they have developed a psychiatric disorder and may question their ability or capacity to return to their previous social, educational and vocational activities (Albiston et al., 1998; Lloyd et al., 1998; Whitehorn et al., 1998).

Social isolation and inactivity are common and persistent problems for people with serious mental illness, and are frequently observed as the most pressing problem experienced by the individual recovering from a first episode (Melle et al., 2005). Psychotic illness can erode a person's self esteem and their social networks. Social skills are lost because of the period of illness and also because the person now has doubts and fears about his or her own ability to interact socially. After a psychotic episode a person may experience:

- Lack of confidence
- A sense of disorganisation
- Lack of motivation
- Loss of self esteem
- Inactivity
- A loss of skills
- Separation from former social groups
- Increased anxiety in social situations

It is crucial that treatment after an acute psychotic episode encompasses interventions that allow the person to maintain a sense of self and avoid the loss of social, educational and vocational skills that could cause disability and disadvantage. Psychosocial rehabilitation has an important role to play in providing a supportive environment, identifying client goals and hope for the future, and emphasising social, academic and/or vocational reintegration into community life (Albiston et al., 1998; Lloyd et al., 1998; Whitehorn et al., 1998).

Defining early psychosis

In the broader context, psychosis now refers to a group of disorders in which there is misinterpretation and misapprehension of the nature of reality reflected in certain symptoms, particularly disturbances in perception (hallucinations), disturbances of belief and interpretation of the environment (delusions), and disorganised speech patterns (thought disorder). An important feature to note is that peoples' competence as a person is called into question, at least temporarily, and consequently their status as a person may appear as undermined. First episode is defined as the first onset of a disorder in the lifetime of an individual. Recovery refers to a temporal period of approximately 18 months following the onset of early psychosis and initial acute treatment phase. However, the critical period for recovery often encompasses the first 5 years post onset.

Stress–vulnerability

The aetiology of psychosis is generally accepted as involving the impact of stress upon a biological predisposition. This is known as stress–vulnerability interaction. The stress–vulnerability model emphasises a set of perceived vulnerabilities, which are genetic, neuronal, life stress and physical. Vulnerability is central to the explanation of psychotic symptoms, where stress is applied to biological vulnerabilities/determinants, which in turn manifest as psychiatric disorder. The greater the individual's level of vulnerability, the less stress is required to trigger the psychosis. Risk factors include being an adolescent, or young adulthood. Distal risk factors include family history, vulnerable personality, poor premorbid adjustment, history of head injury, low IQ, obstetric complications, perinatal trauma, developmental delay and season of birth. Proximal risk factors include life events, substance abuse, and subjective or functional change in the person (Gardiner-Caldwell Communications Ltd, 1997).

Phases of early psychosis

Four phases of early psychosis have been identified (National Early Psychosis Project Clinical Guidelines Working Party, 1998): prodromal, acute, early recovery and late recovery. Early psychosis usually emerges during adolescence or early adult life and tends to be characterised initially by impaired social functioning and non-specific symptoms. These non-specific symptoms are present in the prodrome, and the prodromal phase may have a mean duration of at least 2 years. The prodrome concept is essentially a retrospective concept. The vast majority of people who develop psychosis can be seen in retrospect to have experienced a period of pre-psychotic symptomatology and behaviour change. The prodrome may be considered the earliest form of psychotic disorder, or an at-risk mental state.

Symptoms and signs

Prodromal symptoms and signs may include suspiciousness, appetite changes, depression, loss of energy or motivation, irritability, perception that things around them have changed, mood swings, deterioration in work or study, sleep disturbance, and withdrawal and loss of interest in socialising (National Early Psychosis Project Clinical Guidelines Working Party, 1998).

The acute phase may be characterised by the presence of psychotic features such as delusions, hallucinations and formal thought disorder. The psychotic episode may also occur with comorbid symptoms of depression, obsessive compulsive disorder (OCD), post-traumatic stress disorder (PTSD), anxiety disorders or substance abuse. During the acute phase, the goals of treatment are to resolve the acute symptoms, prevent the development of secondary morbidity, and promote adaptation and psychosocial recovery.

During the early recovery phase, it is important that individual psychoeducation for the client is provided and that family interventions are included in the management plan. Chapter 8 provides a discussion of family psychoeducation. Clients who are in early recovery will benefit from a supportive environment in which they can receive a range of interventions including psychotherapy and psychosocial rehabilitation, which focuses on skill development and social reintegration.

During the late recovery phase, discharge and closure planning are integral components. It is important that linkages should be established for clients with a local

GP, private psychiatrist, and social and vocational services. The key point is that young people need assistance to reintegrate into the community and move beyond the mental health service with the necessary skills to get on with their lives. The focus of the overall management strategy for both the early and late recovery phases is assisting clients to understand and manage psychosis and to develop a range of skills that will enable them to achieve their valued goals and roles for the future.

Risk and protective factors

When working in the area of early intervention it is important to have an understanding of risk and protective factors in order to target interventions appropriately. Risk factors can exacerbate the burden of the existing disorder, while protective factors may reduce the exposure or effect of risk factors (Commonwealth Department of Health and Aged Care, 2000). Risk factors may include social isolation, stigma and discrimination, unemployment, homelessness, substance abuse, adverse life events, lack of support, and lack of access to services and service responsiveness (Office of the Deputy Prime Minister, 2004). Protective factors are increasingly being emphasised for prevention interventions. Protective factors may be individual (e.g. social competence, optimism or problem solving skills), family (e.g. supportive parents, stable family), life events and situations (e.g. economic security, good physical health), and community and cultural factors (e.g. sense of connectedness, networks within the community, participation in community groups, access to support services) (Commonwealth Department of Health and Aged Care, 2000).

Risk factors are those that contribute to a person's vulnerability to relapse. Protective factors are those that mitigate against relapse by enhancing wellbeing. By adopting a strengths based approach, protective factors in life domains (environmental, physical, social and emotional) can be utilised to build resiliency and prevent relapse. Rickwood (2004) stressed the importance of having a focus on protective factors to enhance effectiveness of interventions. She believed that this is essential in order to place relapse prevention within a recovery orientation.

Key principles of intervention

The treatment and support offered to clients and their families should reflect the best available evidence in the field, including the integration of biomedical, psychological and social strategies (Falloon et al., 1998). A comprehensive range of treatment and support services needs to be provided for clients with early psychosis, which should be appropriate to the person's age and stage of development and stage of recovery (Birchwood et al., 1997). All treatment and support services associated with early psychosis prevention and intervention should emphasise positive and realistic outcomes for clients, and maintain an attitude of hopefulness. Positive expectations have been strongly associated with recovery, even at later stages of illness (see Chapter 4).

The potential benefits of early intervention can be summarised as reducing:

- Risk of relapse and suicide
- Need for inpatient care and high cost of treatment
- Disruption to educational, vocational, and social development and personal burden experienced by the individual with the illness
- Disruption and burden to the family
- Burden to the community and economic costs

Strategies for intervention

Psychosocial rehabilitation programmes in early psychosis should focus on:

- The appropriate intervention for the phase of illness
- Directly targeted to the client's needs and goals for the future
- Minimising the trauma associated with the onset of psychosis
- Reducing the development of secondary morbidity
- Enhancing protective factors
- Skills building and consolidation of gains
- Promotion of recovery, and
- Reintegration into the community

The section following discusses a number of useful interventions and strategies in providing early psychosis programmes. These include involving the family, psychotherapy, psychoeducation and group programmes.

Family involvement

Greater emphasis has been placed on the role of the family in the therapeutic process following a client's first episode of psychosis. Families can play a vital role in supporting the client and facilitating engagement in treatment and participation in psychosocial rehabilitation programmes, thereby minimising long-term morbidity.

First episode psychosis can have a very distressing effect on family members as they struggle to come to terms with what has happened within the family. Some of the key components regarding the role of the family in early psychosis include:

- Family interventions need to be developed within a collaborative framework
- Family interventions should be tailored to the needs of each individual family
- The main aims of family intervention should be to empower the family to cope and adjust to the crisis of psychotic illness within the family, and develop problem-solving skills

It must be noted that it is important to clarify the client's wishes regarding the involvement of the family in their recovery. In some instances, clients do not want their families to be involved. The basis for this should always be carefully explored.

Strategies

Strategies for involving the family include:

- Initial contact should be made with the family/carers early in the intervention process of the initial assessment of the client so that crisis intervention, support and psychoeducation can be provided
- The initial interview with the family should explore and gain a clear understanding of the impact of early psychosis on the family, their current level of knowledge of psychosis and services and supports which are available, and identify their current needs
- The family should be part of the ongoing management. A collaborative relationship needs to be established whereby the family is consulted about options and management of the client
- Psychoeducation and support will need to be provided for the family on both an initial and ongoing basis through both individual work and family psychoeducation group programmes, and carer support networks

Lloyd (1999) highlighted the importance of involving both the family and client in a comprehensive programme where the client is involved in psychosocial rehabilitation and the family in psychoeducation. The focus of such a programme should be on the provision of information, support, networks and skill development. She believed that families are able to play a key role in supporting clients and in encouraging their participation in psychosocial rehabilitation.

Psychotherapy

Cognitive therapy interventions may be delivered either individually or in groups. Individual cognitive therapy focuses directly on the positive symptoms (hallucinations or delusional beliefs), the distress it causes and the evidence for that belief, and encourages clients to consider alternative constructions and meanings in a collaborative manner (Drury et al., 1996a). Group cognitive therapy may be conducted in small groups of up to six to eight clients, in which group members can observe inconsistencies and irrationalities in each others' beliefs. They are encouraged to offer alternative explanations for their beliefs and to develop new coping strategies for positive symptoms, including possible relapse. In addition, they are challenged to evaluate their negative beliefs about psychosis and integrate their illness (Drury et al., 1996a). Drury et al. (1996a, 1996b) found that cognitive therapy resulted in a decline in positive symptoms and a reduction in recovery time.

An alternative model of treatment was put forward by Jackson et al. (1998). This is known as cognitively oriented psychotherapy for early psychosis (COPE). In COPE, the focus is not on positive symptoms but rather on assisting people to adjust after their first episode when their symptoms have abated. Psychoeducation and cognitive techniques, are used to challenge self-stigmatisation and self-stereotypes. The person is helped to come to terms in understanding their illness and with pursuing life goals to promote adaptation. Cognitive and behavioural techniques are also used to focus on emergent secondary morbidity such as depression and social anxiety (Jackson et al., 1998).

Hodel et al. (1998) suggested that emotional management therapy (EMT) may be useful as an adjunct to existing therapies and could play a substantial role in secondary prevention. EMT aims to help people develop and refine specific strategies for coping with the impact of the emotional stress in early psychosis. It consists of two parts, one including relaxation techniques, and the other stress coping skills.

Strategies

The goals of psychotherapy in early psychosis are to:

- Form a therapeutic alliance with the client
- Provide education about the nature of the symptoms
- Record negative or distressing thoughts and their context
- Become more conscious of thoughts and assumptions
- Learn alternative strategies to deal with stressful situations
- Promote adaptation and recovery
- Protect and enhance self-esteem
- Focus upon stigma issues and develop effective coping strategies, and
- Utilise cognitive strategies to prevent and reduce secondary morbidity and comorbidity

Psychoeducation

Psychoeducation aims to develop a shared and increased understanding of the illness for both the client and his or her family. Increasing emphasis has been placed on the importance of educating the client and his/her family about the nature and course of the illness. Psychoeducation can be delivered in a variety of modes, such as one-to-one, group sessions or family work. It is important to ensure that the material supplied to clients and their families is appropriate to early psychosis. The content of any written information provided should also be explained (Lloyd et al., 2006). Group programmes are an effective means of imparting information for clients with early psychosis. Psychoeducation sessions in a group format can offer the opportunity for clients to participate in discussions, brainstorming as part of the larger group and role playing.

Psychoeducation should explain:

- The nature of the illness
- The importance of relapse prevention
- The range of treatment options available
- The patterns and variable nature of recovery
- The prospects for the future and what clients and carers can do to influence this
- What agencies and personnel will be involved in their treatment
- What support services are available
- What community services are available (e.g. employment, accommodation) (Lloyd et al., 2006)

Strategies

Strategies in the provision of psychoeducation for clients and families include:

- The material used should be appropriate for clients experiencing early psychosis, and additionally should reflect the individual's requirements and take into account how the individual usually learns or absorbs new information
- Clients and their families should be given initial and appropriate written and verbal information about early psychosis as soon as is practical after diagnosis
- Clients should have access to group programmes and activities that provide education about early psychosis and the opportunity to discuss and assimilate the information

Group programmes

Groupwork interventions for people experiencing early psychosis can be both efficient and effective in promoting recovery and involvement in community life, reducing the development of disability, and facilitating the achievement of personal goals and valued social roles (Albiston et al., 1998). They can play a preventive role in improving recovery levels and preventing decline in psychosocial functioning in vulnerable subgroups (Albiston et al., 1998).

Groupwork interventions complement the other clinical interventions within a biopsychosocial model as they can provide positive outcomes across a number of broad life domains. Members of groups are linked by particular perceptions, motivation and purpose and as such the peer process is central as it provides a forum for the disclosure of personal information. Group participation facilitates the feeling that other people have similar experiences, and learning can occur through observation of others.

In order to respond to the diverse clinical and developmental needs of young people, a wide range of group programmes should be developed. Recovering early psychosis clients need a stable secure base from which to proceed, coupled with a sense of purpose and hope for their future activities. Specific areas to focus on include:

- Coping and stress management skills
- Psychoeducation
- Goal setting
- Activity scheduling
- Vocational and educational planning and training
- Social and recreational skills
- Health promotion
- Lifestyle issues such as substance use and safe sexual practices
- Personal development
- Interaction with people who are further along in recovery and who provide hope and inspiration for the future (Albiston et al., 1998)

Programmes such as those described by O'Toole et al. (2004) and Russell and Lloyd (2004) focused on providing a healthy lifestyle package, which includes nutrition and exercise. In these programmes, the gym was used as a means of promoting structured activity, encouraging socialisation, and as a meeting point for clients prior to attending college courses. Programmes that are designed to address the educational and vocational needs of young people with psychosis need to focus on self development, peer support, illness and medication education, increasing the clients' links with services and agencies such as colleges and employment agencies, and developing work related skills (Lloyd & Bassett, 1997).

Strategies

Strategies for providing a comprehensive range of group programmes specifically tailored to meet the needs of people with early psychosis include the following:

- Group programmes should be available in a range of clinical and community settings; conducting programmes away from health based settings is important in promoting re-integration within the community
- Ideally, group programmes should include partnerships with educational and vocational services within the community
- Group programmes should be specialised for young people only and not include older clients who may have a more chronic picture
- Development of the content of group programmes should be based on the identified needs, goals and aspirations of clients. People in the acute and recovery phases of illness have differing needs, which should be reflected in the types of group programmes available
- Development of any group programme should be based on a thorough planning process, which includes the best available evidence, needs assessment, clear objectives, content areas relevant to early psychosis intervention and establishment of evaluation strategies
- Decisions regarding participation in any group programme should be made collaboratively with the client based on an understanding of the potential benefits for that person

- Processes for engaging and supporting clients in group programmes should be established by the psychosocial rehabilitation practitioners

Text box 13.2 Multidisciplinary focus in early psychosis

- Targeted social, educational and vocational interventions have a major role in meeting the needs of young people
- Multidisciplinary psychosocial group programmes should consist of a range of choices and strategies to enhance the wellbeing of young people
- Families need to be included as partners in care, which supports recovery

Intervention in prodromal psychosis

Despite the substantial support for early intervention in first episode psychosis, when it comes to intervention in prodromal psychosis, there are concerns regarding clinical, ethical and economic benefits (Jackson, 2003; McGlashan et al., 2001; Warner, 2001). The critics suggest that attempting to provide treatment to people who have prodromal features but do not have a clear mental illness is problematic because:

- Risk indicators are sufficiently common to result in high numbers of false positives in any screening exercise
- Early treatment, especially when medication is involved, carries risks as well as benefits
- Involvement of a person in a mental health service or psychiatric diagnosis is potentially stigmatising
- The costs of early intervention services may result in redistribution of resources away from better targeted services

See Pelosi & Birchwood (2003) for further debate on this issue.

Proponents of early intervention with this broader group rely on the Duration of Untreated Psychosis (DUP) hypothesis, which suggests that the earlier the treatment, the better the prognosis. However, opponents argue that the link between DUP and poor outcome may be spurious because it is based on an association between untreated psychosis and poor prognosis, rather than a demonstrated causal link (Verdoux et al., 2001). The reasoning here is that the association may have nothing to do with lack of treatment, but rather may be an artefact of the established relationship between insidious onset and poor prognosis. It is argued that insidious onset psychosis is a poor prognosis subtype and that this subtype is also likely to be untreated for an extended period because the symptoms emerge gradually and so do not come to the attention of treatment services.

Others argue that DUP continues to predict poor prognosis even when confounding factors are taken into account (Harrigan et al., 2003). It is possible that there are two subgroups: those who respond better if treated early and those whose response is relatively poor regardless of when treatment is initiated (Perkins et al., 2004).

In summary, the theoretical basis of clinical intervention in the prodrome as well as the ethical and practical value of such intervention remains a matter of contention. Practitioners who encounter such individuals should take into account the range of potential benefits and disadvantages associated with early clinical intervention and, where appropriate share this information with the client and family members.

Does specialist intervention in early psychosis make a difference?

Melle et al. (2006) reported that suicidality was lower among clients of early intervention programme in Norway compared with similar clients who were treated in standard services. While this was not a controlled trial, the authors concluded that early detection programmes that bring clients into treatment when they have lower symptom levels may reduce suicide risk. McGlashan et al. (2006) found that half the number of clients with prodromal symptoms for schizophrenia developed a full schizophrenic syndrome if they were treated with olanzapine (16%), compared with those treated with placebo (38%). This benefit did not continue after treatment ceased, and the numbers were too small to draw definitive conclusions about the benefits of early treatment. However, while clinical results were promising, one concern was that those on olanzapine had a weight gain of more than 8 kilograms compared with those on placebo.

The EPPIC programme, which has formed the basis of much of the service model described above, has never been subjected to a randomised controlled trial. A quasi-experimental investigation of the impact of the cognitive therapy component (COPE) produced results (Jackson et al., 2001) that the researchers described as 'discouraging', leading them to conclude that this component did not confer any clinical advantage on those who received it compared with those who did not receive it. Four year follow-up (Jackson et al., 2005) confirmed initial findings.

Two UK randomised controlled trials investigating the impact of psychological interventions on early psychosis have reported modest results. The Socrates study (Lewis et al., 2002; Tarrier et al., 2004) showed some initial benefits for cognitive–behavioural therapy in some of the outcome measures compared with supportive counselling or treatment as usual (Lewis et al., 2002) and the authors concluded that the intervention had sped recovery. However at 18 month follow-up (Tarrier et al., 2004), any advantages for cognitive–behavioural therapy over supportive counselling had evaporated, and on some critical measures such as relapse rate there were no advantages for either intervention over treatment as usual.

Another UK group (Kuipers et al., 2004) reported on randomised controlled trial outcomes in a study that compared a specialist early intervention programme that shared a number of features with the EPPIC programme, and treatment as usual. They found that after 12 months, there were no significant differences in outcomes between those who took part in the specialist early psychosis programme and those who received usual treatment. Both groups showed substantial improvement, but there was no evidence that the specialist programme had any specific effect.

Text box 13.3 Evidence base for intervention in early psychosis

- There is a strong consensus around the principles and values associated with psycho-social intervention in early psychosis, but there is not yet an evidence base for the effectiveness of these interventions. The evidence base is therefore the relatively weak 'clinical consensus'
- The DUP hypothesis, which provides the theoretical basis for early intervention, has partial but not definitive empirical support
- Early intervention in psychosis in the context of individualised psychosocial rehabilita-tion is warranted on the existing evidence base, but resource intensive specialist services need systematic evaluation to determine effectiveness
- There is no consensus regarding the merits of intervention in response to 'prodromal' features and this is an area of research focus rather than evidence based practice

The best that can be said at this stage is that it is too early to draw definitive conclusions. (McGorry et al., 2003) and that there are some promising indicators, but more research is needed (Bechdolf et al., 2006). However, there is certainly not a strong basis for the development of intensive early psychosis services that are not under active, well designed evaluation. The preliminary results of the Prevention Through Risk Identification, Management and Education project (McGlashan et al., 2006) raise questions as to the relative benefits of reduced incidence of schizophrenia for a minority of prodromal clients compared with increased risk of weight gain for the majority of prodromal clients.

Conclusion

Early intervention programmes are increasingly becoming a focus in the delivery of mental health services. Psychosocial rehabilitation is an important adjunct to biomedical treatment. A focus of young adulthood is the marking of career and study choices with the forming of individual values, interests and social relation-ships. For young people experiencing early psychosis, the opportunities to achieve their vocational goals and career choices may be interrupted by periods of hospit-alisation, recovery from their illness and managing the symptoms of their illness. The provision of psychosocial rehabilitation as an early intervention strategy is import-ant in secondary prevention.

References

Albiston, D., Francey, S., & Harrigan, S. (1998). Group programmes for recovery from early psychosis. *British Journal of Psychiatry*, 172, 117–121.

Australian Health Ministers. *National mental health plan 2003–2008*. Canberra: Australian Government, 2003.

Bechdolf, A., Phillips, L.J., Francey, S.M., Leicester, S., Morrison, A.P., Veith, V., Klosterkotter, J., & McGorry, P.D. (2006). Recent approaches to psychological interventions for people at risk of psychosis. *European Archives of Psychiatry and Clinical Neuroscience*, 256, 159–173.

Bertolote, J., & McGorry, P. (2005). Early intervention and recovery for young people with early psychosis: consensus statement. *British Journal of Psychiatry Supplement*, 48, s116–119.

Birchwood, M., McGorry, P., & Jackson, H. (1997). Early intervention in schizophrenia. *British Journal of Psychiatry*, 170, 2–5.

Commonwealth Department of Health and Aged Care (2000). *Promotion, prevention and early intervention for mental health – a monograph*. Canberra: Mental Health and Special Programs Branch, Commonwealth Department of Health and Aged Care.

Davis, C., Martin, G., Kosky, R., & O'Hanlon, A. (2000). *Early intervention in the mental health of young people*. Canberra: Promotion and Prevention Section, Mental Health Branch, Department of Health and Aged Care.

Drury, V., Birchwood, M., Cochrane, R., & Macmillan, F. (1996a). Cognitive therapy and recovery from acute psychosis: A controlled trial I: Impact on psychotic symptoms. *British Journal of Psychiatry*, 169, 593–601.

Drury, V., Birchwood, M., Cochrane, R., & Macmillan, F. (1996b). Cognitive therapy and recovery from acute psychosis: A controlled trial II: Impact on recovery time. *British Journal of Psychiatry*, 169, 602–607.

Falloon, I., Held, T., Roncone, R., Coverdale, J., & Laidlaw, T. (1998). Optimal treatment strategies to enhance recovery from schizophrenia. *Australian and New Zealand Journal of Psychiatry*, 32, 43–49.

Gardiner–Caldwell Communications Limited (1997). *The early psychosis training pack*. Cheshire, UK: Gardiner–Caldwell Communications Ltd.

Harrigan, S.M., McGorry, P.D., & Krstev, H. (2003). Does treatment delay in first-episode psychosis really matter? *Psychological Medicine*, 33, 97–110.

Hodel, S., Brenner, H., Merlo, M., & Teuber, J. (1998). Emotional management in early psychosis. *British Journal of Psychiatry*, 172, 128–133.

Jackson, G.E. (2003). The dilemma of early intervention: Some problems in mental health screening and labeling. *Ethical Human Sciences and Services: An International Journal of Critical Inquiry*, 5, 35–40.

Jackson, H., McGorry, P., Edwards, J., Hulbert, C., Henry, L., Francey, S., Maude, D., Cocks, J., Power, P., Harrigan, S., & Dudgeon, P. (1998). Cognitively oriented psychotherapy for early psychosis (COPE). *British Journal of Psychiatry*, 172, 93–100.

Jackson, H., McGorry, P., Henry, L., Edwards, J., Hulbert, C., Harrigan, S., Dudgeon, P., Francey, S., Maude, D., Cocks, J., & Power, P. (2001). Cognitively oriented psychotherapy for early psychosis (COPE): A 1-year follow-up. *British Journal of Clinical Psychology*, 40, 57–70.

Jackson, H., McGorry, P., Edwards, J., Hulbert, C., Henry, L., Harrigan, S., Dudgeon, P., Francey, S., Maude, D., Cocks, J., Killackey, E., & Power, P. (2005). A controlled trial of cognitively oriented psychotherapy for early psychosis (COPE) with four-year follow-up readmission data. *Psychological Medicine*, 35, 1295–1306.

Kuipers, E., Holloway, F., Rabe-Hesketh, S., & Tennakoon, L. (2004). Croydon Outreach and Assertive Support Team (COAST). An RCT of early intervention in psychosis: Croydon Outreach and Assertive Support Team (COAST). *Social Psychiatry and Psychiatric Epidemiology*, 39, 358–363.

Lewis, S., Tarrier, N., Haddock, G., Bentall, R., Kinderman, P., Kingdon, D., Siddle, R., Drake, R., Everitt, J., Leadley, K., Benn, A., Grazebrook, K., Haley, C., Akhtar, S., Davies, L., Palmer, S., Faragher, B., & Dunn, G. (2002). Randomised, controlled trial of cognitive–behavioural therapy in early schizophrenia: acute-phase outcomes. *British Journal of Psychiatry, 181* (Suppl. 43), 91–97.

Lloyd, C. (1999). Interventions for rehabilitation of patients with early psychosis. *British Journal of Therapy and Rehabilitation, 6*, 554–558.

Lloyd, C., & Bassett, J. (1997). Life is for living: A pre-vocational programme for young people with psychosis. *Australian Occupational Therapy Journal, 44*, 82–87.

Lloyd, C., Bassett, J., & Samra, P. (1998). Rehabilitation programmes for early psychosis. *British Journal of Occupational Therapy, 63*, 76–82.

Lloyd, C., Tse, S., & McKenna, K. (2006). Teaching clients with mental illness. In: K. McKenna and L. Tooth (Eds.), *Client education: A practical guide for clinical therapists* (pp. 270–306). Sydney: University of New South Wales Press.

Malla, A., Norman, R., McLean, T., Scholten, D., & Townsend, L.A. (2003). Canadian programme for early intervention in non-affective psychotic disorders. *Australian and New Zealand Journal of Psychiatry, 37*, 407–413.

McGlashan, T.H., Miller, T.J., & Woods, S.W. (2001). Pre-onset detection and intervention research in schizophrenia psychoses: Current estimates of benefit and risk. *Schizophrenia Bulletin, 27*, 563–570.

McGlashan, T.H., Zipursky, R.B., Perkins, D., Addington, J., Miller, T., Woods, S.W., Hawkins, K.A., Hoffman, R.E., Preda, A., Epstein, I., Addington, D., Lindborg, S., Trzaskoma, Q., Tohen, M., & Breier, A. (2006). Randomized, double-blind trial of olanzapine versus placebo in patients prodromally symptomatic for psychosis. *American Journal of Psychiatry, 163*, 790–799.

McGorry, P.D., Yung, A.R., & Phillips, L.J. (2003). The 'close-in' or ultra high-risk model: a safe and effective strategy for research and clinical intervention in prepsychotic mental disorder. *Schizophrenia Bulletin, 29*, 771–790.

Melle, I., Haahr, U., Friis, S., Hustoft, K., Johannessen, J.O., Larsen, T.K., Opjordsmoen, S., Rund, B.R., Simonsen, E., Vaglum, P., & McGlashan, T. (2005). Reducing the duration of untreated first-episode psychosis – effects on baseline social functioning and quality of life. *Acta Psychiatrica Scandinavica, 112*, 469–473.

Melle, I., Johannesen, J.O., Friis, S., Haahr, U., Joa, I., Larsen, T.K., Opjordsmoen, S., Rund, B.R., Simonsen, E., Vaglum, P., & McGlashan, T. (2006). Early detection of the first episode of schizophrenia and suicidal behavior. *American Journal of Psychiatry, 163*, 800–804.

National Early Psychosis Project Clinical Guidelines Working Party (1998). *Australian clinical guidelines for early psychosis.* Melbourne: National Early Psychosis Project, University of Melbourne.

Office of the Deputy Prime Minister (2004). *Mental health and social exclusion.* Wetherby, UK: ODPM Publications.

O'Toole, M., Ohlsen, R., Taylor, T., Purvis, R., Walters, J., & Pilowsky, L. (2004). Treating first episode psychosis – the service users' perspective: A focus group evaluation. *Journal of Psychiatric and Mental Health Nursing, 11*, 319–326.

Pelosi, A.J., & Birchwood, M. (2003). Is early intervention for psychosis a waste of valuable resources? *British Journal of Psychiatry, 182*, 196–198.

Perkins, D., Lieberman, J., Gu, H., Tohen, M., McEvoy, J., Green, A., Zipursky, R., Strakowski, S., Sharma, T., Kahn, R., Gur, R., & Tollefson, G. (HGDH Research Group) (2004). Predictors of antipsychotic treatment response in patients with first-episode schizophrenia, schizoaffective and schizophreniform disorders. *British Journal of Psychiatry*, *185*, 18–24.

Raphael, B. (2000). *Promoting the mental health and wellbeing of children and young people.* Canberra, National Mental Health Working Group, Department of Health and Aged Care.

Rickwood, D. (2004). *Pathways of recovery: Preventing relapse.* Canberra: Department of Health and Ageing.

Russell, A., & Lloyd, C. (2004). Partnerships in mental health: Addressing barriers to social inclusion. *International Journal of Therapy and Rehabilitation*, *11*, 267–274.

Tarrier, N., Lewis, S., Haddock, G., Bentall, R., Drake, R., Kinderman, P., Kingdon, D., Siddle, R., Everitt, J., Leadley, K., Benn, A., Grazebrook, K., Haley, C., Akhtar, S., Davies, L., Palmer, S., & Dunn, G. (2004). Cognitive–behavioural therapy in first-episode and early schizophrenia: 18-month follow-up of a randomised controlled trial. *British Journal of Psychiatry*, *184*, 231–239.

Verdoux, H., Liraud, F., Bergey, C., Assens, F., Abalan, F., & van Os, J. (2001). Is the association between duration of untreated psychosis and outcome confounded? A two year follow-up study of first-admitted patients. *Schizophrenia Research*, *49*, 231–241.

Warner, R. (2001). The prevention of schizophrenia: what interventions are safe and effective? *Schizophrenia Bulletin*, *27*, 551–562.

Whitehorn, D., Lazier, L., & Kopala, L. (1998). Psychosocial rehabilitation early after the onset of psychosis. *Psychiatric Services*, *49*, 1135–1147.

Useful resources

Useful resources on early psychosis include the following:

Gardiner–Caldwell Communications Ltd (1997). *Early psychosis training pack.* Macclesfield: Gardiner–Caldwell Communications Ltd. (Available at www.eppic.org.au)

National Early Psychosis Project Clinical Guidelines Working Party (1998). *Australian clinical guidelines for early psychosis.* Melbourne: National Early Psychosis Project, University of Melbourne.

National Institute for Clinical Excellence (NICE) (2002). *Schizophrenia: Core interventions in the treatment and management of schizophrenia in primary and secondary care.* London: NICE.

Chapter 14

SERVICE EVALUATION

Tom Meehan

Overview of chapter

Service evaluation is central both to the provision of evidence based services and accountability to clients. Whether we deliver programmes developed elsewhere or develop our own programmes, the question of effectiveness arises. Even when a programme has a demonstrated evidence base, we cannot assume that it will be effective with our specific client group and service environment. How do we measure effectiveness as it applies to clients in real-world treatment settings? How do the processes, costs and outcomes of our programmes compare with those of other similar programmes? This chapter sets out the key issues that need to be taken into account by anyone with an interest in the effectiveness of psychosocial rehabilitation services. The design of evaluation studies is a complex and sophisticated field and it is neither practical nor appropriate to attempt to address the range of issues that are raised by the field here. Practitioners and others interested in service evaluation are advised to consult local experts and researchers with evaluation expertise when planning to evaluate their programmes. This chapter should assist you to engage in an informed dialogue with such experts and so contribute to the success of the evaluation process.

Why evaluate services?

Evaluation is a systematic means of learning from experience. Organisations, like individuals, have a capacity for self-deception either through overvaluing or undervaluing their achievements. The evaluation process introduces a dimension of objectivity. Evaluation is critical at all levels of an organisation. At the macro level, it is necessary to ensure ongoing evaluation of the key policy and strategic directions. Each year, governments generate several publications that report on attempts to conduct large scale evaluations. At the micro level, evaluation is more likely to be concerned with establishing whether or not a specific programme should be continued, modified or ceased. Thus, in the rehabilitation field, evaluation studies are frequently conducted to:

- Contribute to decisions about the overall benefits of the programme – which clients tend to benefit from the programme and under what conditions?

- Contribute to decisions about programme expansion, continuation, modification or termination – what works/does not work and why?
- Obtain evidence to secure support for the programme – demonstrate effectiveness
- Obtain evidence to rally opposition to the programme – to challenge the value and worth of the programme
- Gain a better understanding of the processes (interpersonal, social, structural, financial, etc.) impacting on the programme
- Ensure that the programme remains responsive to the needs of the target group (to prevent 'upmarket shift' in service delivery)
- Ensure programme fidelity

Quality assurance, evaluation, or research?

The distinction between research and evaluation is not always clear. Research involves a contribution to knowledge that is not limited by highly specific circumstances. It contributes to a theoretical understanding or set of general principles, which may then be taken into consideration in a specific circumstance. Evaluation is concerned simply with determining whether or not a specific programme or activity had its intended effect. This distinction can be illustrated with respect to a practice example. If we set out to determine whether or not family psychoeducation reduces burden of care, we are engaged in research. If, on the other hand, we want to find out whether or not family members were satisfied with a specific education session, we are engaged in evaluation. However, in practice the boundaries often become blurred because our intentions may involve both research and evaluation. To move beyond evaluation into research, we need to be able to demonstrate that our results in relation to a specific service can be generalised to a wider group of existing services and we need to link service components to underlying theory.

Whereas research and evaluation are typically concerned with outcomes, quality assurance has as its focus service processes. Quality assurance (QA) is concerned with determining whether or not specified processes are being followed within an organisation. The issue of whether or not these processes are associated with particular outcomes then becomes a matter for evaluation. Quality assurance takes as its premise the relationship between processes and outcomes and is concerned with monitoring process integrity. One of the weaknesses of the QA philosophy is that this relationship is often simply supposed and has never been systematically investigated. Ideally, QA processes are concerned with monitoring performance standards and processes that have a demonstrated linkage with consumer outcomes. Some of the differences between the approaches are summarised in Table 14.1.

The measurement of service performance through the benchmarking of mental health is gaining momentum in Australia (Coombs & Meehan, 2003; Eagar et al., 2003) and overseas (Bird et al., 2003; Wait, 2004). The routine collection and reporting of performance data through benchmarking enables services to monitor their progress relative to other similar services. The process enables providers to identify

Table 14.1 Characteristics of quality assurance, evaluation and research

Characteristic	Quality assurance	Evaluation	Research
Purpose	Assess quality	Examine efficiency and effectiveness	Test hypothesis, explain relationships
Origin	Service problem	Service problem/question	Question
Outcome	Feedback	Feedback plus new knowledge	New knowledge
Generalisability of findings	Not generalisable	Depends on study methodology	Usually generalisable
Scientific principles	Important but not essential	Essential	Essential
Dissemination of findings	Internal to organisation	Internal and external	External

service components requiring attention. For example, the cost per patient day in one residential service could be significantly higher than similar services targeting the same population. Since overall outcomes and other variables such as length of stay are similar to the other services, the cost structure of the more expensive programme requires attention.

Benchmarking may be used to compare the performance of units/services in a single organisation (internal benchmarking) or to compare a number of independent units/services (collaborative benchmarking). Benchmarking can also be undertaken with partners coming from different fields (i.e. adult mental health, forensic mental health) but who have an interest in a particular performance indicator (e.g. aggression) – generic benchmarking. Benchmarking partners generally identify a specific process or aspects of performance on which they agree to collaborate. Benchmarking can be used continuously as an ongoing quality assurance process, or it can be used as part of a focused evaluation of a programme or service component.

Eagar and colleagues (2003) have proposed a framework for benchmarking based on work by the Australian Manufacturing Council. This has five related phases:

(1) *Preparation*, in which the following are determined: what to benchmark, and who or what to benchmark against
(2) *Comparison*, which may include the following activities: data collection; data manipulation, construction of indicators, etc.; and comparison of results with benchmarking partners
(3) *Investigation*, that is, identification of practices and processes that result in superior performance
(4) *Implementation*, in which best practices are adapted and/or adopted
(5) *Evaluation*, where new practices are monitored to ensure continuous improvement and, if necessary the whole cycle is repeated

In practice, many benchmarking activities cease at phase 2 and there is little evidence to suggest that the organisations involved move on to explore how the findings can be used to improve service delivery. Producing graphs/tables to highlight the best and worst performers is threatening for some organisations and does little to keep organisations engaged in the process. Thus, the focus of benchmarking needs to be reflection that evolves from service reform and ongoing performance monitoring, as outlined in phases 3–5 above.

Although benchmarking holds considerable potential for promoting improvements in care, attempts to benchmark mental health services in most developed countries have been severely constrained by the lack of adequate data, especially data on clinical improvement/outcomes (Rosenheck & Cicchetti, 1998). Most previous studies have relied on 'outcomes' such as length of stay or rehospitalisation rates, which are proxy measures of client outcome. Australia has introduced routine standardised outcome measures and these have the potential to form a major component of future benchmarking activities.

Evaluation – factors to consider

A review of the rehabilitation literature suggests that a number of different approaches have been used to evaluate rehabilitation programmes. The final approach is usually dictated by the purpose of the evaluation (i.e. deliverables), the amount of funding/resources available, and the experience/orientation of the evaluator. These factors usually determine the complexity and scope of the investigation, the methodology, data collection techniques, selection of subjects and dissemination of findings, etc. In any event, there are a number of issues/questions that the evaluator needs to consider prior to commencement, and these are outlined below.

What constitutes the programme to be evaluated?

Most rehabilitation programmes have a number of related components frequently involving input from the rehabilitation team, clinical team, family members, housing, disability services and peer support groups. The components to be included and/or excluded from the evaluation must be agreed at the outset with the agency/individual requesting the evaluation. Once the programme/intervention has been identified, the evaluator will need to explore the theory underpinning the use of the intervention. For example, a support group for parents should be tied to a theory that explains how parents benefit from group rather than individual support. When an intervention is so loose that it can be explained by almost any theory, it can be difficult to isolate those elements that are critical to its failure or success (Yeaton & Sechrest, 1981). The value of having a written protocol, describing the *who, what, where, when, why* and *how* of the evaluation, cannot be overstated. This should be signed off by the agency requesting the evaluation and the evaluator to prevent misunderstanding and possible conflict at a later date.

How long has the programme being operating?

Most rehabilitation programmes will require some modification during implementation to meet local conditions. Evaluations of programmes in the early stages of implementation may have little impact, as they are likely to change over the evaluation period. By the time the results of the evaluation are available, the programme will have changed so much that the results are irrelevant. Thus, it is desirable that programmes have reached a high level of implementation prior to evaluation.

Why is the programme being evaluated?

A number of factors motivate managers to request evaluation studies. Some of these have already been discussed above. It is clear that a manager may have a real interest in knowing how a particular programme is performing, or he/she may be undertaking the evaluation reluctantly to meet funding requirements or external requests from concerned parties. Indeed, evaluation studies may be commissioned in the context of a larger agenda concerning organisational change or competing demands for resource allocation. In the latter situation, management staff frequently fail to engage with the evaluators and this can lead to criticism of the evaluation and the evaluation findings when they are released. Some managers may not be receptive to negative findings and may try to undermine the integrity of the evaluation. It is useful at the outset to query how negative findings, should they arise, be received. The evaluation should be a collaborative effort on the part of the agency and the external evaluator/s. Thus, it is important to keep senior management informed of progress and seek every opportunity to feed back findings as the evaluation proceeds.

What are the primary questions to be addressed by the evaluation?

When government departments, service managers, and/or clinicians commission evaluation studies, they often have partially formulated questions they want answered. Managers often have a general question about the outcomes of the programme, for example, is our rehabilitation programme working effectively? The problem for the evaluator is to achieve a satisfactory definition of what is meant by 'working effectively'. Different vested interests will have different views on what constitutes effectiveness when applied to a given programme (see Table 14.2).

While the evaluators can provide guidance and direction in setting and refining the evaluation questions, they should ensure that the needs of the service, rather than the evaluators, are being met. Thus, the evaluation should be driven by questions of concern for the service and not simply the collection of data for publications. The final question set is important since it will determine data sources for the evaluation (carers/clients/staff), type of data to be collected (qualitative/quantitative), and the way in which it is collected (observation, survey, interviews, focus groups, etc.).

Table 14.2 Effectiveness as defined by different vested interests

Group	How effectiveness may be defined
Consumer	Improved quality of life
Family	More independence – less of a burden on family
Treatment team	Better clinical functioning – symptom control
Rehabilitation team	Better general functioning – improved opportunities
Programme staff	Rewards from work – greater job satisfaction
Funding body	Cost efficiency – best possible return on investment
Programme management	Throughput – increase in number of clients serviced
Health department	Adherence to policy and procedures – protect public
Academic evaluator	Study yields new/quality data – publications in academic journals

Table 14.3 Different components of programme evaluation and focus of investigation

Type of evaluation	Focus of investigation
Process	Assesses the inputs/activities of the programme – i.e. are all components of the programme available? How satisfied are participants with the programme (e.g. content, structure, materials, facilitators, etc.)?
Impact	Assesses the immediate effects of the programme – does it meet its objectives? For example, is there improvement in knowledge, skill and/or attitude following participation in the programme?
Outcome	Assesses the long-term effects of the programme – does it meet its goal? For example, has the overall delivery of care improved as a consequence of staff attending the programme?

Are there tools/models available to provide a framework for evaluation?

There are now a number of books and websites devoted to research and evaluation. The traditional method of conceptualising an evaluation was to divide the programme under investigation into three separate but related components; process, impact and outcome (Table 14.3). The level of attention devoted to each of the three components depends upon the evaluation question/s.

'Programme logic' expands on the framework outlined in Table 14.1 and Text box 14.1 (i.e. process, impact and outcome) to provide another method of separating a programme into a series of logical components (Bickman, 1987; Funnell, 1997). It is clear that every programme consists of a series of components/elements and the assumed links between these elements of the programme make up its 'logic' (Wholey, 1987). Making this logic explicit provides a clearer picture of how the programme works in practice. From here, it is possible to develop an evaluation

Text box 14.1 Different phases of evaluation: Sam

Over the past 12 months, Sam has become non-compliant with his medication and this has resulted in numerous admissions to acute inpatient care. Sam's case manager has encouraged him to attend a community based medication education group (1 hour each week for 6 weeks).

In terms of 'process' evaluation, one could examine the number of sessions attended by Sam, and his satisfaction with each session/overall programme. Impact evaluation would assess changes in Sam's knowledge of his medications and his attitudes toward taking medications pre- and post-programme. Outcome evaluation would compare the number of admissions in the year prior to the programme with the number in the year following the programme.

Table 14.4 Example of a programme logic evaluation matrix (partially completed)

Outcomes	Measures of success	Factors impacting on success	Performance indicators
Relapse due to non-compliance is reduced	80% of clients compliant with medication	Availability of dosette boxes for clients	Relapse reduced by 50%
↑			
Graduates take medication as prescribed			
↑			
Graduates have improved knowledge, skills and attitude			
↑			
Participants react favourably to programme			
↑			
Appropriate clients are enrolled in programme			
↑			
Training programme is prepared			
↑			
Information about training needs of target group is available			

matrix for a given programme. Table 14.4 provides an example of a programme logic matrix (partially completed) for the evaluation of the medication education programme for non-compliant clients. The 'logic' assumes that each lower outcome has to be achieved before the next higher outcome.

According to Conrad et al. (1999), programme logic models address four domains: (i) the context (background conditions – population, geographic area, and so forth); (ii) underlying theory and assumptions; (iii) the intervention (key activities); and (iv) the outcomes (short, intermediate, and long term). They point out that the development or propositions that set out the relationship between each of these domains enables focused research testing not only whether the programme is achieving the outcomes it aims to achieve, but also the extent to which programme activities contribute to outcomes, the role of external factors and, ultimately, the validity of the theory that underlies the programme. Programme logic models can be used as tools to assist in the development of indicators of programme fidelity.

Programme logic models are of value where programmes lack an identified theory, where outcomes are not explicit, or where the causal relationship between programme activities and programme outcomes is not clearly articulated. The development of a programme logic model identifies gaps in information, assumptions or unstated relationships. The University of Wisconsin (USA) provides a useful website on aspects of programme logic for those wishing to acquire a better understanding of the tool. The site is located at: http://www.uwex.edu/ces/pdande/evaluation/evallogicmodel.html

What design/approach will be used?

Evaluation studies usually follow three commonly used designs:

- 'Pre-test/post-test design', where data collected prior to implementation of a (rehabilitation) programme (baseline) are compared to data collected following implementation (possibly on a number of occasions) to assess the degree of change derived from the programme.
- 'Matched pairs design', where people attending a programme are matched on some characteristic (e.g. diagnosis, duration of illness, age and gender). One group is exposed to the programme/intervention while the other acts as a control. Differences between both groups can be contrasted to determine if exposure to the programme leads to improved outcomes.
- 'Randomised controlled trial' design, where people seeking treatment are randomly assigned to a defined (rehabilitation) programme/intervention, or some other intervention, or possibly no intervention. Random assignment of people to the different groups eliminates selection bias and increases generalisability, making it the most powerful of all possible designs. The use of a no-treatment control group may raise ethical issues, since a group is deprived of the programme for the sake of evaluation. This problem is commonly addressed by randomly assigning participants to the active programme or a waiting list for the programme as a control. This provides a reasonable solution, since the people on the waiting list will eventually receive treatment when vacancies occur in the programme. An even better solution is to randomly assign participants to the new programme or 'treatment as usual'. This enables the evaluator to determine whether the new programme really adds value to existing programmes.

Data collection – quantitative versus qualitative?

Evaluation data may be collected through the use of quantitative or qualitative methods or, indeed, a combination of both methods (i.e. triangulation). Quantitative studies focus on 'numbers' and use standardised measures which can be applied to larger samples and offer the advantages of reliability, straightforward analysis procedures and generalisability of results. By way of example, data collected through the use of scales such as the Global Assessment of Functioning Scale (GAF) and the Health of Nation Outcomes Scales (HoNOS), etc., is classified as being quantitative, since these scales provide a 'score' to represent the phenomenon under investigation. On the other hand, qualitative studies focus on how people interact with their environment and other individuals. Findings are usually described in words rather than numbers. Qualitative methods include field studies (observations of people in natural settings), participant observation, structured/unstructured interviews with 'key' informants, focus/discussion groups, in-depth interviews (where people describe their feelings, perceptions, attitudes, etc.) and case histories. As qualitative studies can generate a lot of information, this can be difficult to manage and interpret. A 1-hour interview, for example, can take up to 4 hours to transcribe and yield 20 pages of text. In general, qualitative studies are useful in exploratory work where little or no previous research has been conducted. Qualitative evaluations provide a conceptual map or theoretical understanding of the phenomenon under study. These theories can than be 'tested' through the use of quantitative methods. Thus, both approaches compliment each other.

Which data collection instruments should be used?

When the decision is made to collect quantitative data, there is a major advantage in using measures that have been developed and tested in previous research. Such measures usually have established psychometric properties (i.e. reliability, validity and sensitivity to change) and any data collected using these measures can be cross-referenced to normative samples (McLellan & Durell, 1996). Even in situations where an appropriate measure cannot be found, it is better to modify an existing measure (that will preserve many of its original psychometric properties), than to embark on the development of a new measure. Reports on new scales are being published on a daily basis and it is important to undertake a thorough literature search before proceeding. The search for existing measures will therefore form part of the strategy for quantitative research. This can be a time consuming process and is one of the reasons why people may decide to create their own measure.

In any event, evaluation instruments should meet recognised 'psychometric' properties such as validity, reliability and sensitivity to change. A measure is said to be valid when it measures what it purports to measure: a measure of depression should assess depression, and not some related condition such as anxiety. A reliable measure will produce the same results on repeated application so long as the client hasn't changed (i.e. test retest reliability). Inter-rater reliability is achieved when it produces the same results when used by different staff. An instrument that can identify small changes in functioning between assessments is said to be sensitive to change. Many of the instruments currently used in the mental health field have been previously used on 'normative' samples and therefore have what is known as 'norms' for these samples. For example the Beck Depression Inventory has norms for males and females. An evaluator can therefore make judgments about the depression levels in a specific study group by comparing the obtained scores with those of the 'normed' sample.

How will data be analysed?

Most evaluations generate large amounts of data and the way in which this is to be managed needs to be considered prior to commencement of the study. If a statistician is required to assist with data analysis, consult this person prior to data collection. A statistician can provide useful insights in to the way in which data are to be arranged for ease of analysis. The analysis of interview and focus group data requires a different set of skills and expertise and should be subjected to a level of rigour appropriate to the particular approach taken.

How will findings be reported?

The content and structure of the final report will usually vary according to the audience. Busy senior management usually require a brief summary of the final report (Executive Summary) to be prepared in addition to the main report. It may also be useful to organise an oral presentation for senior staff. Permission from the funding agency will be required prior to the publication of findings in scholarly journals or other media.

What staff input will be required for the different phases of the evaluation?

Most evaluations involve the collection, analysis and reporting of data. Agreement on what agency staff and evaluation staff will contribute to the evaluation should be reached prior to commencement of the study. Many evaluations do not have allocated funding and staff are required to contribute to the evaluation in addition to their normal duties. Even in studies that are funded, staff are frequently required to conduct client assessments, etc., since they have most knowledge of client functioning.

How will opposition to the evaluation be managed?

Opposition to research/evaluation by practitioners providing the service or programme under investigation is common. Evaluation studies have been criticised by practitioners for being irrelevant (not meeting the needs of programme staff), unfair (not considering the needs of service users), and unused (having little influence over planning and decision making) (Weiss, 1983). Practitioners may feel threatened by what the findings might reveal and may believe that their individual performance is being assessed. Practitioners will be aware that many clients in the mental health field with severe disabilities may not improve significantly and they will be concerned that this may reflect on their ability. They may also be aware that some of their programmes are ineffective in achieving clinical outcomes but nonetheless are valued by clients. Engaging key practitioners in planning for the evaluation and ensuring that all staff and clients are adequately informed of the evaluation and its objectives will help to offset resistance.

Ethical considerations

Research and evaluation that is formally conducted within universities and/or hospitals will usually require approval by an Ethics Committee. These committees are designed to protect the rights of individuals participating in research and, indeed, the researcher. Committee membership usually includes academics, researchers, legal representatives, member of the clergy, a member of the public and a consumer representative. Routine quality assurance processes are not usually subject to ethical review. However, it is important to clarify requirements with the local ethical committee before undertaking evaluation. Even where a formal ethical review is not required, any person planning to undertake research or evaluation should keep in mind some basic ethical considerations.

Is the evaluation worthwhile?

Most research will impinge on an individual's life to some degree. Even if the extent of the intrusion or demand on time is small, the evaluator should be able to demonstrate that there are good reasons for making such demands. Evaluators should always have a clear understanding of how a proposed study will be of benefit to participants, to service users, to the organisation or to the advancement of knowledge.

Does the evaluation have adverse effects or consequences for participants?

The collection of data for research and evaluation purposes can be a source of distress and even burdensome for some people. For example, having participants recall aspects of their childhood may be traumatic for people who were exposed to abuse in childhood. How will the evaluator manage information that may incriminate the participant? For example, during an interview a participant admits to having committed a serious crime. The evaluator will need to have a clear plan for responding to any unintended adverse effects and a clear explanation of any predictable adverse effects.

Have participants provided informed consent?

There are two parts to this, both of which are more subtle than might seem at first glance. Providing adequate and reasonable information is sometimes quite difficult, especially if there are concerns about the impact that knowledge about the study will have on information provided. The key is to ensure that people have sufficient information about the general nature of the study and about the demands that will be made on them, to enable them to decide whether or not to participate. Consent means that people make a free choice and are not in any way coerced into participating. In particular it is important that participants are not led to believe that refusal will result in denial of services or treatment. It is also important that participants understand that they may change their mind during the course of the study and withdraw without giving a reason.

Are participants protected from breaches of confidentiality?

It is important to specify forms of protection against inadvertent release of confidential information. This will include locked storage of records, separation of identifiers such as names from information records, disguise of identifying information in published reports and undertakings to report group data rather than individual data. Some forms of research and evaluation by their nature raise greater ethical concerns and require more intense scrutiny than others. In general, any research or evaluation that involves the collection of data from vulnerable groups such as children, people whose illness significantly impairs comprehension or judgment, and people from ethnic minorities, will be subjected to close scrutiny. Surveys of staff raise fewer ethical concerns than surveys of clients, because it can be assumed that staff will have fewer difficulties understanding the request being made of them and making an informed decision about participation.

Evaluation: example from the field (Project 300)

In 1995, the Government of Queensland (Australia) launched a project to resettle up to 300 people with long-term mental illness from institutional care into community housing – hence the title 'Project 300'. Each individual accessing Project 300 was provided with a support 'package' consisting of mental health services, disability support services, and normal community housing, in keeping with an assessment of their needs. Clinical supports were provided by local mental health services, while lifestyle support services were provided by non-government disability agencies.

In early 1996, Meehan et al. (2001) were contracted to evaluate the resettlement programme. The evaluation had two main objectives:

(1) To evaluate the quality of life for the individuals following the move to the community and to identify whether this conforms to acceptable standards in the community.
(2) To evaluate the contributions of housing, disability support services, informal support networks and access to mental health services, to the person's quality of life and the process of change in which they are engaged.

The evaluation used a combination of qualitative and quantitative approaches to ensure a comprehensive evaluation was conducted. The *qualitative* component of the evaluation involved in-depth interviews with a convenient subsample of 55 clients who were willing and able to participate. These people were interviewed in hospital 6 weeks prior to their discharge and again at 6 weeks and 6 months post-discharge. This interview data provided valuable insight from the clients' perspective into the challenges of resettlement in the community.

The *quantitative* component of the evaluation employed a number of standardised scales (Life Skills Profile, HoNOS, BPRS, and Wisconsin Quality of Life Index) to monitor changes in a number of domains. The initial assessment carried out 6 weeks prior to discharge provided baseline data for comparison with subsequent follow-up assessments at 6, 18 and 36 months.

The use of both qualitative and quantitative techniques did complicate data collection and interpretation, but provided a more comprehensive analysis of the programme. It was clear that the clients who participated in the interviews valued the opportunity to be able to provide feedback directly to the evaluation team.

Evaluation and clinical practice – bridging the gap

A major problem in any clinical work is that clinicians continue to use interventions that have been shown in evaluation studies to provide little or no effect (Sackett et al., 1997). Clinicians frequently argue that the volume of information is too vast for them to be able to explore and that they have neither the skills nor time to do this. The introduction of the Internet, and databases such as *Cochrane* have clearly made this task easier. However, even when interventions are shown to be clinically effective, they are rarely sustained beyond the period of external funding (Sullivan et al., 2005). Moreover, in countries where the collection of data for clinical decision making (e.g. outcomes data) is mandated, compliance with collection protocols remains poor.

Many clinicians argue that standardised measures are frequently subjective (Gilbody et al., 2005) and do little to address issues of importance to clients (Lakeman, 2004). Others see the collection of evaluation data as a paper exercise with little relevance to clinical practice (Walter et al., 1998) or the improvement of client outcomes (Kazis et al., 1990). These negative perceptions tend to hinder the potential for evaluation data to drive clinical decision making. A recent North American study (Garland et al., 2003) suggests that even when evaluation data derived from outcome measures are collected routinely and available to staff, the majority never use it in the planning and monitoring of client treatment. Our own research (Meehan et al., 2005) found that competing workloads, lack of support from senior medical staff, questionable evidence to support the collection of evaluation data, and fear of what the data might reveal hampers efforts to establish a culture driven by evidence.

Notwithstanding the above issues, the end users of evaluation and research findings should exercise a degree of caution when incorporating evaluation findings into

Table 14.5 Differences between efficacy and effectiveness studies

Efficacy studies	Effectiveness studies
Usually a set number of sessions	Keeps going until the patient improves
Interventions usually set and provided in a set order according to a manual	Interventions change to meet needs of client – difficult to maintain fidelity
Patients enter efficacy studies by the passive process of random assignment to treatment and with the knowledge of what is to be offered in the study	Patients enter treatment they actively seek with a therapist they screened and chose. Public patients have little choice of provider
Patients in efficacy studies are selected through a long set of exclusion/inclusion criteria. Intervention is usually focused on one primary problem	Patients usually have multiple problems, and intervention is geared to relieving parallel and interacting difficulties
Intervention is usually focused on specific symptom reduction and whether the disorder ends	Intervention is focused on improvement in the general functioning of patients

their practice. One of the key problems is that programmes that have been shown to provide significant outcomes during controlled conditions/trials (efficacy studies) may not produce the same positive results in real world conditions (effectiveness studies). Thus, while efficacy studies answer the question, 'Can a programme work in routine clinical practice?' effectiveness studies address the question, 'Does it work in routine clinical practice?' For example, a skill development programme would use techniques known to be efficacious in a controlled environment; however, the programme may or may not be effective when applied in usual care conditions.

In relation to psychotherapy, Seligman (1995) discussed some of the gaps that exist between 'laboratory' style research (efficacy) and its application in the field (effectiveness): see Table 14.5.

Conclusion

Research, evaluation and quality assurance are distinct but interrelated processes designed to provide objective information about the performance of programmes. Research and evaluation have as their focus outcomes, whereas quality assurance is concerned more with the processes used to achieve outcomes. Research is concerned with answering fundamental questions and testing theories, whereas evaluation and quality assurance are more concerned with the operation of specific services. At each level, ethical issues and matters of strategy and design must be considered. The information produced though research and evaluation does not always meet the expectations or wishes of those who commissioned or conducted the work. However, it should assist rational decision making and planning for service improvement. Efficiency and effectiveness studies rely on different design strategies and have competing implementing conventions. The development of hybrid designs (incorporating some elements of both) may assist in bridging the gap between evaluation and clinical practice.

References

Bickman, L. (1987). The functions of program theory. In: L. Bickman (Ed.), *Using program theory in evaluation. New directions for program evaluation* (pp. 5–18). San Francisco: Jossey–Bass.

Bird, S., Cox, D., Farewell, V., Goldstein, H., Holt, T., & Smith, P. (2003). *Performance indicators: Good, bad, and ugly.* Royal Statistical Society Working Party on Performance Monitoring in the Public Services: Cambridge.

Conrad, K.J., Randolph, F.L., Kirby, M.W., & Bebout, R.R. (1999). Creating and using logic models: Four perspectives. *Alcoholism Treatment Quarterly, 17,* 17–31.

Coombs, T., & Meehan, T. (2003). Mental health outcomes in Australia: Issues for mental health nurses. *International Journal of Mental Health Nursing, 12,* 163–164.

Eagar, K., Burgess, P., & Buckingham, B. (2003). *Towards national benchmarks for Australian mental health services. ISC Discussion Paper No 4.* Canberra: Commonwealth Department of Health and Aging.

Funnell, S. (1997). Program logic: An adaptable tool for designing and evaluating programmes. *Evaluation News and Comment, 6,* 5–17.

Garland, A., Kruse, M., & Aarons, G. (2003). Clinicians and outcome measurement: What's the use? *Journal of Behavioural and Health Services Research, 30,* 393–405.

Gilbody, S., House, A., & Sheldon, T. (2005). Outcome measures and needs assessment tools for schizophrenia and related disorders. *The Cochrane Library, 1.* Wiley.

Kazis, L., Callahan, L., Meenan, R., & Pincus, T. (1990). Health status reports in the care of patients with rheumatoid arthritis. *Journal of Clinical Epidemiology, 43,* 1243–1253.

Lakeman, R. (2004). Standardized routine outcome measurement: Pot holes in the road to recovery. *International Journal of Mental Health Nursing, 13,* 210–215.

McLellan, T. & Durell, J. (1996). Outcome evaluation in psychiatric and substance abuse. In: L. Sederer & B. Dickey (Eds.), *Outcome assessment in clinical practice* (pp. 34–44). Baltimore: Williams & Wilkins.

Meehan, T., O'Rourke, P., Morrison, P., Posner, N., & Drake, S. (2001). *Outcomes for long-stay patients discharged under the Project 300 programme: Follow-up at 6 & 18 months post discharge* (final report). Brisbane: Queensland Health.

Meehan, T., McCombes, S., Hatzipetrou, L., & Catchpoole, R. (2005). Introduction of routine outcome measures: staff reactions and issues for consideration. *Journal of Psychiatric and Mental Health Nursing, 13,* 581–587.

Rosenheck, R., & Cicchetti, D. (1998). A mental health program report card: a multi-dimensional approach to performance monitoring in public sector programs. *Community Mental Health Journal, 34,* 85–106.

Sackett, D., Richardson, W., Rosenberg, W., & Haynes, R. (1997). *Evidence-based medicine: How to practice and teach EBM.* New York: Churchill Livingstone.

Seligman, M. (1995). The effectiveness of psychotherapy. The consumer reports study. *American Psychologist, 50,* 965–974.

Sullivan, G., Duan, N., Mukherjee, S., Kirchner, J., Perry, D., & Henderson, K. (2005). The role of services researchers in facilitating intervention research. *Psychiatric Services, 56,* 537–542.

Wait, S. (2004). *Benchmarking: A policy analysis*. London: The Nuffield Trust.

Walter, G., Cleary, M., & Rey, J. (1988). Attitudes of mental health personnel towards rating outcome. *Journal of Quality Clinical Practice, 18,* 109–115.

Weiss, C. (1983). The stakeholder approach to evaluation: Origins and promise. In: A. Bryk (Ed.), *Stake-holder based evaluation* (pp. 26–36). San Francisco: Jossey–Bass.

Wholey, J. (1987). Evaluability assessment: Developing program theory. In: L. Bickman (Ed.), *Using program theory in evaluation. New directions for program evaluation No. 33* (pp. 77–92). San Francisco: Jossey–Bass.

Yeaton, W., & Sechrest, L. (1981). Critical dimensions in the choice and maintenance of successful treatments: Strength, integrity, and effectiveness. *Journal of Consulting and Clinical Psychology, 49,* 156–167.

Chapter 15

THE WELLBEING AND PROFESSIONAL DEVELOPMENT OF THE PSYCHOSOCIAL REHABILITATION PRACTITIONER

Robert King and Chris Lloyd

Overview of chapter

In this chapter we consider how stress and burnout have been conceptualised in relation to human services work. We then examine the various sources of stress and the evidence that indicates they are specific risks for people working in psychosocial rehabilitation. In each case we identify strategies likely to assist in preventing or reducing stress. We discuss the role of clinical supervision as a strategy for addressing workplace stress and enhancing professional satisfaction. Finally, we look at the importance of professional development and areas that are important to address in designing professional development programmes, namely recovery, rehabilitation, social inclusion and evidence based practices.

Conceptualising stress and burnout

Mental health practice has been identified as potentially stressful (Bassett & Lloyd, 2001; Cottrell, 2001; Edwards et al., 2000a, 2000b). It has been suggested that mental health practitioners are more adept at looking after the mental health of their clients than they are at attending to their own mental health needs. Developing and maintaining wellbeing in a work role is a complex matter. This involves identifying and dealing with sources of stress, preferably before they become noxious. It also involves developing skills that make the work more successful and the job more satisfying.

Stress is usually defined as an environmental or internal demand that overloads the coping capacities and resources of the person. The stress – coping – strain model proposes that strain (the subjective experience and impact of stress) is a function of the relationship between stressors and coping capacities (Fogarty et al., 1999). Higher coping capacities enable increased management of the same level of objective stress without the experience of strain.

The primary focus in this chapter is on forms of stress that are most commonly encountered in a psychosocial rehabilitation context. There are two broad categories of stress that are especially relevant:

- Traumatic stress that is either direct and immediate as a result of 'critical incidents', or that is vicarious or secondary as a result of indirect exposure to the stress of a client
- Occupational stress and burnout, a chronic stress condition associated with the total work environment and its interaction with individual vulnerabilities and problems, rather than specific direct or indirect events

Traumatic stress is characterised by acute stress symptoms (arousal, intrusion and avoidance) whereas occupational stress and burnout are characterised by dissatisfaction, absenteeism, reduced productivity, career damage and loss of self-esteem. While the two forms of stress are not necessarily related, it is possible to get a double dose and it may be that one form of stress increases susceptibility to the other.

Noy (2004) proposed a three level model of trauma-related stress:

- *Alert*: the first phase is characterised by heightened alertness and anxiety in preparation for a noxious event
- *Impact*: the immediate post-impact phase is characterised by dissociation, denial and avoidance of stress linked stimuli
- *Post-traumatic*: the post-trauma phase is characterised by attempts to make sense of the experience, to adapt and to reconstruct life in the context of the trauma

Stress that does not involve major trauma may still be conceptualised within this framework as prolonged experience of the alert phase, or as chronic impact and post-traumatic symptoms associated with multiple low or moderate level psychological traumas rather than a single major event. Thus, absenteeism and seeking other forms of employment may be seen as avoidance of stress linked stimuli in the impact phase.

Another widely used conceptual model focuses on 'strain' as the impact and subjective experience of stressors, mediated by individual coping capacity. The stress – coping – strain model proposes that degree of strain is a function not just of the intensity of the stress but also of the coping capacity of the individual (Fogarty et al., 1999). This is supported by evidence that symptoms of psychological distress among healthcare professionals can be attributed both to personal vulnerabilities to anxiety and depression and to work and non-work related conflicts and stresses (Weinberg & Creed, 2000). The implication is that effective prevention or intervention requires attention both to reduction of stressors and to enhancement of individual coping capacity (Cottrell, 2001). Issues associated with prevention of stress related problems and intervention following experience of traumatic stress or burnout are discussed in greater detail below.

Acute stress associated with critical incidents

Critical incidents are unexpected traumatic events, usually with serious outcomes. They may or may not involve clients. Examples include a client assaulting a staff member, a fire in the workplace, a robbery with violence in the workplace, suicide of a client in the workplace, a client assaulting another client in the workplace (Sacks et al., 2001). Of these, assaults by clients on staff present the greatest risk.

Assaults on staff are reasonably common in mental health workplaces (Blow et al., 1999); however, the risk of assault is higher in inpatient settings than community settings where most psychosocial rehabilitation takes place (Antai-Otong, 2001; Flannery et al., 2000). Therefore the risk of assault in most rehabilitation settings is relatively low. However, low frequency can actually increase the impact, because one of the components of psychological trauma is that the person is unprepared. While nurses are the most frequent victims of assault, the evidence suggests that any kind of practitioner, including more experienced and senior staff, are at risk of assault (Flannery, 2004).

Aside from any physical injuries that may result from an assault, some form of post-traumatic stress symptom (intrusion, avoidance or arousal) is highly likely following workplace assault. For example, Matthews (1998) found that 62 of 63 workers who had been assaulted in the course of their work in community residences for people with mental health or developmental disability problems showed evidence of post-traumatic symptoms.

Secondary traumatic stress (STS), vicarious traumatisation, and compassion fatigue distinctions are sometimes drawn between these conditions (Jenkins & Baird, 2002) but the terms are most commonly used interchangeably (Sabin-Farrell & Turpin, 2003). Here, the term STS will be used for simplicity. STS is characterised by traumatic stress symptoms of intrusion, arousal and avoidance and in this respect is similar to the acute stress syndrome resulting from critical incidents and described above. The important difference is that STS does not result from direct exposure to assault or other frightening or dangerous event. Rather, STS results from indirect exposure via another person's account of a traumatic event. While the mechanism of STS is not fully understood it is likely that it is the capacity of people, through use of imagination, empathy or identification, to put themselves in the position of another person that creates this vulnerability. It is as if the listener has actually experienced the same event as the immediate victim. It is possible that the very skills that make for effective interpersonal communication in a rehabilitation environment also create this vulnerability to experience of another person's trauma (Figley, 1995).

There is uncertainly about the prevalence of STS among mental health practitioners because of limited empirical evidence and lack of agreement as to measurement (Sabin-Farrell & Turpin, 2003). However, Meldrum et al. (2002) found that just under 18% of a sample of 300 Australian case managers reported symptoms of intrusion, avoidance and arousal at post-traumatic stress disorder level of intensity, which they attributed to client work. Boscarino et al. (2004) found even higher rates of STS for a sample of just under 200 social workers who worked with people exposed to the World Trade Center attacks of 2002. Meldrum et al. (2002), Bride et al. (2004) and Boscarino et al. (2004) found that the extent of STS symptoms was significantly related to the extent of exposure to people who had experienced trauma, but in each study the relationship was modest, suggesting that a variety of personal and environmental factors in addition to exposure to trauma victims contribute to STS.

Occupational stress and burnout

Occupational stress and burnout among mental health and related workers has been more extensively studied than has either acute post-traumatic stress or secondary traumatic stress. There are a variety of measures, including one specifically developed for mental health professionals (Cushway et al., 1996). By far the most widely used measure is the Maslach Burnout Inventory (Maslach et al., 1996). The Maslach Burnout Inventory conceptualises occupational stress and burnout as having three components: emotional exhaustion, depersonalisation and lack of personal accomplishment.

There is a clear pattern of occupational stress and burnout among mental health professionals that is characterised by moderately high emotional exhaustion, moderate to low depersonalisation and high personal accomplishment (Edwards et al., 2000b; Lloyd & King, 2004; Robinson et al., 2003). In other words, the typical mental health professional is stressed by work demands but is not typically burnt out by the nature of the work itself. The greatest sources of emotional exhaustion among mental health professionals are organisational issues and demands (Robinson et al., 2003; Taylor & Barling, 2004) and home–work conflicts (Cushway et al., 1996), rather than client contact. However, concerns about violent patients and inadequate staff resources may be a significant source of stress for nurses (Cushway et al., 1996; Taylor & Barling, 2004). For many mental health professionals, a high sense of the worth of the work they are doing (personal accomplishment) mitigates stress associated with emotional exhaustion.

While workload has been identified as a significant stressor (Cottrell, 2001), there are mixed findings regarding the relationship between objective indicators of workload, such as client caseload and stress (Coffey & Coleman, 2001; King et al., 2000). It may be that when practitioners are experiencing stress, workload feels unmanageable even when it is not unreasonably high. Stress can reduce efficiency, meaning that a stressed practitioner may struggle with a caseload that a non-stressed practitioner will find manageable.

Other factors that have been identified as contributing to stress are workplace relationships (Cottrell, 2001), job insecurity and unsupportive line management (Edwards et al., 2001). Although client work in itself appears to be protective, there is evidence that some client groups are more stressful to work with than others (Cottrell, 2001). Work with older people has been found to be less stressful than work with other client groups.

Managing acute and secondary traumatic stress

The most effective means of minimising traumatic stress is to reduce exposure, as the risk of both acute stress associated with critical incidents and STS is directly related to exposure. In the case of acute stress the most effective prevention strategy is to reduce the likelihood of assault, as this is the most common cause of acute stress. The evidence suggests that the implementation of service-wide dispute resolution and de-escalation training appears to be helpful (Hodgson et al., 2004). However, training the individual does not impact on risk for that person. This suggests that organisational climate and culture are major factors in risk reduction.

There is evidence that the greatest risk of assault is from unfamiliar clients (Hodgson et al., 2004; Trenoweth, 2003). This means that practitioners should exercise more than usual care when working with someone for the first time or while the relationship is developing. In practice, being alert to agitation, intoxication and paranoid ideation is of a high priority. Clients in such states should be given adequate space and, where possible, interactions should include another staff member. Denial of service, acute psychosis and overstimulation have been found to be the most common precipitants of assaults on staff (Flannery et al., 2006). It is likely that rehabilitation practitioners will need to deal with denial of service situations and acute psychosis. Maintaining a quiet and respectful demeanour will minimise risk of overstimulation in such circumstances and probably reduce risk of assault.

In the case of STS, while supervision is not, in itself, protective (Meldrum et al., 2002), supervisors may be able to reduce risk by ensuring that the caseloads of rehabilitation practitioners are not dominated by people with high exposure to trauma. Some practitioners develop a particular interest in working with trauma victims and such people should be made aware of the risks of STS and educated as to warning signs such as:

- Recurrent intrusive thoughts or images about experiences that clients have reported
- Recurrent dreams related to experiences that clients have reported
- Disturbances of mood or feelings of anxiety prompted by thoughts or memories of experiences that clients have reported
- Avoidance of anything that might activate thoughts or memories of experiences that clients have reported
- Irritability, sleep disturbance or concentration problems that have no other reasonable explanation

There is a substantial and somewhat controversial literature concerning the value of critical incident stress debriefing (CISD) after a critical incident has occurred (Antai-Otong, 2001; Jacobs et al., 2004). CISD is a procedure whereby critical incident victims are encouraged to reconstruct the event, the circumstances surrounding it and their thoughts and emotional and physiological reactions, usually in a group setting with other people affected by the incident. It is primarily a psychoeducational intervention that is designed to assist people to 'normalise' their responses and also detect and seek specialist help when responses are more extreme than normal, or continue beyond the normal duration.

Early advocates for CISD recommended mandatory debriefing of all staff exposed to a critical incident. However, research into outcomes from single session debriefing suggested that it was more likely to be harmful than helpful (Rose et al., 2002) and, as a result, the use of CISD is now typically voluntary. The evidence suggests that most people exposed to critical incidents choose not to avail themselves of CISD when it is offered (Macnab et al., 2003), and it has been argued that CISD may be of more value to people who have had secondary exposure than to primary victims of critical incidents (Jacobs et al., 2004).

It is likely that the most useful intervention, when a practitioner has been exposed to a critical incident such as an assault, is to encourage the person to self monitor for distressing intrusion, avoidance and arousal and to seek help early if such symptoms become prominent. While mandatory single session debriefing does not appear to be helpful, there is some evidence that brief psychological interventions in response to early signs of post-traumatic stress can reduce symptoms (Bisson et al., 2004). So far, there have been no high quality studies of psychological interventions specifically designed to reduce STS. However, the similarity in the symptoms profile means that it is likely that interventions that are successful in reducing post-traumatic stress disorder symptoms will also be effective with STS.

Managing occupational stress and burnout

A great deal is known about the extent and sources of occupational stress among mental health practitioners; however, the evidence base for effective prevention or intervention is relatively weak (Edwards & Burnard, 2003b; Mimura & Griffiths, 2003). There is some evidence that personal support and cognitive and behavioural strategies can assist people to manage stress at the individual level (Edwards & Burnard, 2003a; Mimura & Griffiths, 2003), but much of what follows is based on principles that would appear to derive logically from the findings about sources of occupational stress rather than from an empirical literature concerning effectiveness.

Given the evidence that high levels of occupational stress involve complex interactions between individual and environmental factors, careful assessment of the sources of stress and multilevel interventions are required (Weinberg & Creed, 2000). Individual vulnerabilities such as depression and anxiety and extra-work stresses such as personal problems need to be addressed at the individual level, whereas organisational factors require system level interventions.

Consistent with the stress – coping model, interventions can be conceptualised as operating at three levels:

- Primary (preventative) interventions designed to reduce stressors
- Secondary (resilience) interventions designed to enhance coping capacity
- Tertiary (clinical) interventions designed to assist people to recover from stress-induced symptoms (strain)

Table 15.1 Matrix of organisational stress management interventions

	Primary stress reduction	**Secondary stress management**	**Tertiary stress treatment**
Individual (Individual perspective)	Personal stress profile feedback	Healthy lifestyle	Counselling
	Time management	Reflection	Psychotherapy
	Career consultation	Clinical supervision	Occupational health interventions
	Assertiveness	Mentorship	Physical wellness: diet, exercise, addictions
	Communication skills	Buddy systems	Lifestyle work
	Psychoeducation	Relaxation	
		Home/work interface	
		Support mapping	
		Biofeedback	
		Imagery	
Group (Team perspective)	Team building	Group development, diagnosis and intervention	Therapeutic remedial team work
	Team role analysis		Work group role negotiation
	Boundary clarification	Clinical team supervision	
		Dependency/skill mix	
		Workload analysis and review	
Organisation (Systems perspective)	Individual performance review	Workload management	Therapeutic consultancy
	Professional development record	Mission clarification	Reorganisation
	Job descriptions and role	Risk analysis and management	Organisational transformation programmes
	Clarification	Employee participation	Employee assistance programmes
	Participation and empowerment		Process redesign
	Schemes		Cultural change work, e.g. combating 'presenteeism'

Reproduced with permission from Cottrell (2001), p. 160.

Cottrell (2001) argued that primary, secondary and tertiary interventions can be provided at individual, team or system level, generating a 3 × 3 matrix of approaches to the management of workplace stress, which is outlined in Table 15.1. While the boundaries between types of intervention are more fluid in practice than the matrix suggests, it is a useful tool for identifying the factors that impact on workplace stress and designing interventions at the appropriate level.

When designing interventions, opportunity and leverage are important factors. Opportunity is concerned with the feasibility of interventions. Interventions may be effective in principle but impossible to implement in practice. Leverage is concerned with the impact of interventions. Some interventions may have a much greater capacity to reduce stress than others.

In the case of traumatic stress, as discussed above, there is evidence that victims often elect not to take up the offer of tertiary interventions even when they are available. Furthermore, there is limited evidence of effectiveness when people do avail themselves of psychological treatments. This means that both opportunity and leverage are relatively low. Reducing risk of assault, a primary intervention, may present greater opportunity and superior leverage as an intervention to reduce stress.

In the case of occupational strain, there is evidence that the level of occupational stress, but not the personal coping resources, is critical with respect to the intentions of rehabilitation counsellors to change jobs (Layne et al., 2004). This suggests that, if the aim is to reduce staff turnover, it is likely to be more effective to intervene at the organisational level to reduce stress factors than to build resilience at the individual level.

Clinical supervision as a case study of response to occupational stress

Clinical supervision has acquired a prominent place in mental health practice, especially in the UK (Butterworth et al., 1997) and Australia (Strong et al., 2003). As a result both of government and professional association policies, clinical supervision models and practices have been developed and implemented for the mental health nursing workforce and there is a substantial literature concerning the merits of supervision.

According to Proctor (1994), supervision has restorative, normative and formative functions. This means that it has potential as a stress intervention at primary, secondary and tertiary levels. At the primary level, the normative functions ensure that practitioners utilise procedures and approaches that maximise safety and minimise risk of assaults or other identifiable stressors. At the secondary level, the formative function assists practitioners to develop clinical skills and responses to clients that build personal resilience and capacity to cope with adverse situations. At the tertiary level, supervision provides the practitioner with a safe environment in which to debrief, identify strains associated with work and get assistance with accessing specialist therapeutic interventions when they are necessary.

Others have collapsed the restorative and formative functions of supervision to produce two rather than three fundamental dimensions of supervision, often termed administrative or managerial (normative), and clinical (restorative and formative) (Schultz et al., 2002; Yegdich, 1999a). The administrative function provides a guarantee of accountability, work performance and work safety. It is often linked with the management of junior or unqualified staff who lack the skills and judgement to work independently. The supervisor may give clear direction on work performance and insist that this direction be followed.

The clinical function supports the complex emotional and cognitive processes that are fundamental to working with clients. The supervisor may well be a senior practitioner, perceived to have high levels of expertise, but the supervisor does not assume responsibility for the work of the practitioner receiving supervision. Rather, the supervisor provides an opportunity for the practitioner to review and reflect on the rehabilitation work and to develop a level of objectivity that enables new thinking and creative solutions. This is both a means of reducing the impact of stressful events that have already taken place and an opportunity to learn strategies that will enable more effective interventions in the future. The supervisor may provide advice or even model interventions, but it is for the practitioner to decide whether or not to follow this advice and how to implement ideas developed in supervision.

The supervisory relationship has been conceptualised as having similarities to and differences from the processes of a therapeutic relationship. It is similar in that it requires an effective alliance characterised by core components of equality, safety and challenge (Weaks, 2002). However, there are somewhat different boundaries in a supervisory relationship and while there are different views as to the proper location of these boundaries, there is agreement that they are different from those of the therapeutic relationship (Yegdich, 1999b) and that supervision involves less investigation of the internal private world of the practitioner than would be the case in a therapist–client relationship.

There is evidence that clinical supervision, whether provided individually or in groups, is valued by a range of health and rehabilitation professionals (Lindahl & Norberg, 2002; Weaks, 2002), both for the emotional support it provides and for the opportunity it provides for development of practitioner skills. However, some practitioners, in particular nurses, are wary of clinical supervision because of concerns that it will become contaminated by more administrative considerations (Cole, 2002; Cottrell, 2002). This has led some to argue that administrative and clinical supervision should be rigidly separate. However others have taken the view that it is possible to achieve both quality improvement that meets administration goals and lifelong learning within a single supervisory process (Clouder & Sellers, 2004; Howartson-Jones, 2003; McSherry et al., 2002).

It has been argued that clinical supervision it an effective intervention for both prevention of stress and response to the effects of stress (Butterworth, 1992; Cottrell, 2001). However, the limited empirical data are at best inconclusive. Some studies have failed to find any relationship between supervision and reduced work-related stress (Meldrum et al., 2002; Pålsson et al., 1996) and some have reported a mixed picture (Bégat et al., 2005; Teasdale et al., 2001). Hyrkas (2005) concluded that the results of a Finnish survey indicate that supervision is beneficial in respect of job satisfaction and stress; however, her data suggest that the greatest benefits were for the supervisors rather than the supervisees. There has been surprisingly little research into the impact of supervision on outcomes for clients; however, one well designed study (Bambling et al., 2006) found a substantial supervision effect on psychotherapeutic treatment of depression. Evidence of a more general supervision effect on practitioner effectiveness could be expected to reduce burnout through enhancing the protective personal accomplishment dimension. Until further well designed and adequately powered studies are undertaken, the effectiveness of clinical supervision in stress reduction must be considered at best promising. Teasdale et al. (2001) suggested that supervision may have a more strategic function with junior rather than experienced practitioners.

Professional development

Delivering effective recovery-focused rehabilitation has required a shift in thinking to reflect current rehabilitation beliefs, goals and practices (Casper et al., 2002). It has also become necessary to utilise a recovery approach (Mental Health Commission, 2001) with providing services that promote the social inclusion of people with mental illness (Office of the Deputy Prime Minister, 2004). Additionally, there is the challenge of integrating evidence-based practices and the recovery vision (Anthony et al., 2003; Frese et al., 2001).

The providers of psychosocial rehabilitation need an appropriate educational and professional background to ensure that they develop the necessary skills in being able to assess each individual's role functioning in the community; develop strengths-based assessment; develop community partnerships; provide effective clinical interventions; and utilise evidence-based practice. Targeted continuing education is believed to add value to mental health interventions and is a fundamental component of professional development (NSW Health Department, 2002). The aim of staff education and training is to build awareness and skills in the areas of rehabilitation philosophy, recovery and policy directions. When designing professional development programmes, consideration needs to be given to practitioners' attitudes, beliefs, values and skills. For example, Borkin et al. (2000) developed a questionnaire designed to assess attitudes towards recovery-related outcomes such as empowerment, satisfaction with services and life, improved quality of life, increased opportunities and environmental impacts. They suggested that this tool could be used for educational and training purposes to measure indicators of change in beliefs following educational interventions. They also suggested that it could be used in professional development as a focus of discussion.

It has previously been identified that mental health professionals often have a negative and pessimistic view of people diagnosed with mental illness, and this has been a barrier to providing a recovery-oriented approach to rehabilitation (Andresen et al., 2003). The relationship between the attitudes of mental health professionals and education and training was a focus of a project conducted by Deakin University (Deakin Human Services Australia, 1999). This particular project highlighted the importance of involving consumers and carers in education and training in order to change the attitudes and values of mental health practitioners. Having consumer and carer input into professional development activities will enable a better understanding of the needs of people living with mental illness and how practitioners can provide for their needs. The Deakin project concluded that education and training should cohere around two guiding principles: 'Mental health professionals need to learn about and value the lived experience of consumers and carers', and 'Mental health professionals should recognise and value the healing *potential in the relationships between consumers and service providers and carers and service providers.'* (p. 1). Happell et al. (2003) conducted a study examining consumer involvement in the education of mental health practitioners, and found that the majority of respondents felt that consumers should be involved in the planning and delivery of staff education and professional development sessions.

Conclusion

Workplace stress is a highly complex phenomenon that includes both traumatic stress (immediate and secondary) and strain and burnout associated with a wide range of organisational and personal stressors. There is evidence that mental health practice carries risks of all forms of stress. The development of effective interventions to reduce stress must take into account the complexity of stress and also decisions concerning the level of intervention: primary, secondary or tertiary.

There has been an historical tendency to develop and implement responses to stress before the development of an evidence base to support these interventions, and some interventions widely considered to be effective have subsequently been found to have limited value. While there are promising approaches and strategies, the evidence base for the effectiveness of stress reduction interventions, including clinical supervision, remains modest and the development of this evidence base remains a priority. In a rapidly changing practice environment, the practitioner's own continuing professional development is a key component of both professional competence and work-related wellbeing.

References

Andresen, R., Oades, L., & Caputi, P. (2003). The experience of recovery from schizophrenia: Towards an empirically validated stage model. *Australian and New Zealand Journal of Psychiatry, 37,* 586–594.

Antai-Otong, D. (2001). Critical incident stress debriefing: A health promotion model for workplace violence. *Perspectives in Psychiatric Care, 37,* 125–134.

Anthony, W., Rogers, E., & Farkas, M. (2003). Research on evidence-based practices: Future directions in an era of recovery. *Community Mental Health Journal, 39,* 101–114.

Bambling, M., King, R., Schweitzer, R., & Raue, P. (2006). Clinical supervision: its influence on client-rated working alliance and client symptom reduction in brief treatment of major depression. *Psychotherapy Research, 16,* 317–331.

Bassett, H., & Lloyd, C. (2001). Occupational therapy in mental health: Managing stress and burnout. *British Journal of Occupational Therapy, 64,* 406–411.

Bégat, I., Ellefsen, B., & Severinsson, E. (2005). Nurses' satisfaction with their work environment and the outcomes of clinical nursing supervision on nurses' experiences of well-being – A Norwegian study. *Journal of Nursing Management, 13,* 221–230.

Bisson, J.I., Shepherd, J.P., Joy, D., Probert, R., & Newcombe, R.G. (2004). Early cognitive–behavioural therapy for post-traumatic stress symptoms after physical injury. Randomised controlled trial. *British Journal of Psychiatry, 184,* 63–69.

Blow, F.C., Barry, K.L., Copeland, L.A., McCormick, R.A., Lehmann, L.S., & Ullman, E. (1999). Repeated assaults by patients in the VA hospital and clinic settings. *Psychiatric Services*, 50, 390–394.

Borkin, J.R., Steffen, J.J., Ensfield, L.B., Krzton, K., Wishnick, H., Wilder, K., & Yuangarber, N. (2000). Recovery Attitudes Questionnaire: Development and evaluation. *Psychiatric Rehabilitation Journal*, 24, 95–102.

Boscarino, J.A., Figley, C.R., & Adams, R.E. (2004). Compassion fatigue following the September 11 terrorist attacks: A study of secondary trauma among New York City social workers. *International Journal of Emergency Mental Health*, 6, 57–66.

Bride, B.E., Robinson, M.M., Yegidis, B., & Figley, C.R. (2004). Development and validation of the Secondary Traumatic Stress Scale. *Research on Social Work Practice*, 14, 27–35.

Butterworth, T. (1992). Clinical supervision as an emerging idea. In: T. Butterworth & J. Faugier (Eds.), *Clinical supervision and mentorship in nursing* (pp. 230–239). London: Chapman and Hall.

Butterworth, T., Carson, J., White, E., Jeacock, J., & Bishop, V. (1997). It is good to talk, an evaluation of clinical supervision and mentorship in England and Scotland. Manchester: The School of Nursing Studies, University of Manchester.

Casper, E.S., Oursler, J., Schmidt, L.T., & Gill, K.J. (2002). Measuring practitioners' beliefs, goals, and practices in psychiatric rehabilitation. *Psychiatric Rehabilitation Journal*, 25, 223–234.

Clouder, L., & Sellers, J. (2004). Reflective practice and clinical supervision: An interprofessional perspective. *Journal of Advanced Nursing*, 46, 262–269.

Coffey, M., & Coleman, M. (2001). The relationship between support and stress in forensic community mental health nursing. *Journal of Advanced Nursing*, 34, 397–407.

Cole, A. (2002). Someone to watch over you: Clinical supervision. *Nursing Times*, 98, 22–25.

Cottrell, S. (2001). Occupational stress and job satisfaction in mental health nursing: Focused interventions through evidence-based assessment. *Journal of Psychiatric and Mental Health Nursing*, 8, 157–164.

Cottrell, S. (2002). Suspicion, resistance, tokenism and mutiny: Problematic dynamics relevant to the implementation of clinical supervision in nursing. *Journal of Psychiatric and Mental Health Nursing*, 9, 667–671.

Cushway, D., Tyler, P.A., & Nolan, P. (1996). Development of a stress scale for mental health professionals. *British Journal of Clinical Psychology*, 35, 279–295.

Deakin Human Services Australia (1999). *Learning together: Education and training partnerships in mental health*. Canberra: Commonwealth Department of Health and Aged Care.

Edwards, D., Burnard, P., Coyle, D., Fothergill, A., & Hannigan, B. (2000a). Stress and burnout in community mental health nursing: a review of the literature. *Journal of Psychiatric and Mental Health Nursing*, 7, 7–14.

Edwards, D., Burnard, P., Coyle, D., Fothergill, A., & Hannigan, B. (2000b). Stressors, moderators and stress outcomes: Findings from the All-Wales Community Mental Health Nurse Study. *Journal of Psychiatric and Mental Health Nursing*, 7, 529–537.

Edwards, D., Burnard, P., Coyle, D., Fothergill, A., & Hannigan, B. (2001). A stepwise multivariate analysis of factors that contribute to stress for mental health nurses working in the community. *Journal of Advanced Nursing*, 36, 805–813.

Edwards, D., & Burnard, P. (2003a). A systematic review of stress and stress management interventions for mental health nurses. *Journal of Advanced Nursing*, 42, 169–200.

Edwards, D., & Burnard, P. (2003b). A systematic review of the effects of stress and coping strategies used by occupational therapists working in mental health settings. *British Journal of Occupational Therapy*, 66, 345–355.

Figley, C.R. (1995). Compassion fatigue: Towards a new understanding of the costs of caring. In: B.H. Stamm (Ed.), *Secondary traumatic stress: Self care issues for clinicians, researchers, and educators* (pp. 3–27). Lutherville, MD: Sidran Press.

Flannery, R.B. Jr. (2004). Characteristics of staff victims of psychiatric patient assaults: Updated review of findings, 1995–2001. *American Journal of Alzheimer's Disease and Other Dementias*, 19, 35–38.

Flannery, R.B. Jr., Fisher, W., Walker, A., Kolodziej, K., & Spillane, M. (2000). Psychiatric patient assaults on community staff: Preliminary inquiry. *Psychiatric Services*, 51, 111–113.

Flannery, R.B. Jr., Laudani, L., Levitre, V., & Walker, A.P. (2006). Precipitants of psychiatric patient assaults on staff: Three-year empirical inquiry of the assaulted staff action program (ASAP). *International Journal of Emergency Mental Health*, 8, 15–22

Fogarty, G.J., Machin, A., Albion, M.J., Sutherland, L.F., Lalor, G.I., & Revitt, S. (1999). Predicting occupational strain and job satisfaction: The role of stress, coping, personality, and affectivity variables. *Journal of Vocational Behavior*, 54, 429–452.

Frese, F., Stanley, J., Kress, K., & Vogel-Scibiia, S. (2001). Integrating evidence-based practices and the recovery model. *Psychiatric Services*, 52, 1462–1468.

Happell, B., Pinikahana, J., & Roper, K. (2003). Changing attitudes: The role of consumer academics in the education of postgraduate psychiatric nursing students. *Archives of Psychiatric Nursing*, 17, 67–76.

Hodgson, M.J., Reed, R., Craig, T., Murphy, F., Lehmann, L., Belton, L., & Warren, N. (2004). Violence in healthcare facilities: Lessons from the Veterans Health Administration. *Journal of Occupational and Environmental Medicine*, 46, 1158–1165.

Howartson-Jones, I. (2003). Difficulties in clinical supervision and lifelong learning. *Nursing Standard*, 17, 37–41.

Hyrkas, K. (2005). Clinical supervision, burnout and job satisfaction among mental health and psychiatric nurses in Finland. *Issues in Mental Health Nursing*, 26, 531–556.

Jacobs, J., Horne-Moyer, H.L., & Jones, R. (2004). The effectiveness of critical incident stress debriefing with primary and secondary trauma victims. *International Journal of Emergency Mental Health*, 6, 5–14.

Jenkins, S., & Baird, S. (2002). Secondary traumatic stress and vicarious trauma: A validational study. *Journal of Traumatic Stress*, 15, 423–432.

King, R., Le Bas, J., & Spooner, D. (2000). The impact of caseload on mental health case manager personal efficacy. *Psychiatric Services*, 52, 364–368.

Layne, C.M., Hohenshil, T.H., & Singh, K. (2004). The relationship of occupational stress, psychological strain, and coping resources to the turnover intentions of rehabilitation counselors. *Rehabilitation Counseling Bulletin*, 48, 19–30.

Lindahl, B., & Norberg, A. (2002). Clinical group supervision in an intensive care unit: A space for relief, and for sharing emotions and experiences of care. *Journal of Clinical Nursing*, 11, 809–818.

Lloyd, C., & King, R. (2004). A survey of burnout among Australian mental health occupational therapists and social workers. *Social Psychiatry and Psychiatric Epidemiology*, 39, 752–757.

Macnab, A., Sun, C., & Lowe, J. (2003). Randomized, controlled trial of three levels of critical incident stress intervention. *Prehospital and Disaster Medicine*, 18, 367–371.

McSherry, R., Kell, J., & Pearce, P. (2002). Clinical supervision and clinical governance. *Nursing Times*, 98, 30–32.

Maslach, C., Jackson, S., & Leiter, M. (1996). *Maslach Burnout Inventory*. Palo Alto, California: Consulting Psychologists Press, Inc.

Matthews, L.R. (1998). Effect of staff debriefing on posttraumatic stress symptoms after assaults by community housing residents. *Psychiatric Services, 49*, 207–212.

Meldrum, L., King, R., & Spooner, D. (2002). Secondary traumatic stress among mental health case managers. In: C. Figley (Ed.), *Treating compassion fatigue* (pp. 85–106). New York: Brunner–Routledge.

Mental Health Commission (2001). *Recovery competencies for New Zealand mental health workers*. Wellington: Mental Health Commission.

Mimura, C., & Griffiths, P. (2003). The effectiveness of current approaches to workplace stress management in the nursing profession: An evidence based literature review. *Occupational and Environmental Medicine, 60*, 10–15.

Noy, S. (2004). The traumatic process: Conceptualization and treatment. *Prehospital and Disaster Medicine, 19*, 37–45.

NSW Health Department (2002). *Framework for rehabilitation for mental health*. Sydney: NSW Health Department.

Office of the Deputy Prime Minister (2004). *Mental health and social exclusion*. London: ODPM Publications.

Pålsson, M.B., Hallberg, I.R., Norberg, A., & Bjorvell, H. (1996). Burnout, empathy and sense of coherence among Swedish district nurses before and after systematic clinical supervision. *Scandinavian Journal of Caring Sciences, 10*, 1926.

Proctor, B. (1994). Supervision – competence, confidence, accountability. *British Journal of Guidance and Counselling, 22*, 309–318.

Robinson, J.R., Clements, K., & Land, C. (2003). Workplace stress among psychiatric nurses. Prevalence, distribution, correlates, and predictors. *Journal of Psychosocial Nursing and Mental Health Services, 41*, 32–41.

Rose, S., Bisson, J., & Wessely, S. (2002). Psychological debriefing for preventing post traumatic stress disorder (PTSD). *The Cochrane Database of Systematic Reviews, Issue 2*. Art. No. CD000560. DOI: 10.1002/14651858.CD000560.

Sabin-Farrell, R., & Turpin, G. (2003). Vicarious traumatization: Implications for the mental health of health workers? *Clinical Psychology Review, 23*, 449–480.

Sacks, S., Clements, P., & Fay-Hillier, T. (2001). Career perspectives: Care after chaos: Use of critical incident stress debriefing. *Perspectives in Psychiatric Care, 37*, 133–136.

Schultz, J.C., Ososkie, J.N., Fried, J.H., Nelson, R.E., & Bardos, A.N. (2002). Clinical supervision in public rehabilitation counseling settings. *Rehabilitation Counseling Bulletin, 45*, 213–222.

Strong, J., Kavanagh, D., Wilson, J., Spence, S.H., Worrall, L., & Crow, N. (2003). Supervision practice for allied health professionals within a large mental health service: Exploring the phenomenon. *Clinical Supervisor, 22*, 191–210

Taylor, B., & Barling, J. (2004). Identifying sources and effects of carer fatigue and burnout for mental health nurses: A qualitative approach. *International Journal of Mental Health Nursing, 13*, 117–125.

Teasdale, K., Brocklehurst, N., & Thom, N. (2001). Clinical supervision and support for nurses: An evaluation study. *Journal of Advanced Nursing, 33*, 216–224.

Trenoweth, S. (2003). Perceiving risk in dangerous situations: Risks of violence among mental health inpatients. *Journal of Advanced Nursing, 42*, 278–287.

Weaks, D. (2002). Unlocking the secrets of 'good supervision': A phenomenological exploration of experienced counsellors' perceptions of good supervision. *Counselling and Psychotherapy Research, 2*, 33–39.

Weinberg, A., & Creed, F. (2000). Stress and psychiatric disorder in healthcare professionals and hospital staff. *The Lancet, 355*, 533–537.

Yegdich, T. (1999a). Clinical supervision and managerial supervision: Some historical and conceptual considerations. *Journal of Advanced Nursing, 30*, 1195–1204.

Yegdich, T. (1999b). Lost in the crucible of supportive clinical supervision: Supervision is not therapy. *Journal of Advanced Nursing, 29*, 1265–1275.

Useful resources

Pages and links developed by Steve Cottrell and Georgina Smith devoted to clinical supervision. http://www.clinical-supervision.com/

Pages and links maintained by the Australasian Society for Traumatic Stress Studies. http://www.astss.org.au/

INDEX